International Trade, Welfare, and the Theory of General Equilibrium

This essential volume reflects the continuing and enduring utility of general equilibrium as a framework of analyses. It attempts to reiterate that understanding the broad and holistic consequence of economic events and policies go beyond the standpoint of partial equilibrium theory. Cutting across areas of research, general equilibrium (GE) perspectives in terms of small-scale GE models following the theory of Ronald Jones can help readers develop informed judgement regarding critical policies. These include but are not limited to several areas of specific interest—the interaction of financial factors with international trade and implications for the 'real sectors' of the economy, the impact of labor market reforms on the unorganized sectors in developing and transition economies, the non-uniform effects of inflation and deflation on internal and external factor flows, and the sought-after relation between foreign investment and skill accumulation.

Sugata Marjit is Reserve Bank of India Professor of Industrial Economics at the Centre for Studies in Social Sciences, Calcutta (CSSSC), Kolkata, India; Fellow, CESIfo, Munich, Germany; and Project Director at the Centre for Training and Research in Public Finance and Policy, Kolkata, India.

Saibal Kar is Professor of Economics at the Centre for Studies in Social Sciences, Calcutta (CSSSC), Kolkata, India and Research Fellow at the Institute of Labor Economics, Bonn, Germany.

International Trade, Welfare, and the Theory of General Equilibrium

Edited by
Sugata Marjit
Saibal Kar

CAMBRIDGE
UNIVERSITY PRESS

CAMBRIDGE
UNIVERSITY PRESS

University Printing House, Cambridge CB2 8BS, United Kingdom

One Liberty Plaza, 20th Floor, New York, NY 10006, USA

477 Williamstown Road, Port Melbourne, vic 3207, Australia

314 to 321, 3rd Floor, Plot No.3, Splendor Forum, Jasola District Centre, New Delhi 110025, India

79 Anson Road, #06–04/06, Singapore 079906

Cambridge University Press is part of the University of Cambridge.

It furthers the University's mission by disseminating knowledge in the pursuit of education, learning and research at the highest international levels of excellence.

www.cambridge.org
Information on this title: www.cambridge.org/9781108473873

First published 2018

Printed in India by Nutech Print Services, New Delhi 110020

A catalogue record for this publication is available from the British Library

ISBN 978-1-108-47387-3 Hardback

Contents

Figures and Tables

Introduction

Sugata Marjit and Saibal Kar

'It is an absolute miracle of clarity and to-the-point-ness'

– Robert M. Solow, Nobel Prize in Economics, 1987

The General Equilibrium model of international trade has profoundly impacted various sub-disciplines of economics such as development economics, public economics, and environmental economics, among many others. These models continue to inspire younger generations of researchers and are used as essential tools for evaluation of policies. It began with the celebrated contribution of Ronald W. Jones in the *Journal of Political Economy* in 1965. The following excerpt from a letter written by Robert Solow to Ronald Jones on February 11, 2004, is a testament to the incisiveness and depth of the formulation:

> In the course of working again on the elasticity of substitution I found myself rereading your 1965 article on 'The Structure of Simple General Equilibrium Models.' In case no one has told you this before, it is an absolute miracle of clarity and to-the-point-ness. Every graduate student in economics should be given a copy. The discipline would be better off. (Robert M. Solow, Winner of Nobel Prize in Economics in the year 1987, Comment on R. W Jones [1965], 'The Structure of Simple General Equilibrium Models', published in the *Journal of Political Economy*).

The excerpt from Solow's letter to his student says it all. His paper on the structure of simple general equilibrium models continues to serve as a theoretical workhorse for many scholars. In 2015, a group of scholars, both senior and young, gathered at the Centre for Studies in Social Sciences, Calcutta, to celebrate 50 years of publication of the article. The event engaged with discussions on a host of contemporary topics in international trade theory and policy highlighting the use of a general equilibrium framework. Central ideas and themes that emerged from these discussions are presented in this volume as cohesive and comprehensive chapters to celebrate a landmark and to record the influence of the idea of general equilibrium in theory and policy. Given that the core theory has ramified along various dimensions, the topics studied in this volume are naturally diverse.

We have classified 12 chapters in 6 sections to accommodate possible questions and coverage that the theory of simple general equilibrium espouses. These sections look at the use of general equilibrium techniques for analyzing adjustments towards free trade—for understanding the economy-wide implications of skill acquisition and its impact on income and wage inequality. It also includes how movement of productive resources, both labor and capital, influence well-being when moulded into the structures of general equilibrium models. In addition it comprehends the patterns of production organization in open economies and quantifies the implications of public policies, such as taxation, on labor and non-labor income. In terms of geographical coverage, the applications deal with both developed and developing country characteristics and experiences, making this volume relevant and interesting for a large readership.

The volume opens with an essay by Ronald Jones that draws attention to the history of his research. His anecdote records his interaction with a young economic historian of Rochester, later the Nobel laureate Robert Fogel, on applying simple general equilibrium theory to understand causes and consequences of history. Later, with the encouragement of Lionel McKenzie, Jones sharpened his focus on research in trade and general equilibrium. His chapter outlines the major topics of his research and analyzes major results in simple terms, reminding us of how some of these topics remain equally vibrant and engaging even today. This chapter will be helpful for graduate students as a snapshot of basic and enduring elements of trade theory.

Jones' chapter is followed by a discussion on the structure of optimal trade agreements and sequencing of liberal trade policies by Eric Bond (Chapter 2). It is an innovative application of two sector model where there are adjustment costs in reallocating workers from one sector to the other. The welfare function of the government considers a trade-off between efficient reallocation of resources and grievances of the workers who suffer due to trade liberalization. The chapter traces the optimal time path for tariff, keeping in view that in absence of distortions, adjustment costs per se do not hurt the optimality of free trade in two large countries. However, given that private moving cost is less than the social cost, there will be excessive flow of resources from one sector to the other. Here, tariff can be used as a second-best instrument to slow the adjustment process in both countries. The result changes if the factor could anticipate the tariff impact and this is the source of distortion. In that case, a tariff may not be a suitable policy instrument. Existence of externalities in the adjustment process may explain the phase-in periods of trade policy but distortions arising from misperceptions are less likely to be cured by tariff.

The formation of Free Trade Areas (FTAs) often stands as a major stumbling block towards achieving global free trade. Noritsugu Nakanishi in Chapter 3 presents an interesting and rigorous mechanism to examine if the initial level of tariff prevailing in a set of countries engaging in free trade agreements within specific networks turn out to be a facilitator or hindrance to global free trade. This chapter contributes to the vast literature on FTAs and customs unions by considering FTAs' network formation games and applications of graph theory in explaining the adjustment process towards global free trade. The farsightedness of countries affects dynamic global general equilibrium outcomes. It is shown that not all FTAs turn out to be closed networks of bilateral trade associations depending on farsightedness of individual countries and the welfare locus of such countries in the von Neumann-Morgenstern stable networks. Adjustment to higher or lower tariffs with the formation of trade associations could forestall global free trade or act as the stepping stone towards lowering global tariff barriers.

The impact of international trade and factor movements on local indicators of development has received substantial importance in related literature. One such issue—between-skill wage movements—is, however, not obvious in many cases and subjected to various conditions prevailing in the country in question. Depending on whether capital flows in to offer support to the prevailing stock of capital or the economy has strong fundamentals for capital accumulation at a reasonable rate are important determinants of the between-skill wage movements. Priya Brata Dutta shows in Chapter 4 that an exogenous rise in capital stock lowers skilled to unskilled wage ratio in both static and dynamic structures. Rashmi Ahuja's chapter (Chapter 5) is more specific, studying what type of capital inflow has an impact on skill formation among the resident population and what would be expected in terms of skilled–unskilled wage gap in such an economy. This chapter shows that inflow of foreign capital as a source of direct investment in higher education increases the stock of skill only if the education sector is capital intensive. The argument is based on the premise that unless the education sector absorbs capital speedily and utilizes that towards skill generation, the inflow would not be productive. As a counterfactual, one could consider a situation where the skill generation sector does not have capital and even if it is made available, the prevalent technology does not allow absorption and utilization to the best possible outcomes, and inflows remain unproductive. Conversely, if capital flows into the production sector, it expands and draws in other resources from the skill formation sector. Consequently, skill formation, as a second-round adjustment, suffers, and the existing skilled workers tend to relocate to production houses. The lack of enthusiasm for skill acquisition is then corroborated by the shrinking of this sector. The discussion based on a static framework does not exactly reflect these possibilities, but one could utilize the direction of outcomes to beget finer implications.

In Chapter 6, Uprety and Lahiri discuss a quintessential and unresolved issue, and a fairly contentious one too—does foreign aid to the nations, which send skilled migrants to the richer countries, reduce the flow of such migration? Intuitively, it should, since foreign aid, if properly utilized, should lead to more productive endeavors creating jobs and increasing income in the host country. They, however, find an exactly opposite result—foreign aid unambiguously raises emigration. The intuition follows the channels of relative shifts in demand and supply of skilled product and the authors show that there are both pull and push factors. The working of an inter-country general equilibrium system is nicely modelled to vindicate a stylized fact that billions spent as foreign aid in Africa, Latin America, and Asia could not contain skilled migration from South to the North. The authors focus entirely on flow of factors, while proposing future research on trade in goods. It is likely that skilled wage should increase in the aid-receiving country to some extent, but that may happen in the donor country as well, even after trade and migration leads to another interesting outcome such as rising inequality as done in more traditional general equilibrium models (for example, in Marjit and Kar, 2005).[1]

With relation to labor mobility, Anwesha Aditya shows in Chapter 7 that the implications of trade liberalization policies like tariff reduction and factor flows increases the product variety for the export basket. If a country exports horizontally differentiated product varieties, then tariff reduction and capital inflow will lead to increased variety when the import-competing homogeneous good is relatively skilled labor intensive. Conversely, immigration of labor (both skilled and unskilled) will lower the number of varieties. The result offers an explanation of asymmetric policy responses for product variety when subjected to commodity trade, capital inflow, and immigration of labor. The proposed outcomes may generate gains at the extensive margin in the short run and growth prospects in the long run. Mitra, Chaterjee, and Gupta, in Chapter 8, use a similar structure with a composite export sector, a product differentiated import competing sector, and a non-traded research and development sector. A shift in the policy regime from no capital mobility to full capital mobility increases research and development activity while also raising the number of differentiated import competing goods. This seems to capture some empirical reality in developing countries, where the expansion of varieties and brand names ranging from automobiles to potato chips has been remarkable. The results would acquire more credence if the linkages between trade reform and income growth leading to greater purchasing power in such countries are traced and analyzed.

---

[1] S. Marjit and S. Kar, 'Emigration and Wage Inequality', *Economics Letters* 88, no. 1(2005): 141–145.

Beladi, Chakrabarti, and Marjit (Chapter 9) continue an exploration of the general equilibrium framework in oligopolistic structure through the general oligopolistic equilibrium (GOLE) model. The structure is a mix of the industrial organization and GE framework initially investigated by Peter Neary as referred to in the chapter. In a GOLE model, they analyze how vertically integrated firms can explain cross-border mergers and informational trade. Cross border mergers will mitigate the effect of vertical integration on the extensive margins of trade and move the industry toward directions of comparative advantage. The impact of a merger on the extensive margin of a firm will be magnified when merger takes place between two disintegrated firms across borders compared to a merger between a disintegrated firm in one country and a vertically integrated firm in another country. They clearly point out that the relationship between exports and merger should depend on the extent of the vertical structure of the industry.

The subject of production organization is central to tracing the impact of trade at the firm level. Meghna Dutta, in Chapter 10, writes a detailed review of how globalization has led to increased competition among firms. In a bid to remain competitive, firms often resort to production re-organization. The idea of production reorganization remains essential as it allows firms to obtain multiple benefits, such as lower cost of production, better availability of resources, and lesser time taken to produce a commodity. Production reorganization in turn has increased the magnitude of trade in intermediate goods. The identification and association of various agents that produce the consorted effects of production re-organization on the economy are categorically described and analyzed in this chapter. Subsequently, it studies the relationship between production organization and wage inequality in the presence of cross-border investments.

Recourse to tools for correcting distortions in most economies takes the form of taxes and subsidies. The need to address imbalances owing to external shocks originating from regime shifts in external and internal barriers to trade, for example, is closely connected with the objective of a social planner for a given economy. General equilibrium structures, closely reflecting specific characteristics of respective countries have evolved not only to accommodate adjustment tools, but also to comprehend welfare implications of first best policies or those of lower orders. In Chapter 11, Sarbajit Chaudhuri examines the usefulness of the Pigouvian tax policy in dealing with negative production externalities in the presence of labor market distortion using a two-sector full-employment model for a small open developing economy. The core result shows that the socially optimal Pigouvian tax rate may not be necessarily positive and that it crucially hinges both on the degree of labor market frictions and on the magnitude of negative externality that production of environmentally hazardous commodities, that this economy is assumed to produce, generates.

The final one by Marjit, Marjit, and Kar (Chapter 12) provides a new perspective on how to use a general equilibrium framework in evaluation of critical government policies when certain welfare policies have strong and adverse feedback effects. They consider the case where income support policies for unskilled workers financed through taxing skilled workers can lead to effective double taxation. Such policies increase the reservation pay-off of the unskilled worker and lead to a direct cost increase for tax payers who hire unskilled workers for support. This could find ample support and evidence in case of day-care facilities, or hired attendants for older and ailing dependents in a family, and such. The disjuncture of this idea from the natural evolution of higher productivity and the consequent wage premium even for relatively unskilled workers in developed countries is particularly appealing for many developing countries of the south. Furthermore, the changing patterns of cultural and social practices of household support workers in some developed countries can also be explained in terms of the incidence of such public policies, rather than as outcomes of growth. It is shown that welfare policies could lead to some sort of double taxation in a simple Nash bargaining model.

Such general equilibrium approach to policy evaluation opens the door for classifying policies that contain an intrinsic element of double taxation. Pure welfare transfers that do not lead to an increase in costs of production or help to reduce the costs due to productivity effect as opposed to those which are accompanied by policies that increase such cost need to be debated at a greater extent. In this example, the authors highlight an often untold and politically incorrect phenomenon. Interestingly, such policies lead to inequality among the tax payers, the less well-off suffers more than the rich. The regressive nature of the policy leads to an interesting twist to populist vote bank policies. Future extensions of the discussion shall incorporate a fully developed Nash-bargaining solution of the household problem in the presence of labor mobility across sectors and even borders. The exodus of low-skilled workers could create similar pressure on the labor market, which again could be different from natural evolution of the labor market, but a likely outcome of certain public policies. The objective is to observe the impact of double taxation on inter- and intra-group inequality when other factors of production play important roles.

Exploring disparate topics and finding a common thread to bind them together even within the sub-discipline of a field can often be an arduous task. This volume, on the contrary, has naturally benefitted from the pervasiveness of the structure of general equilibrium models. The chapters have utilized many direct and implied results of the structure while carving out independent arguments through the length and breadth of this volume. No less importantly, the authors have spontaneously and enthusiastically supported the plan to present their discussions together in a volume, where the blending of the early innovation to the persistence and creativity of later generations has been smooth and complete.

The editors duly appreciate the authors for their insights and well-articulated contributions as chapters to this volume. The Indian Council of Social Science Research facilitated the event without hesitation and the support of Ministry of Higher Education, Government of West Bengal is duly acknowledged. We thank Srijan Banerjee for research assistance. The comments of anonymous reviewers helped to focus and organize the chapters better. Efforts of the editorial team of Cambridge University Press are sincerely appreciated.

Thoughts and Remarks after 50 Years of Simple General Equilibrium Models

Ronald W. Jones

Introduction

'The Structure of Simple General Equilibrium Models,' published in 1965, has been a popular paper, although it was not my first article. I will first explain as to why this paper was written and then I shall make some remarks about general equilibrium models as used in the theory of International Trade.

Early in the 1960s, at the University of Rochester, we hired Robert Fogel who was finishing his graduate work at Johns Hopkins University. At Rochester, our new department was led by our new Chairman, Lionel Mckenzie. Fogel was at the early stage of his career with focus on economic history. He wanted to use basic economic theory in his work, which at that time, focused on explaining the importance of the development of railroads and how it contributed to the growth in the United States in the mid-nineteenth century while the West was being developed. This was a novel idea among economists studying economic history, but was not generally welcomed by scholars of History. Lionel developed our department by hiring young scholars who would focus on areas such as Labor, International Trade, or other applied areas, and would also expose how basic economic theory was essential in explaining major results in applied areas. Lionel asked me to explain to Bob some of the essentials of General Equilibrium Theory that might be useful to Bob's research. I agreed, explaining to Bob that I would try to make it simple for him and making it simpler would also help me gain a better insight of the theory.

Simplifications

As ascertained by my paper, I thought that traditional approaches to the subject matter found in GE theory were more complicated than need be. Apart from similar questions that mathematical theorists were most concerned about, such as, assumptions leading to *existence*, economists would be more interested in observing causes behind a new equilibrium with spillover effects. The mathematical formulations are preoccupied with establishing conditions that support assumptions for ensuring *existence* of competitive markets. It simultaneously produces well-defined *equilibria* that are *stable*, perhaps *unique,* and those which reveal interesting *normative* properties. Economists have always been more interested in applying how changes that may take place in one market would cause new equilibria to be established in other markets, that is, *general* equilibrium as opposed to *partial* equilibrium. For example, if a pre-existing equilibrium situation is disturbed by a presumed increase in the price of some commodity, how are quantities of other produced commodities changed; in addition, what impact does it have on the returns to factors such as wage rates for labor or price adjustments in capital markets, as well as to the rearrangements made to the allocation of factors to different occupations. To make it simpler, assume only two commodities are produced, each with the use, say, of labor and capital, with both capable of moving freely from one occupation to another, and all being employed in the new equilibrium. If it is assumed that only for one commodity the price changes, in this 2 × 2 model (the Heckscher–Ohlin form found frequently in the theory of International Trade), the following eight unknowns are to be found: two new factor prices, two alterations in commodity outputs, and the changes in the amounts each of labor and capital used in producing each of the pair of commodities. This assumes other things are *given*: the total supplies of labor and of capital, as well as the technology whereby labor and capital are used in production (where technologies allow relative differences in the amounts of labor and capital used in each sector and changes in techniques if factor prices change). As suggested in the 1965 paper, the search for equilibrium changes when a commodity price for one sector is raised can be *simplified.* This is because the amount of labor (and of capital) allocated to each of the sectors is a product of 'how much' production changes in each sector (the output changes, which is already a pair of specified variables) and the 'how' variables, which is the amount of labor (and of capital) required to produce a *unit* of each commodity, (the a_{Lj}'s and a_{Kj}'s, each is dependent on the changes in the factor price ratio, w/r).[1] This alteration leads to the following eight equations of change: a pair of full employment equations, a pair of equations matching the relative change in average costs to the relative change in commodity prices, and four statements linking input changes to changes in factor prices (from the definitions of elasticities of substitution in each sector). Finding solutions become easier because it involves solving only four

---

[1] In earlier days, much attention was paid to changes in the *marginal product* of a factor, say labor, as more of this factor was used along with a fixed amount of another factor, say land, with the outcome revealing *diminishing returns* to the variable factor, that is, diminishing marginal products of labor.

sets of two equations in each. Furthermore, the 'duality' features link factor input changes, as they affect outputs that are similar in form to the effect of commodity price changes on factor prices. All this enables making the eight-equation system easier to comprehend.

An early use of general equilibrium theory was the well-known article in 1941 by Wolfgang Stolper and Paul Samuelson. It enquired about the effect that a country engaged in international trade could have, on its own wage rate, if it were to raise a tariff on imports. This was under the assumption that local production of the importable commodity was more labor-intensive in production than found in its export sector. Their proof depicted how, at Home, such a tariff would cause resources, both labor and capital, to move into the sector producing importables, which is the assumed labor-intensive sector. This would cause the marginal product of labor to increase in the production of importables, as well as raising the capital/labor ratio used to produce exportables. Consequently, the *real* wage rate would have to increase, regardless of taste patterns in consumption. Although not emphasized for many years, the necessity of such a strong result comes from an assumption often made, as a result of which its significance has frequently been lost sight of: production of *each* commodity requires inputs of *both* factors of production. This assumption may be alternatively phrased as follows: there is (assumed) that there is *no joint production*. This means, in each sector, the relative price change of the *single* good produced in that sector must be an *average* of the *two* input price changes. Suppose Good 1, the import-competing product, increases in price and Good 2's price does not change. Since each relative price change must be a positive average of the two factor price changes, the relative return to one factor must increase more than the price of Good 1, and the relative change in the return to the other factor must be less than zero (the change in the price of Good 2). The big winner must be the wage rate, because x_1 is the labor-intensive commodity and the change in the big loser (capital) must be negative (i.e., lower than the price change for Good 2).

A similar result may be observed when we consider the possibility that one of the inputs, say capital, is blessed by an increase in volume, whereas the other input—labor—has not changed in volume. Suppose the commodity prices are held constant. In such a case, the factor prices are also held constant, and therefore even the techniques of production (capital/labor ratios used in each sector). The similarity that this scenario shares with the Stolper–Samuelson result is striking: output of the capital-intensive commodity expands by a greater relative amount than the relative change in overall capital supply, and the output of the labor-intensive commodity must actually *decrease*, as suggested by the famous *Rybczynski* effect.[2]

---

[2] T. M. Rybczynski, 'Factor Endowments and Relative Commodity Price, *Economica* 22 (1955): 336–341.

Technical Progress: The Lack of the Role of Bias When Using Calculus

Now consider the possibility of technical progress, which was the last topic in the 1965 paper. If technical progress is assumed to exist only in the labor-intensive sector, the effect on the wage rate would be similar to that of a price increase in the labor-intensive sector, with a constant price in the capital-intensive sector. Indeed, if both commodity prices were to remain constant, there would nonetheless be a magnified increase in the wage rate, coupled with an actual decline in the return to capital. The Trade economists also agreed that if calculus is used as a technique, then this result would *not* depend on the lack of any *bias* in the manner in which the first commodity is produced. Labor economists questioned the result that the real wage rate must rise (*a' la* Stolper–Samuelson result), if there were a bias that was saving on the required use of labor (compared with capital) at initial factor prices. However, the *calculus* result, that the real wage gain holds *regardless* of any factor bias in the improvement of technology is correct—just as, in equations (3d) and (4d) of the 1965 paper, any factor bias is of second order importance. However, labor economists might be concerned with technical progress that is *finite* in size. *For finite changes, factor bias does indeed have a role to play.*

Figure 1.1 illustrates a three-commodity setting, in which there is finite technical progress in the second commodity. The technological link between the wage/rental ratio and the capital/labor ratio that would be used in production before technical progress takes place is shown by the three upward sloping curves. The more heavily drawn schedule reveals how increases in the economy's capital/labor endowment ratio would, if this ratio was very small, result in only the first commodity being produced. The dark horizontal line connecting the curves for the first two commodities illustrates that before technical progress, the economy would be producing two commodities, 1 and 2, and factor prices would thus be completely determined by the given commodity prices (for the given technology). If K/L ratio increases sufficiently, the economy would concentrate on producing only the second commodity. (An even higher endowment of capital to labor would eventually result in the economy producing both commodities, 2 and 3). If Figure 1 were to show the effects of technical progress in Commodity 2 that had *no* bias, at any given wage/rent ratio, production of the second commodity (if it were still produced) would remain as it would be prior to the technical progress. However, the dark segment along Commodity 2's upward sloping profile (showing that only the second commodity would be produced) would be extended at *both* ends as a result of Commodity 2's price rise. The technical progress in the second commodity would signal that Commodity 2 would be the only commodity produced for a wider range of K/L ratios. However, if we assume that the technical progress in the second commodity was *biased*, in the sense that it was purely *saving capital* per unit of labor, the upward sloping curve for the second commodity would be shifted to the left. Consequently, the step-like function in Figure 1.1 would contain the dotted curve profile.[3] I assume that initially the economy was producing both commodities, 1 and 2, so that progress took place in the capital-intensive sector. The dashed lines in Figure 1.1 illustrate how the step-like section is altered by technical progress.

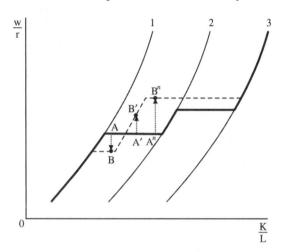

Figure 1.1 Biased technological progress

Figure 1.1 shows three possible positions, **A**, **A'**, and **A"**, for the initial situation in which production takes place for both commodities, 1 and 2. Consider these one at a time. If **A** is the initial production point, the economy produces relatively little of the second commodity, which is the commodity in which technical progress takes place (the relatively capital-intensive commodity). The subsequent lowering of the wage/rental rate is what trade economists would predict (because Good 2 is relatively the capital-intensive commodity at **A** using the calculus technique). However, if initially production takes place at **A'**, the relative wage rate actually would rise, with the *bias* effect, favoring labor. This would dominate the effect of the progress taking place in the capital-important sector of the economy, if there was no bias. An even stronger effect would take place if initially the economy was producing mostly Commodity 2, at **A"**. The economy would then stop producing the labor-intensive first commodity and start producing a small amount of Commodity 3 (as well as Commodity 2), which is even more capital-intensive than the other two. This would help raise the wage rate further than if at **A'**.

---

[3] This diagram appears in Jones (2008), and I apologize for switching attention from purely *labor-saving* progress to purely *capital-saving* progress.

Before proceeding without answering questions concerning possible views of labor economists that could differ from those of trade economists (if they are relying on the use of differential calculus), I suggest a scenario that may be surprising. Suppose we have an economy producing many commodities in competitive markets, and *all* sectors of the economy are blessed with the same degree of technical progress. Suppose such progress is not of the type with *no bias*, but rather is *labor saving of* a severe form: in each industry there is not only the same overall extent of progress, but also the progress is completely labor saving for every commodity.[4] By this, it is meant that at initial factor prices, every industry would use *less* labor per unit of output, but the same amount of capital. Could it be possible that *real* wages nonetheless could increase? The answer would be 'Yes'. Technical progress increases *real* national income, and if progress is, as assumed, purely labor saving, the demand for labor would fall in every industry at the initial factor prices. However, the ensuing fall in the wage rate encourages further hiring of labor. In addition, if the *elasticity of substitution* between capital and labor is sufficiently high in every sector, even with a fall in the wage/rent ratio, the *real wage* could rise. In such a scenario, how high would the elasticity have to be? Consider the average across all sectors for the elasticity of substitution between labor and capital. If this average is greater than unity (the famous Cobb–Douglas case), the real wage rate *must* rise—labor shares in the overall benefit to the society, even though not as much as capital.[5] (The critical value for the elasticity of substitution is the ratio of capital's share in the economy relative to labor's share, which is usually supposed to be around ½). I think such a result might be a little surprising—perhaps not only to labor economists.

The Specific Factor Model, Calculus, and the Gains from Trade

Let me direct your attention to an older type of general equilibrium model, the so-called Specific Factor model. The formal study of this model for use in international trade was discussed in 1971, a few years after my 1965 paper.[6] This model assumes that in each sector there is a factor of production used in all sectors (usually labor), as well as a factor of production used nowhere else in the economy (e.g., different qualities or types of land or capital). Most economists would agree that it is a simpler general equilibrium model than the Heckscher–Ohlin model.

---

[4] Note this is different from what is illustrated in Figure 1.1.

[5] See Jones (1996).

[6] See Jones (1971) and Samuelson (1971). Samuelson refers to this as the Ricardo–Viner model. Indeed this was the model used in Jones (1996) to discuss the possibility that labor could gain even if in all sectors technical progress was purely labor saving in bias.

However, consider how the two models compare in their answers to the question regarding the change in the wage rate caused by an increase in the price of a single produced commodity. This comparison was performed using calculus to obtain the answer, with all other commodity prices as well as factor endowments held fixed. Next, let us consider the two-commodity case (Industries 1 and 2). In the Heckscher–Ohlin case, the answer depends on a single aspect of technology, *viz.*, which commodity is produced with more labor-intensive techniques. If Commodity 1 is relatively labor-intensive, an increase in its price must unambiguously raise the real wage rate. Thereby, let us focus, now, on the Specific Factor model.[7] An increase in p_1 will raise the wage rate, w, by a fraction of the relative price rise. This fraction is the product of *three* further terms, two of which refer to two different aspects of technology. Letting a 'hat' over a variable denotes the *relative* change in that variable, for example, dp_1/p_1 is shown as $\hat{p}_1$, so that

(1) $\hat{w}_1 = \theta_1 \, (i_1 \, s_1) \, \hat{p}_1$

The i_1 term and the s_1 term display a pair of *technological* aspects of the production of the first commodity compared with the average in the economy. The i_1 term refers to the ratio of the relative amount of labor employed in the first industry, λ_{L1}, to the share in national industry that is represented by the first industry, θ_1. The term s_1 refers to a different aspect of technology, *viz.*, how does the elasticity of demand for labor in the first industry, denoted by γ_{L1}, compare with the economy's overall elasticity of demand for labor, denoted by γ_L, which is the weighted average of the two elasticities, $(\lambda_{L1} \, \gamma_{L1} + \lambda_{L2} \, \gamma_{L2})$. The ratio of γ_{L1} to γ_L is greater than one if and only if technology is more flexible in the first industry. Finally, the θ_1 term is the share of the value of national income representing the output of the first sector.

The Specific Factor model differs from the Heckscher–Ohlin 2 × 2 model (or the $n \times n$ model). The difference is that, in the Heckscher–Ohlin model, the only aspect of technology that affects the change in the wage rate is the ranking of the sectors by labor intensity. The *flexibility* of technology in one sector versus the other has no bearing on the result of how much the wage rate changes. In the Heckscher-Ohlin setting, what is probably more surprising is the absence of the *importance* in the national income represented by output in the industry blessed by a commodity price increase. It does not seem to matter if Industry 1, say, is the sector producing hairpins or if it is the sector producing steel. Does this reflect a failure by the Heckscher–Ohlin model to make common economic sense? The answer would be 'No'. Rather, it suggests that *the calculus may not be appropriate for revealing the importance of certain aspects that are related to 'small' changes*

---

[7] Details can be found in the Supplement to Chapter 5, S-17–S-22. Caves, R., J. Frankel, and R. Jones. 2007. *World Trade and Payments*. Tenth edition. Pearson.

(all changes in the differential calculus are 'small'). These, as the label says, are changes that are termed '*secondary* smalls'.

For a useful basic example, consider one of the most important results in the field of economics: the gains from trade. Imagine a country that is in autarky; such a situation could arise by not having any trade with the other countries. International trade could result in gains only if the set of commodity prices in the world market *differs* from those of a country in an autarkic state. However, what would be the outcome under the circumstances outlined in the forthcoming statement? Home is representative of a country in which, among its own inhabitants, internal trade suggests an equilibrium. This equilibrium is represented by a *tangency* of a line whose slope reveals the relative commodity prices in autarky, with an indifference curve, which is also tangent to the point of production on the country's production possibility curve. What would happen if the world price ratio would be different to that at Home, but only by an infinitesimal amount? The 'gain' to the country would be considered a *second-order small*. Gains from trade depend on the world price ratio differing by a *finite* amount from autarky, and such gains are easily portrayed by a simple diagram. This is another example of how finite changes are sometimes required to illustrate relationships that are not identified using the techniques of differential calculus. What is perhaps surprising is that the Specific Factor model, which is simpler than the Heckscher–Ohlin model, shows explicitly the variety of elements available in technology and the importance, in national income, of the output of a sector that has benefited from a price increase. These are elements that are absent (to Heckscher–Ohlin) *when applying calculus*, but become important if changes are finite (as they always are).

In my opinion, the use of general equilibrium models in the field of International Trade Theory is especially important because it allows only *some* markets to be open to trade among countries, whereas other markets are not. Changes that take place in markets present worldwide bring about changes not only to markets that are open to many countries, but also to markets that are open strictly within countries. For example, early Ricardian models assumed that final commodities are often freely traded among countries, whereas factors of production such as labor, land, and capital are not mobile between countries. '*Comparative* advantage' is considered important while explaining world trade models because the models are based on a presumption that at least some factors of production have purely national markets. However, this does not mean that changes in the prices of traded commodities have no impact on returns to labor or other factors of production or on so-called 'non-traded' goods. In world markets, suppose there is an increase in the price of 'Commodity 13', with Home not producing any of it. But if Home consumes some of that commodity, its demand for imports will be negatively affected by the price rise, and this can cause shifts in demand for Home-produced goods. However, this, in turn, can cause changes in wage rates and other returns to factors of production. Alternatively, Home may be a producer, and may indeed be an exporter of Commodity 13. Consequently, the increase in price of Commodity 13 would cause Home's real income to increase, and with it, its demand for some commodities; however, this could also perhaps result in a reduction in its demand for item 13. More modern trade theories do consider international movements for some factors of production, for example, movements of labor between countries in the European Union. The Ricardian trade model assumes only labor was used in production, and for this reason, this model is still useful if the question of interest is whether a country as a whole is worse off or better off because of changes in world markets.

Paradoxical Results

Two important aspects are found in most general equilibrium models used in International Trade theory. They sometimes lead to propositions that are so reasonable that others might say they do not need to use such models—they are too obvious. Alternatively, the GE models may lead to some results that are surprising—even considered *paradoxical*. The models themselves provide the *tools* needed to understand the results; therefore, on understanding the results, the models no longer seem so paradoxical.

Let me illustrate a situation I experienced as an undergraduate (some years ago) at Swarthmore, when I had to take an oral exam (as well as a written exam) given by Professor Kermit Gordon (Williams College). He asked if I was familiar with the Stolper–Samuelson paper. I eagerly replied that Yes, I was. He outlined the following situation: one country levies a tariff on imports that are produced locally by labor-intensive techniques. He questioned as to what would happen to the wage rate. My immediate answer was that it would increase. Thereafter, the following was his next question: what would be the outcome if we were to suppose that the exporting country *retaliates* by raising a tariff on our exported commodity. My first instinct was to say that the wage rate might fall or not increase as much (because, in general, *retaliations* tend to *undo* a previous change), but fortunately, before I did reply, I realized that retaliation under such a circumstance would drive the market even *further* away from free trade; therefore, the wage rate would increase even further. (My changes in expression as I perceived the change in my thought brought a smile on his face even before I had uttered a reply.)

I will point out a few other surprising cases from the history of using GE even in very small-scaled models. The first case that comes to mind is the so-called Metzler (1949) paradox. Metzler paradox also refers to a scenario in which a country levels a tariff on imports. In this scenario, the country is large, and its tariff so weakens the world demand for the imported good that the world price falls even *more* than the amount of tariff. Subsequently, the tariff did not serve to raise the domestic price of the protected commodity, that is, the tariff was not *protective*. This argument was partly responsible for changes in the scenario of the original Stolper–Samuelson result. Consequently, the following was the basic question raised: what effect does an increase in the *domestic commodity* price have on the wage rate if that commodity is labor-intensive? This implies that the Stolper–Samuelson result should question the effect of a given price increase rather than that of a tariff that may not be protective.

Focusing on the Specific Factor model, the first observation made is that, an increase in any commodity price (with other commodity prices kept constant) makes all other industries (each using a different fixed capital) surrender some of their labor (the only mobile factor); subsequently, that one industry expands and all others contract. This statement deserves agreement. At this point, consider instead as to what would happen to factor prices if all commodity prices are constant but one industry (call it Industry 1) gets an increase in its supply of the capital factor, which is used only in that industry, with no changes in the amount of capital used in any other industry. The effect is illustrated as follows: the wage rate is driven up a little (no surprise), and the returns to each and every type of capital will fall. However, one needs to contemplate of the following question: Does the returns to the kind of capital that has increased, fall by more than all the other kinds of capital that remained constant in supply? This may not be necessarily so—it all depends on a simple comparison: if the distributive share of labor in some other industry (say Industry 8) is greater than the labor's share in Industry 1, the return to (specific) capital is driven down by relatively more in Industry 8 than the relative share of specific capital in Industry 1, despite the fact that only the supply of K_1 has increased. There has been no change in any commodity price (by assumption); therefore, in every industry (i) the distributive factor share-weighted average in factor price changes must be zero: $\theta_{Li} w + \theta_{Ki} r_i = 0$. All industries in the country face the same increase in the wage rate; therefore, those industries in which labor's distributive share is greater than Industry 1 must face a reduction in its returns to capital that is *greater* than in the first country, despite the fact that the supply of its capital has not increased. Many other instances can be cited in which results may be quite surprising. For some of these, I refer readers to my fairly recent paper on 'Sense and Surprise in Competitive Trade Theory' Jones (2011).

Higher Dimensional Models

International Trade models often consider only a limited number of countries, commodities produced, and productive factors. The assumption is that small-scale

GE models can capture the characteristics of larger-scale models. However, let us contemplate whether such an assumption would be applicable to three of the most often used models in Trade Theory: the Ricardo model, the Sector-specific model, and the Heckscher–Ohlin model.[8]

First, let us consider The Ricardo Model. It was first published in the early nineteenth century.[9] The model was intended to make use of the concept of *comparative advantage*, explaining how all countries can gain by moving from autarky to free trade in markets with a number of countries. The scenario Ricardo considered is still applicable today as in the following illustration: two countries (say England and Portugal), each capable of producing two commodities (wine and cloth), with a single input, labor, of different capabilities on comparing the two countries; however, there is strict homogeneity within each country. As Ricardo admitted, if each country had a unique commodity in which its labor would require less input per unit output than is required in the other country, considered as the case of 'Absolute Advantage' for each country, there would clearly be an improvement for each country, because it would need to concentrate on producing the good that requires less labor. However, what would be the scenario if one country (say Portugal) is better at producing both commodities than the other country (say England)? Ricardo's great contribution was to argue that open trade between countries could nonetheless result in gains for *both* countries. The necessary background for this assumption is that labor cannot move from country to country, only commodities can get traded. As a consequence, Portuguese labor obtains a higher wage rate than that in England. Both countries gain from international trade. With a_j^i denoting the quantity of labor required to produce a unit of commodity (j) in country (i), Ricardo revealed that England has a *comparative advantage* in producing cloth, while Portugal has a *comparative advantage* in producing wine. This can be represented as follows (with P standing for Portugal, E for England, C for cloth, and W for wine):

(2) $\quad a^E_C / a^E_W < a^P_C / a^P_W$

Trade patterns of production that conform to comparative advantage could also be suggested for a scenario in which only two commodities are produced. However, many countries exist by ordering the kind of ratios shown in (2) by moving from lowest country relative cost of producing cloth compared with wine to the highest country ratio (the world's worst relative producer of cloth). Alternatively, a similar kind of ordering would be possible if there were only two countries but many

---

[8] The reader will find this issue (and others) discussed in Jones, 'On the Value of Small-scale GE models' (2015).

[9] The first edition of David Ricardo's work is *The Principles of Political Economy and Taxation*, 1817.

commodities. To better represent this illustration, consider that the ranking in (2) could also be written as (2') as follows:

(2') $a^E_C / a^P_C < a^E_W / a^P_W$

Each ratio is that of a particular commodity for England (in the numerator) and for Portugal (in the denominator). With more than a pair of commodities, rank the ratios (one for each commodity) from the lowest to highest, similar to the two-country case in (2).

What these suggestions reveal is that the concept of rankings by comparative advantage can easily be applied to the many-country case (with only two commodities), as in (2), or the scenario in which there are many commodities but only two countries (as suggested by (2')). Recently, a somewhat different approach was used that allowed a study of comparative advantages in a trading world consisting of many countries *and* many commodities.[10] Instead of making the change from equation (2) to equation (2'), it is suggested to cross multiply the elements in equation (2) to get equation (2") as follows:

(2") $a^E_C \, a^P_W < a^P_C \, a^E_W$

For the two-country, two-commodity case, the two products found in equation (2") refer to the two possibilities, in which there is one country assigned only to wine and the other only to cloth. Only one of these outcomes could be a possibility in markets that are purely competitive. The inequality states that the efficient assignment in which one country produces wine and one country produces cloth is also that assignment which *minimizes the product* of the labor assignments in that *class* of assignments. Of course, this is the same as shown in (2), but with a comparison of *products* instead of a comparison of *ratios*.

Consider a higher dimensional case with, say, three countries and three commodities, and focus on all the possible assignments in which each country is completely specialized. First, consider the class of complete assignments in which all three countries are specialized. In such a scenario, all three countries are capable of producing the first commodity, and, therefore, none can produce the second commodity or the third commodity. There is only one contender in such an assignment class. In the next class, suppose there is one country assigned to produce Commodity 1, two countries to produce Commodity 2 and no country to produce Commodity 3. There are three contenders in this class of complete assignments. In addition, there is another type of complete specialization in which one country produces the first commodity and the other two produce the third commodity. Similarly, there are assignments where one country produces the second commodity, and the others produce the first commodity. Alternatively, it

---

[10] The procedure is explained in Jones (1961).

could also be that one country produces the second commodity, and both of the others produce the third commodity. Finally, there is an assignment where all three commodities are produced—with one country producing each. There are three ways to produce the first commodity, two ways to produce the second, and only one way to produce the third. That is, there are six possible assignments in which all three commodities are produced. According to my calculations, are a total of 27 possible assignments in the classes of complete assignments in the 3 × 3 situation. The winner in each assignment is the contender that minimizes the product of labor input coefficients. Isn't this complicated? Perhaps, but nowadays, it is so much easier as these calculations are performed by computers. Of course, it is possible that one or two countries are producing a *pair* of commodities. Alternatively, it might also be possible that a single country produces all three commodities. However, these are all varied combinations of the single winner, where you have specified how many countries are assigned to each commodity in that *class* of assignments. Figure 1.2 illustrates the *world transformation schedule* for the case in which there are three countries and only two commodities. Let us first consider that all three countries produce linen. The country with the greatest comparative advantage in producing cloth compared with linen is Country 1. At point **A**, there is a range of the relative price of cloth in terms of linen that would have Country 1 specialized in producing nothing but cloth and the other two countries producing nothing but linen. If the relative price of cloth increases sufficiently, Country 2 will start producing cloth and, at **B**, both countries, 1 and 2 produce cloth and Country 3 still produces linen.

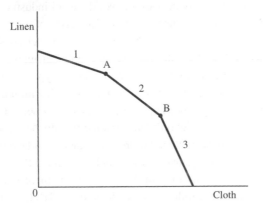

Figure 1.2 World transformation schedule

The 3 × 3 case discussed earlier supports a three-dimensional world transformation surface made of points, lines, and 'flats' along which two of the countries are producing a good in common as well as another (different) commodity. There are 10 *classes* of complete specialization, and within each class, the winning combination is the one that minimizes the product of labor coefficients for all its members.[11] The class that has each country specialized completely in a different commodity so that all three are produced has six possible contenders. The winner, of course, is the one that exhibits the lowest product of labor coefficients.

Let us now focus on the other two cited models, the Specific Factor model and the Heckscher–Ohlin model. An interesting article by Fred Gruen and Max Corden (1970) captures a particularly simple way of providing multi-commodity, multi-factor versions of both these models. They assumed an economy with three commodities and three factors of production, but in only two *sectors*. One sector, the manufacturing sector, produces only one product, textiles, using labor and capital. The other sector is the agricultural sector, with two commodities, wheat and wool, that use labor that is homogeneous and mobile between sectors as well as a different form of 'capital', which they call 'land'. They asked the following question: suppose the economy (they used Australia as an example) imports textiles, and if the economy levies a tariff on imports, could its terms of trade *deteriorate*? In Trade Theory, the common response would be that if ever the terms of trade change, the terms of trade would turn in favor of the tariff-levying country. They explained this phenomenon as follows: as the domestic price of textiles increases, it attracts labor from agriculture, whereas 'capital' is specific to each sector, and therefore, does not move to textiles. As agriculture loses some labor, the output of the more labor-intensive good in agriculture (wheat) falls, but the output of the other commodity in agriculture (wool) actually expands (the Rybczynski effect). Australia is an important producer in the world's wool industry, and the price of wool would fall—leading to a deterioration of its terms of trade.

To move to higher dimensions of the Gruen–Corden model, consider an economy initially disconnected from world trade (i.e., a country in autarky). This economy produces everything it consumes, using a homogenous type of labor that is used in all sectors and is freely mobile between sectors as well, with n different types of 'capital'. When world trade opens up, the country may observe that in all *sectors* many industries disappear, with only the commodity with the greatest comparative advantage in each sector surviving. Alternatively, there may be *one* sector in which a *pair* of industries survives (just as wheat and wool did in the agricultural sector in the Gruen–Corden scenario).[12] In this scenario, if there is (only) one sector that has two commodities produced, it is a form of the Heckscher–Ohlin $\{(n+1) \times$

---

[11] Details are found in Jones (1961).

[12] That is, more commodities produced in the economy in which commodity prices are given in world markets cannot exceed the number of productive factors, because each (competitive) equilibrium must bring average costs equal to commodity price. The number of factors (n + 1) determined in the economy cannot exceed the number of price equal to cost equations.

(n+1)} model, whereas if each sector produces only a single (best) commodity, the economy is of the Specific Factor type.

Using these model specifications, the economy that has what can be described as a Heckscher–Ohlin *nugget,* that is, a (single)sector with two commodities produced (with two factor inputs), is *more* dependent on the array of world commodity prices, with *(n + 1)* commodities produced locally. Such a case is a scenario in which the *economy* produces only *n commodities* but still has *(n + 1)* local factor prices to be determined, as does a many-commodity Sector-specific model. In the Heckscher–Ohlin case, for small changes, only one technological feature (factor-intensive comparisons) links local non-traded factor prices to world commodity prices. In the Sector-specific model, the economy has *(n+1)* factor prices to be determined, but only *n* given world commodity prices to help in the solution. In this scenario, let us recall our discussion on the difference between models of the 2×2 Heckscher–Ohlin case and the Specific Factor case, as illustrated in equation (1). In the latter case, other characteristics of the local economy, namely the *flexibility* of the economy's technology (the s_1 term) and the *importance* in the economy of the commodity whose price has changed (the θ_1 term), are also features of the local economy that influence factor returns.

To analyze the Gruen–Corden model for higher dimensions, let us start by assuming that there are *n* sectors in an economy engaged in trade, with each sector producing only a *single* commodity, a commodity produced with labor and a type of capital specific to that single commodity. Suppose the world price of some commodity, *j*, that is produced in this economy increases. The price rise in sector *j* is passed on to the factors used in its production, leading to the following alignment as shown in (3):

(3) $\hat{r}_j > \hat{p}_j > \hat{w} > 0 = \hat{p}_t$ (for all $t \neq j$) $> \hat{r}_t$

Of the two factors used to produce commodity *j*, capital is specific and is not used in other commodities, whereas labor is used in all sectors, so that the increase in the wage rate is less than the price rise, and the return to capital is greater. All other sectors, where prices have not increased, must experience a fall in the return to their specific capital, because the wage rate has increased, but the price has not.

This scenario of the effect of changes in world markets on factor markets can be compared to the form of the Heckscher–Ohlin model, as suggested by Gruen and Corden. Herein, *(n + 1)* commodities are produced, with commodity *(n + 1)* produced in the *n^{th}* sector as well as commodity *n*, similar to the Gruen–Corden case for the agriculture sector producing wheat and wool. In making this comparison, there are two different kinds of commodity prices to consider. The first is an increase in price for a commodity, *j*, *not* produced in the *n^{th}* sector. In this case, there is *no* change in the wage rate because factor prices are completely determined by changes in the prices of goods, which is n or $(n + 1)$. Therefore, the price changes are as shown in (4):

(4) $\hat{r}_j > \hat{p}_j > \hat{w} = 0 = \hat{p}_t$ (for all t ≠ j) $> \hat{r}_t$ (for all $t ≠ j$)

Compared with the changes in (3), the increase in the returns to sector-specific capital in the jth sector is not as great because the wage rate stays the same, in which case there is no change in any return to capital, except for that in the favored j^{th} sector.

The situation is different if the price change is for either commodity produced in the nth sector, because in that case, the wage rate is affected by the price change. However, in a direction that depends upon whether the price change is for the capital-intensive commodity (assumed to be commodity n) or commodity $(n + 1)$, the labor-intensive sector is in the nth sector. Suppose it is the price of the capital-intensive good in the nth sector that increases, it leads to changes as shown in (5):

(5) $\hat{r}_n > \hat{p}_n > 0 = \hat{p}_t$ (for all $t ≠ n$) $> \hat{w}$

Compared with (4), the return to specific capital in the favoured sector (r_n) increases by a *greater* relative amount because the wage rate falls (because the price change takes place in the capital-intensive commodity (n) in the 2×2 *nugget*). With the fall in the wage rate in all other commodities, the return to capital in those commodities also increases, which is a severe form of *complementarity* among different types of capital. The big looser is labor. The outcome would be rather different if the price increase were for the labor-intensive commodity in the nugget sector, that is commodity $(n + 1)$, as shown in (6):

(6) $\hat{w} > \hat{p}_{(n+1)} > 0 = \hat{p}_t$ (for all $t ≠ (n + 1)$) $> \hat{r}_n$

For such a scenario, labor is the big winner, and the return to capital used in the nth sector is the big looser. If the price increase is for one of the commodities produced in the nugget found in the nth sector of the economy, it is noticed that for this form of the many-sector Heckscher–Ohlin model, the change in factor returns is *more* severe than in the Specific Factor model, in which fewer commodities are produced in world markets.

Conclusion

The scholars in the discipline of International Trade have always been inquisitive about a country's economy when the country moves from autarky to free trade with other countries without completely surrendering their privacy in all markets. Earlier, economists generally assumed that commodity markets were global and factor markets were determined mostly in local markets. Nevertheless, trade, just within a country, could still benefit from general equilibrium models, but the use of such models to study International Trade has resulted in an additional set of questions in markets featuring competitive equilibria. This might be because some markets are local, whereas others are global. This suggestion gives rise to another query: when global markets exhibit changes, what is the effect on other markets, some of which exhibit strictly national markets? The famous paper by Stolper and Samuelson (1941) focused on the effects of real wages of disturbances in tariff levels to commodities that are imported from global markets. This paper helped to promote the usefulness of general equilibrium in competitive markets. International markets are often more competitive than national markets, especially in recent years. Because, with the increase of 'globalization,' transport costs and other costs inhibiting international trade are being reduced. In my paper, Jones (1965), I focused on the methods of analysis in general equilibrium. Consequently, herein, I have attempted to make observations on some of the issues that are addressed in general equilibrium models.

References

Caves, R., J. Frankel, and R. Jones. 2007. *World Trade and Payments.* Tenth edition. Pearson.

Jones, R. 1961. 'Comparative Advantage and the Theory of Tariffs: A Multi-Country, Multi-Commodity Model.' *Review of Economic Studies* 28(3): 161–75.

_____. 1965. 'The Structure of Simple General Equilibrium Models.' *Journal of Political Economy* 73: 557–72.

_____. 1971. 'A Three Factor Model in Theory, Trade and History.' In *Trade, Balance of Payments and Growth,* edited by J. Bhagwati, R. W. Jones, R. Mundell, and J. Vanek. Amsterdam: North-Holland Publishing.

_____. 1974. 'The Small Country in a Many Commodity World.' *Australian Economic Papers* 13: 225–36.

_____. 1996. 'International Trade, Real Wages and Technical Progress: The Specific Factors Model.' *International Review of Economics and Finance* 5(2): 113–24.

_____. 2008. 'Key International Trade Theorems and Large Shocks.' *International Review of Economics and Finance* 17: 103–12.

_____. 2011. 'Sense and Surprise in Competitive Trade Theory.' *Economic Inquiry* 48(1): 1–12.

_____. 2015. 'On the Value of Small-Scale GE Models.' *International Journal of Economic Theory* 11: 155–68.

Metzler, L. 1949. 'Tariffs, the Terms of Trade, and the Distribution of National Income.' *Journal of Political Economy* 57: 1–29.

Rybczynski, T. M. 1955. 'Factor Endowments and Relative Commodity Prices.' *Economica.*

Samuelson, P. 1971. 'Ohlin was Right.' *Swedish Journal of Economics* 73: 365–84.

Stolper, W. and P. Samuelson. 1941. 'Protection and Real Wages.' *Review of Economic Studies* 9: 58–73.

2

Adjustment Costs and Trade Liberalization

Eric W. Bond

Events such as the negotiation of international trade agreements and the entry of China into international markets may require a significant reallocation of resources in a country. The reallocation is from import-competing sectors to exportable sectors. For example, Carneiro (2014) finds that adjustment costs in Brazil could represent between 14 and 42 per cent of the gains from trade, and that the adjustment process can take five years or longer. The question of how economic policy can be used to facilitate this reallocation is important. This is so because ineffective management of the transition can undercut the gains from trade liberalization and undermine the political support currently seen for international trade.

The purpose of this chapter is to characterize the optimal path for tariff rates following the negotiation of a trade agreement between two countries, wherein each country incurs costs for moving resources from import-competing to exportable sectors. It is assumed that these countries can commit to a path for tariffs in the agreement, and that their governments have chosen policies to maximize national welfare. The question we address is as to what form the phase-in period for tariff reductions should take. At one extreme end is the 'big bang' approach, which has been advocated for transition economies. This approach would call for tariffs to be eliminated immediately once an agreement is signed. The alternative is a gradualist approach, which has been the approach more frequently applied in trade agreements. In this approach, the agreed tariff reductions are phased in over a pre-specified period. The analysis in this chapter will focus on how the answer to this question depends on the efficiency of the adjustment process in the countries.

The model analyzed in this chapter is one in which factors located in the import-competing and exportable sectors are fixed in the short run, but can move between sectors in the long run by incurring a resource cost for moving between sectors. The short-run model is similar to the specific factors model of international trade, which was presented in the classic paper by Ronald Jones (1971), and has become the workhorse model in the political economy of trade literature. The model presented herein adds a dynamic element by considering the relocation decision of workers between sectors and allowing for heterogeneity in the tradable goods sectors. As a result, workers may differ in their timing to move out from an import-competing sector or into an exportable sector during a period of trade liberalization.

This chapter is related to several strands of literature that examine the optimal timing for tariff reductions in the presence of adjustment costs. One branch of the literature has examined the optimal path of unilateral trade liberalization for a small open economy when the objective function is the maximization of national welfare. Mussa (1978) examines the adjustment process in a small open economy with a Heckscher–Ohlin production structure and adjustment costs for moving capital between sectors. He obtained the seminal result that when the objective of the government is to maximize the value of output, the competitive path maximizes the discounted value of output when expectations of capital owners are rational. Without distortions, the 'big bang' policy is optimal, because it sends the correct signals to resource owners in the case of a closed economy. In a subsequent paper, Mussa (1982) further develops this model by considering the role of government policy when there are distortions in the adjustment process, which prevent the competitive path from being socially optimal.

Karp and Paul consider a small open economy model with externalities in the adjustment cost process, such that workers do not incur the full social cost of their decision to move between sectors. In this case, the optimal policy will depart from immediate free trade to mitigate this distortion. If the government can commit to a time path for tariffs, the optimal policy will involve the phasing in and phasing out of tariffs in order to mitigate the congestion of workers who are moving between sectors. They also consider the scenario in which the government cannot commit to tariff rates. The approach in this chapter differs from that taken by Mussa and Karp and Paul. The difference lies in the consideration of a trade agreement between two large countries and in the heterogeneity of the mobile factor.

A second strand of the literature has focused on the role played by the government's commitment to tariff rates in a trade agreement wherein there are adjustment costs for moving workers between sectors. Furusawa and Lai (1990) consider the scenario in which countries cannot commit to future trade tariff rates; therefore, the trade agreement must be self-enforcing in nature. They show that the most cooperative tariff that can be sustained under a trade agreement will decline as workers in each country leave the import-competing industry; therefore, the agreement will involve gradual tariff reductions over time.

A final strand of the literature focuses on the role of political constraints. Maggi and Rodriguez-Clare [7] consider a political economy model wherein the government is unable to commit to tariff rates when dealing with a domestic special interest group; therefore, the trade agreement serves as a commitment mechanism for the country. Maggi and Rodriguez-Clare highlight the role played by tariff ceilings under a trade agreement because negotiated tariff ceilings act as a constraint on the negotiation between the government and the interest group, when considering the setting of the tariff.

A similar paper that considers political economy constraints is Bond (2015). This paper deals with a two-country model wherein the government initially puts extra weight on the welfare of factor owners in the import-competing sector. In such a scenario, the optimal path of tariffs when the government can commit to tariff rates involves a gradual tariff reduction that trades on the desire to compensate factor owners against the efficiency cost of slowing the movement of resources out of the import-competing sector. The model presented here differs for the aforementioned model in that the model focuses on the objective function that introduces adjustment costs in the exporting country and allows for heterogeneity of factor owners. Most importantly, the objective function is national welfare maximization and focuses on distortions in the adjustment process.

The first section presents the short run equilibrium in a symmetric two-country trade model with an initial allocation of labor in each country, and description of the adjustment technology. The second section characterizes the adjustment path for an optimal trade agreement between the two countries, starting from an initial protectionist equilibrium. It is shown that Mussa's result on the optimality of immediate elimination of tariffs holds in the two-country model in the absence of distortions. When the distortions take the form of externalities in the adjustment process, an immediate movement to free trade is not optimal, and the tariff can be considered as the second best policy instrument. Static expectations about future prices is also considered. The last section offers some concluding remarks.

The Model

We consider a symmetric two-country model in which factors in the importable and exportable sectors are, in the short run, locked in place due to past decisions. However, in the long run, these same factors are mobile in and out of their respective sectors by incurring a cost of moving. We begin by characterizing the short-run equilibrium for the given initial allocation of workers between sectors, and then introduce the dynamic adjustment process. The quasi-fixity of factors in the model is useful for analyzing the efficient transition path for trade liberalization.

The model considers three goods and preferences for these goods are identical across countries and can be represented at a point in time by the quasi-linear utility function as follows:

$$U(D_1, D_2, D_N) = \sum_{i=1}^{2} u(D_1) + D_N$$

where u(.) is a strictly concave function. Good N is the numeraire good that absorbs all income effects, with the demand for good $i \subset \{1,2\}$ given by $D_i = D(p_i)$.

There are two types of labor in each country, denoted by **m** and **x**, with an equal supply of each type in each country, which we normalize to 1. In the home country, a unit of type **m** labor can produce either a_1 units of Good 1 or 1 unit of the numeraire Good N. Productivity of **m** workers in Sector 1 is assumed to be heterogeneous and takes values in the interval $[\underline{a}_m, \bar{a}_m]$. The distribution function for productivity in Sector 1 given by a continuous function denoted $F_m(a_1)$. A type x worker can produce either a_2 units of Good 2 or 1 unit of Good N, where $a_2 \in [\underline{a}_x, \bar{a}_x]$. The distribution function for productivity of type **x** workers in Sector 2 is given by the continuous function $F_x(a_2)$. Workers are assumed to know their productivity in each sector where they can work, with the distribution function for x workers having a relationship of first-order stochastic dominance with respect to that for m workers, $F_m(a) > F_x(a)$ for $a \subset [\underline{a}_m, \bar{a}_x]$.

In the foreign country, the identification between workers and sectors is reversed as follows: *x* workers can produce Good 1 in the foreign country and m workers can produce Good 2. The distribution of productivities among *x* and m workers is assumed to be common across countries, which in light of the symmetry in demand across countries will give the home country a comparative advantage in production for Good 2 and for the foreign country in Good 1.

Short-Run Equilibrium

At the beginning of each period, the allocation of workers between sectors is determined by past decisions. Workers produce output during the period, and at the end of the period make a decision as to whether to incur a moving cost and move to the other sector where they are employable. Because workers know their productivity type, we assume that the initial allocation of workers to production of Good 1 takes the form $[a_m, \bar{a}_m]$ in the home country and $[a_x^*, \bar{a}_x]$ in the foreign country.

The supply of output in Sector 1 in the respective countries at a point in time will be as follows:

$$X_1(a_m) = \int_{a_m}^{\bar{a}} af_m(a)da \quad X_1^*(a_x^*) = \int_{a_x^*}^{\bar{a}} af_x(a)da$$

where $f_i(a) = dF_i(a)$ is the density function for labor of type i = x, m. We can then denote the excess demand functions for Good 1 in the respective countries as

$$M_1(p_1, a_m) = D_1(p_1) - X_1(a_m) \quad M_1^*(p_1^*; a_x^*) = D_1(p_1^*) X_1^*(a_x) \tag{1}$$

Observe that the above assumptions result in a separability between sectors, which allows us to solve for the price of Good 1 independently of trade policy in

Sector 2. Therefore, in the subsequent discussion, we will focus on behavior in Sector 1, with results for Sector 2 following in accordance to symmetry.

The assumption on the distribution of productivity among type m and x workers ensures that $M_1(p, a) > M_1^*(p, a)$, which with costless labor mobility between sectors will ensure that the foreign country has comparative advantage in Good 1.[1] Assuming that trade barriers take the form of a specific tariff, t, which is imposed on the import-competing sector, the equilibrium foreign price for Good 1 can be solved using the world market clearing condition,

$$M_1(p_1^* + t, a_m) + M_1^* (p_1^*, a_x^*) = 0 \qquad (2)$$

The market clearing condition yields a solution for the foreign price, $\tilde{p}^* (t, a_m, a_x^*)$, with the home country given by $\tilde{p}(t, a_m, a_x^*) = \tilde{p}^* (t, a_m, a_x^*) + t$. The equilibrium price functions have the following properties that will be useful below:

$$\tilde{p}_t^* = \frac{-D'(p)}{D'(p) + D^{*\prime}(p^*)} \in (-1, 0) \qquad \tilde{p}_{a_m}^* = \tilde{p}_{a_m} = \frac{-a_m f_m(a_m)}{D'(p) + D^{*\prime}(p^*)} > 0$$

$$\tilde{p}_{a_x^*}^* = \tilde{p}_{a_x^*} = \frac{-a_\infty^* f_\infty(a_\infty^*)}{D'(p) + D^{*\prime}(p^*)} > 0 \qquad \tilde{p}_t = 1 + \tilde{p}_t^* \in (0, 1) \qquad (3)$$

The immediate impact of an increase in the tariff by the home country is a simultaneous increase in the home country price and a decrease in the foreign country price for Good 1. Increases in productivity of the marginal worker in either country reflects an outflow of workers from Sector 1, which reduces the supply of Good 1 and raises its world price.

Because labor is sector specific in the short run, an increase in home tariff raises wages of m workers at home by the same proportion as the increase in p_1. Consequently, it reduces wages of x workers in foreign country by the same proportion as the decrease in p_1^*.

Trade Liberalization and Transition

The initial equilibrium is assumed to involve positive tariffs in each country. Such a scenario would exist if, for example, the initial equilibrium was the outcome of

---

[1] If workers are costlessly mobile between sectors, an m worker in home will work in sector 1 if $p_1 \geq a_1^{-1}$ and an x worker in foreign will work in sector 1 if $p_1^* \geq a_1^{-1}$. The autarky price in home is determined by the condition that $M_1(p, 1/p) = 0$. Since $\frac{\partial M_1}{\partial p_1} < 0$ and $\frac{\partial M_1}{\partial a} > 0$, we have $M_1(p, 1/p) > M_1^*(p, 1/p)$, which ensures that the home country's autarky price of good 1 will be higher.

a non-cooperative tariff setting game because the Nash equilibrium of this model will exhibit a terms of trade-driven prisoner' dilemma.

The initial equilibrium will have employment in sector 1 of ability levels $\left[a_{m,0} = \dfrac{1}{(p_0^* + t_0)}, \bar{a} \right]$ in home and $\left[a_{x,0} = \dfrac{1}{p_0^*}, \bar{a} \right]$ in foreign, where p_0^* is the

solution to $M\left(p * + t_0, \dfrac{1}{p * + t_0} \right) + M * \left(p*, \dfrac{1}{p *} \right) = 0$. Trade liberalization will

result in an outflow of workers from sector 1 in home and in inflow of workers to sector 1 in foreign. It will be assumed that $\bar{a}_m \tilde{p}\left(0, \bar{a}_m, \bar{a}_m \right) > 1$, which ensures that there is positive output of good 1 in the home country in the free trade equilibrium.

To model the transition from the short-run specific factor model to the long-run equilibrium, we extend the model by considering an infinite number of time periods indexed by s. We assume that workers moving between sectors incur resource costs of relocating to the new sector. Letting I_s denote the number of workers moving between sectors at time s in a country, the cost to the country of moving these workers is given by a convex function $G(I_s)$. This function can represent the physical cost of moving location and searching for a job in the other sector, as well as training costs that might be incurred in the new job.

We focus on the case where the goal of the trade agreement is to maximize sum of welfare of the two countries, where welfare is defined to be the present value of the sum of consumer surplus, producer surplus, and tariff revenue.[2] Due to the separability of sectors, the path of tariffs for Sector 1 is determined by the sum of payoffs from Sector 1 alone. Therefore, we will focus on payoffs in Sector 1 in the subsequent discussion.

Surplus from the home country importable sector in a given period is the sum of consumer surplus, $S(p) = u(D(p)) - p$, surplus earned by m workers in Sector 1,

$\Pi\left(p, a_m\right) = \int\limits_{a_m}^{\bar{a}} \left(ap - 1\right) f_m\left(a\right) da$ and tariff revenue, tM(p; am). This yields the

home payoff function for Sector 1 as follows:

$$V(t, a_m, a_x^*) = S(\tilde{p},) + \Pi(\tilde{p}, a_m) + tM(\tilde{p}, a_m) \tag{4}$$

Observe that an increase in the home tariff has both terms of trade and trade volume effects, $V_t = -M\left(\tilde{p}, a_m\right) \tilde{p}_t^* + tM_p\left(\tilde{p}, a_m\right) \tilde{p}_t$, so that the home country's optimal tariff is positive.

---

[2] In the symmetric model we consider this without loss of generality, because it will be equivalent to maximizing welfare of each individual country. With asymmetries, this objective requires the ability to make transfers of Good N between countries.

Welfare of the foreign country exportable sector is the sum of foreign consumer surplus and surplus earned by foreign x workers in sector 1, $\Pi^*\left(p^*, a_x^*\right) =$ $\int_{a_x^*}^{\bar{a}}\left(ap^* - 1\right)f_x\left(a\right)da$. Foreign surplus from its export sector will be $V^*\left(t, a_m, a_x^*\right)$

$= S(\tilde{p}) + \Pi^*\left(\tilde{p}, a_x^*\right)$. The foreign welfare function has the property that

$V_t^* = -M_1^*\left(p_1^*, a_x^*\right)dp_t^* < 0$, which reflects the adverse effect of the home tariff

on foreign's terms of trade.

World welfare from sector 1 in a given period is the sum of home and foreign welfare,

$$W\left(t, a_m, a_x^*\right) = V\left(t, a_m\right) + V^*\left(t, a_x^*\right) \tag{5}$$

Differentiation of the world welfare function yields properties that will be useful as follows:

$$W_t\left(t, a_m, a_x^*\right) = tD'\left(\tilde{p}\right)\tilde{p}_t$$

$$W_{a_m}\left(t, a_m, a_x^*\right) = \left(1 - a_m\tilde{p}^*\right)f_m\left(a_m\right) \tag{6}$$

$$W_{a_x^*}\left(t, a_m, a_x^*\right) = \left(1 - a_x^*\tilde{p}^*\right)f_x\left(a_x^*\right)$$

For a given allocation of labor in Sector 1, we obtain the standard result, that is, world welfare is maximized with t = 0. The home country terms of trade gain is simply a redistribution between countries, so tariff increases will reduce world welfare by reducing the volume of trade. As a result, reciprocal trade liberalization has the potential to benefit both countries. A movement of labor out of Sector 1 in either country will increase world welfare if the wage in Sector N exceeds the marginal revenue product of a worker in Sector 1 when evaluated at world prices. The world price is the relevant measure for the value of a unit of labor in Sector 1. This is so because the world price represents the social value of a unit of Good 1.

Trade Agreements and Optimal Adjustment

We begin by characterizing the optimal policy for a social planner that can choose a time path for tariffs, which is as follows:

$$t = \left\{t_0, \ldots\right\}$$

In addition, the minimum productivity level of a worker in Sector 1 in each country is also characterized as follows:

$$a_{m,1} = \left\{a_{m,1}, \ldots\right\} \text{ and } a_{x,1}^* = \left\{a_{x,1}, \ldots\right\}$$

These characterizations help to maximize world welfare, given an initial allocation $\left\{ a_{m,0}, a_{x,0}^* \right\}$ of workers in Sector 1. We then consider a scenario where the social planner's only instrument is the tariff.

Letting $\beta \in (0, 1)$ denoted the per period discount factor, the present value of world surplus in sector 1, net of adjustment costs, will be

$$\Omega\left(t, a_{m,1}, a_{x,1}^*\right) = \sum_{s=0}^{\infty} \left[W\left(t_s, a_{m,s}, a_{x,s}^*\right) - G\left(I_s\right) - G*\left(I_s^*\right) \right] \beta^s \tag{7}$$

Since the social planner is able to choose the allocation of labor between sectors, the optimal tariff policy is the solution to $W_t\left(t, a_m, a_x^*\right) = 0$, which from (6) requires $t_s = 0$ for all s. Free trade is optimal in all periods because the only effect of $t \neq 0$ is to distort the allocation of the good in consumption between countries.

Assuming that the initial allocation of labor is such that $\beta(1 - a_{m,0} p * (0, a_{m,0}, a_{x,0}^s))/(1 - \beta)$ and $\beta(a_{m,0} p * (0, a_{m,0}, a_{x,0}^s) - 1) / (1 - \beta)$ exceed $G'(0)$, the planner can raise welfare by moving some workers into sector 1 in foreign and out of sector 1 at home. We will have a_m non-decreasing and a_x^* non-increasing along the optimal path, so $I_s = F_m\left(a_{m,s+1}\right) - F_m\left(a_{m,s}\right)$ and $I_s^* = F_x\left(a_{x,s}^*\right) - F_x\left(a_{x,s+1}^*\right)$. The necessary conditions for choice of labor allocation to sector 1 in period s in the respective countries are

$$\left(1 - a_{m,s} \tilde{p} * \left(0, a_{m,s}, a_{x,s}^*\right)\right) + G'\left(I_s\right) - G'\left(I_{s-1}\right) / \beta = 0 \tag{8}$$

$$\left(a_{x,s}^* \tilde{p} * \left(0, a_{m,s}, a_{x,s}^*\right) - 1\right) + G'\left(I_s^*\right) - G'\left(I_{s-1}^*\right) / \beta = 0$$

If the planner moves the worker with ability $a_{m,s}$ out of sector 1 at home at the end of pe'riod $s - 1$, a moving cost of $G'(I_{s-1})$ is incurred. It the planner delays the move until the end of period s, there is a productivity loss of $\left(1 - a_{m,s} \tilde{p} * \left(0, a_{m,s}, a_{x,s}^s\right)\right)$ in period s plus a moving cost of $G'(I_s)$ at the end of periods s. The necessary condition (8) requires that the planner be indifferent between moving at $s - 1$ and delaying until s on the optimal path. A similar interpretation applies to the necessary condition for moving labor into sector 1 in the foreign country. The steady state employment levels in the respective sectors can be obtained by solving (8) for a_m and a_x^* at $I_S = I_S^* = 0$.

We can illustrate the optimal policy for two specific examples of adjustment cost. Suppose first that the adjustment cost function is linear, $G(I) = \gamma I$. The necessary conditions in this case require that

$$\gamma = \beta\left(1 - a_{m,s}p*\left(0, a_{m,s}, a_{x,s}^*\right)\right) / (1 - \beta) \tag{9}$$

$$\gamma = \beta\left(a_{x,s}^* p*\left(0, a_{m,s}, a_{x,s}^*\right) - 1\right) / (1 - \beta)$$

for all s, which means that the present value of the wage differential between sectors equals the constant marginal cost of moving. A similar interpretation applies for the foreign country, where workers is sector N have an incentive to move to sector 1. if a pair $\left\{a_m, a_x^*\right\}$ solve (9) at some time s' then it applies for all s. In this case all movement of labor will occure at the end of period 0. so that the employment levels jump immediately to the steady state levels $\left\{a_m^s, a_x^{*s}\right\}$ that solve (9).

Will $\gamma > 0$, the ability of the marginal worker in sector 1 will not be equalized in the steady state, because the historical location of workers affects the return to working in sector 1 relative to sector N.

Differentiatin (9) yields the following comparative statics result:

$$\frac{da_m^s}{d\gamma} = \frac{\left(\tilde{p} + a_x^* \tilde{p}_{\infty \infty^*} + a_m \tilde{p}_{a_x^*}\right)(1 - \beta)}{\Delta\beta} < 0$$

$$\frac{da_x^{*s}}{d\gamma} = \frac{-\left(\tilde{p} + a_m \tilde{p}_{a_m} + a_x^* \tilde{p}_{a_m}\right)(1 - \beta)}{\Delta} > 0 \tag{10}$$

where $\Delta \equiv -\left(p^e + a_m p_{a_m}^e + a_x^* p_{a_x^*}^e\right) p^e < 0$. Increase in γ raises the cost of moving between sectors, which will lower the threshold productivity for remaining in sector 1 at home and raise the threshold productivity for moving into sector 1 in foreign.

A second example is one with quadratic adjustment costs and a uniform distribution of ability for each type of labor, $G(I) = gI^2/2$ and $F_i(a) = \dfrac{a_i - \underline{a}_i}{\bar{a}_i - \underline{a}_i}$ for $i \in \{m, x\}$. In this case $G'(I_s) - G'(I_{s-1})/\beta = -g\left(a_{m,s+1} + (1-\beta)a_{m,s} - a_{m,s-1}\right)/\left(\beta\left(\bar{a}_m - \underline{a}_m\right)^2\right)$, so that the adjustment process will be pair of second order difference equations. The socially optimal policy results in gradual adjustment of labor in each country, with equalization of factor returns between Sectors 1 and N achieved asymptotically. With strictly convex adjustment costs, it pays to delay movement of more productive workers in order to take advantage of the lower moving costs that result from delay.

Privately Optimal Adjustment

We now consider the decentralized solution, where the countries set tariffs in the trade agreement and the workers make location decisions to maximize the present value of their wage income net of adjustment costs.

Let $c_{s'}(s)$ denote the expected moving cost faced by a type m worker in the home country at time $s > s'$ and $p_s^e(u)$ the price expected to prevail at time $u > s'$ based on information available at time s. We denote lifetime income, discounted to time s, of a worker of ability a who moves from sector 1 to N at time $s > s'$ by

$Y_{s'}(a, s) = \sum_{u=s'}^{s} a p_{s'}^e(u) \beta^{u-s'} + \sum_{u=s+1}^{\infty} \beta^{u-s'} - c_{s'}(s) \beta^{s-s'}$. The optimal time to move

from sector 1 for a worker with ability a based on information at time s' is $\hat{s}_{s'}(a) = $

arg max$_s$ $Y_{s'}(a, s)$. A necessary condition for a worker in sector to move at time s

$- 1$ is that moving at $s - 1$ yield a higher payoff than delaying for another period,

$Y_{s-1}(a, s) - Y_{s-1}(a, s - 1) = \beta\left(a p_{s-1}^e(s) - 1\right) + c_{s-1}(s - 1) - c_s(s)\beta < 0$.[3]

Assuming that expectations are common across all workers, $Y_{s-1}(a, s) - Y_{s-1}(a, s-1)$ is increasing in a. If a worker with ability a finds it optimal to move at time $s - 1$, then so would all workers of ability $a' < a$.

The set of workers moving between sectors at the end of period $s - 1$ at home will be an interval of workers $[a_{m,s-1}, a_{m,s}]$, with the marginal worker at time s being the one who was indifferent between moving at $s - 1$ and delaying the move until $\underline{s}$ as follows:

$$a p_{s-1}^e(s) - 1 + c_{s-1}(s - 1) - c_s(s) / \beta = 0 \qquad (11)$$

The impact of the tariff reduction on m workers will be greatest on those with the largest values of a who remain in the import-competing sector, since they have the greatest degree of sector specificity.

If workers have perfect foresight, $p_{s'}^e(s)$ and $c_{s'}(s)$ are independent of s' for all s and s' and the choice of time of leave will be independent of s'. With perfect foresight, workers have no regrets about the time of their moving decisions. When workers do not have perfect foresight, we have two possibilities that involve ex-post regret on the part of workers on the timing of their move. One possibility is that workers are overly optimistic about the benefits of moving, so that some would have

---

[3] This condition will also be sufficient if $\beta\left(a p_{s-1}^e(s') - 1\right) + c_{s-1}(s' - 1) - c_s(s')\beta$ is non-increasing in s', which can be interpreted as requiring the returns to delay to be non-increasing. If the cost of moving is a constant in all periods, this condition will be satisfied if the expected price be non-increasing over time.

been better off by delaying their move for another period.[4] The other possibility is that workers are overly pessimistic about the returns from moving, and would have preferred to move one period earlier.

In the foreign country, the lifetime income discounted to time s_o of a worker who moves to Sector 1 at time $s \geq s'$ is $Y_{s'}^*(a, s) = \sum_{u=s'}^{s} \beta^{u-s'} + \sum_{u=s+1}^{\infty} a p_{s'}^{*e}(u)\beta^{u-s'} - c_s^* \beta^{s-s'}$. In this case high ability workers have a greater value of moving between sectors than low ability workers, so the optimal entry time to sector 1 in the foreign country is non-increasing in a. The set of workers moving between sectors at time s will be an interval of abilities $\left[a_{x,s}^*, a_{x,s-1}^*\right]$, with $a_{x,s}^*$ determined by the condition

$$a_{m,s} p_s^{*e} - 1 + c_{s-1}^*(s) - c_{s-1}^*(s-1)/\beta = 0 \tag{12}$$

The biggest winners in the exportable sector are those with the highest ability. When the planner's only policy instrument is the path of tariffs specified in the trade agreement, the social planner is unable to choose the time paths $a_{m,1}$ and $a_{x,1}^*$ directly.

The optimization problem for the decentralized solution is to maximize the objective function (5) subject to the constraints (11) and (12) that determine the timing of worker moves between sectors.[5]

Comparing the rules for worker moves in the decentralized solutions with those from the socially optimal solutions, (8), it can be seen that they will coincide if

$$p_s^e = p_s^{*e} = p*\left(0, a_{m,s}, a_{x,s}^s\right), c_s = G'\left(I_s\right) \text{ and } c_s^* = G'\left(I_s^*\right)$$

for all s. If workers rationally anticipate the prices that will prevail in future periods and the costs of adjustment they face equal the marginal social cost of moving workers, then the decentralized moving constraints will not bind, and the optimal policy will be immediate free trade. Observe that the optimality of free trade when there are no distortions in the adjustment process is the same as that obtained by Mussa (1978) for the small country case. The results are similar because the objective function of the trade agreement eliminates the incentive to manipulate the terms of trade along the optimal path.

---

[4] We assume that moving costs are sufficiently high such that workers who regret the move do not find it profitable to move back.

[5] There will also be mobility constraints arising from the potential for home workers in the N sector to move to Sector 1 and for foreign workers in Sector 1 to move to Sector N. Under the assumptions made herein, the path of prices will be monotone, and these additional mobility constraints will be slack throughout the adjustment process.

Distortions with Constant Marginal Moving Costs

To illustrate the role of expectations and distortions in the adjustment process, we continue to analyze the case in which workers face constant marginal costs of adjustment. The case with constant marginal costs of adjustment is useful for identifying the role of distortions, because all movement of labor occurs at the end of period 0 in the socially optimal solution. The question that we address in this section is whether a given distortion would result in too little or too much movement of labor between sectors relative to the social optimum if the trade agreement were to be set at $t_s = 0$ for all s. This case provides some intuition about how departures from immediate free trade might affect welfare in the presence of distortions. The necessary conditions for the optimal policies in the general case are presented in the Appendix.

We first consider the case in which the private cost of adjustment between sectors is a constant, γ^p, that may differ from the social cost of the search. Suppose that worker anticipate a free trade policy forever and forecast future prices according to $\tilde{p}(t, a_m, a_x^*)$ with perfect foresight about future employment levels. With these assumptions, we obtain the same steady state as in (9) with γ replaced by γ^p. Thereafter, we can use the comparative statics result (10) to show that when $\gamma > \gamma^p$, the employment level in Sector 1 at home will be too low relative to the socially optimal level, and that in a foreign country, the employment level in Sector 1 will be too high relative to the socially optimal level. When workers do not bear the full social cost of moving, there is too much movement between sectors.

The most efficient method for dealing with this problem would be to tax movement between sectors by an amount $(\gamma - \gamma^p)$. This results in workers facing the full social cost of their decision. This would be equivalent to directly choosing the employment levels in the planner's problem. In the absence of this labor market intervention, the tariff can be used to reduce the amount of movement out of the import-competing sector at home and into the exportable sector in foreign. In the case of constant marginal costs, this tariff would be a constant over time. In the case of strictly convex adjustment costs, the tariff would be phased out over time.

An export tax in the foreign country would have the same effect of slowing mobility as would a tariff because the export tax would raise the home price and reduce the price in the foreign market. Thus, the export tax is a redundant policy instrument in this case. It should be emphasized, however, that the tariff/export tax is a second-best instrument. This is so because it also has the effect of distorting the consumption decision. Because the tariff at time 0 has no effect on the location decisions for $s > 0$, the optimal policy would involve $t_o = 0$ even when $(\gamma \neq \gamma^p)$. This result is analogous to that obtained by Karp and Paul (1994) on the phasing in of protection in the optimal agreement, and is based on the assumption that the signing of the trade agreement comes as a surprise to workers. If in practice there is a delay between the signing of the agreement and its actual implementation, then t_o will have an impact on worker's decision while considering location.

A second type of distortion arises if workers do not have perfect foresight about future prices. Consider a scenario in which the expectations of workers in each country are static, so that a free trade policy will result in an expected price of $p_L^e = p_L^{*e} = \tilde{p}\left(0, a_{m,0}, a_{x,0}^*\right)$. Since $a_m^S > a_{m0}$ and $a_x^{*S} < a_{x0}^*$, workers with static expectations fail to take into account the impact pact of labor reallocations on the world output of sector 1 in period 1. Suppose that the $\tilde{p}\left(0, a_{m,0}, a_{x,0}^*\right) > \tilde{p}\left(0, a_m^S, a_x^{*S}\right)$,

which means that with static expectations there will be too many workers in Sector 1 in both the home and foreign countries relative to the social optimum. Tariff imposed in period 0 would mitigate the oversupply of workers in Sector 1 in foreign. However, this would worsen the oversupply of workers in home. The tariff represents a poor policy instrument for dealing with an expectations-driven distortion in the two-country case. Better policy instruments would be ones that allowed the producer price of Good 1 to move in the same direction in both countries.

In contrast to the case with distortions in moving costs, the tariff in period 0 has an impact on the worker's decision while considering location. Such an outcome persists even if the agreement comes as a complete surprise. With static expectations, the period 0 price affects beliefs about future prices, which could result in the choice of $(t_0 \neq 0)$ in the optimal agreement.

Conclusion

This chapter has characterized the optimal time path for tariffs in a trade agreement with two large countries. This is done under the assumption that the objective of the government is to maximize national welfare. It was observed that immediate free trade is optimal in the absence of distortions. Such a result continues to hold good in the presence of adjustment costs in both countries and heterogeneity of factor owners. In the presence of distortions as a result of externalities in the adjustment process in both countries, immediate free trade will result in an inefficiently high level of movement between sectors in both countries, especially when the private cost of moving is lesser than the social cost. In this case, the tariff can be used as a second-best instrument to slow adjustment in both countries.

In a scenario where the distortion is as a consequence of static expectations on the part of factor owners, it results in them anticipating a price of the home importable that is too high in the case of immediate free trade. Moreover, there will be too little movement of factors out of import-competing sectors and too much movement into exportable sectors. In this case, the tariff will not be as effective an instrument for dealing with the distortion, and the adjustment process will be delayed.

Can this analysis be used to explain the presence of the phase-in periods for tariff reductions that are included in virtually all bilateral and multilateral trade agreements? The existence of externalities in the adjustment process is a potential justification for the inclusion of phase-in periods, although they are better handled by factor market policies. On the other hand, distortions arising from misperceptions about the gains from moving do not give a clear argument for gradual phase-outs of tariff protection.

Appendix

The optimization problem is to maximize (5) subject to the labor mobility constraints (11) and (12).

$$
\max_{t, a_{m,1}, a^*_{x,1}} L = \sum_{s=0}^{\infty} [W(t_s, a_{m,s}, a^*_{x,s}) - G(I_s) - G^*(I^*_s) + \lambda_s \left((1 - a_{m,s} p^e_{s-1}(s))\right)
$$

$$
+ c_s - c_{s-1} / \beta) + \lambda^*_s \left((a^*_{x,s} p^{*e}_{s-1}(s) - 1) + c^*_s - c^*_{s-1} / \beta\right)]\beta^s
$$

$$(13)$$

where $\lambda(\lambda^*)$ is the current value multiplier associated with the home (foreign) labor mobility constraint. The multiplier has the interpretation of being the impact on welfare of increasing the worker's cost of moving at the end of period s relative to s – 1. The multiplier will be negative if labor is moving too rapidly relative to the social optimum. Therefore, an increase in the cost of delay to workers will tighten the constraint. The multiplier will be positive if labor is moving too slowly relative to the social optimum.

In the case where workers have perfect foresight about future prices, the necessary conditions for choice of t_s, $a_{m,s}$ and $a^*_{x,s}$ are

$$
\left(t_s D'(\tilde{p}) - \lambda_s a_{m,s}\right)\tilde{p}_t + \lambda^*_s a^*_{x,s}\tilde{p}^*_t = 0 \tag{14}
$$

$$
\left(1 - a_{m,s}\tilde{p}\right) + G'(I_s) - G'(1_{s-1}) / \beta - \lambda_s \left(\tilde{p} + a_{m,s}\tilde{p}_{am}\right) + \lambda^*_s a^*_{x,s}\tilde{p}^*_{am} = 0 \tag{15}
$$

$$
\left(a^*_{x,s}\tilde{p}^* - 1\right) + G'(I^*_s) - G'(I^*_{s-1}) / \beta - \lambda_s a_{m,s}\tilde{p}_{a_\infty} + \lambda^*_s \left(\tilde{p}^* + a^*_{x,s}\tilde{p}^*_{a_x}\right) = 0 \tag{16}
$$

In the case where demand is linear with slope –b, we can rewrite (14) as follows:

$$
t_s = \left(\lambda_s a_{m,s} + \lambda^*_s a^*_{x,s}\right) / b
$$

The tariff will be positive in period of s if $\lambda_s a_{m,s} + \lambda_s^* a_{x,s}^* < 0$, which occurs when the social planner wants to delay movement of labor between sectors. A tariff raises the price of price of Good 1 at home and lowers it abroad, which tends to slow the movement of labor in each country.

Substituting from (11) and (12) into (15) and (16) and using (3) yields the following:

$$\left(G'(I_s) - G'(I_{s-1}) / \beta\right) - \left(c_s - c_{s-1} / \beta\right) = \lambda_s \tilde{p} + \left(\lambda_s a_{m,s} - \lambda_s^* a_{x,s}^*\right)\tilde{p}_{a_m} \quad (17)$$

$$\left(G'(I_s^*) - G'(I_{s-1}^*) / \beta\right) - \left(c_s^* - c_{s-1}^* / \beta\right) = \lambda_s \tilde{p}^* + \left(\lambda_s a_{m,s} - \lambda_s^* a_{x,s}^*\right)\tilde{p}_{a_x}^*$$

For the case of constant marginal adjustment costs, the left hand side of each equation in (17) becomes $\left(\gamma^P - \gamma\right)(1 - \beta) / \beta$, so there is a presumption that $\left(\gamma^P - \gamma\right) = \text{sgn}\,\lambda = \text{sgn}\,\lambda^*$. When the private cost of moving is less than the social cost, world welfare is maximized by using a tariff to slow the movement of labor between sectors. In addition, note that in the case of constant marginal adjustment costs, the left-hand side will be a constant for all s. Therefore, the adjustment to the steady-state level can be achieved in one period. We can also consider a scenario in which factor owners do not have perfect foresight. If expectations are static, we have $p_{s-1}^e(u) = \tilde{p}\left(t_{s-1}, a_{m,s-1}, a_{x,s-1}^*\right)$ for all $u \geq s$. Assuming that $c_{s'}(s) = G'(I) = \gamma$ for all s and s' and $D'(p) = -b$, the necessary conditions for choice of t_s with the static expectations is $t_s = \beta\left(\lambda_{s+1} a_{m,s+1} + \lambda_{s+1}^* a_{x,s+1}^*\right) / b$

The difference from the case with perfect foresight is that with static expectations, an increase in the tariff at s affects the exit decisions in home and foreign in period s + 1 rather than s.

The necessary conditions for choice of $a_{m,s}$ and $a_{x,s}^*$ are

$$a_{m,s}\left(\tilde{p}\left(t_{s-1}, a_{m,s-1}, a_{x,s-1}^*\right) - \tilde{p}*\left(t_s, a_{m,s}, a_{x,s}^*\right)\right) = \lambda_s \tilde{p}\left(t_{s-1}, a_{m,s-1}, a_{x,s-1}^*\right)$$

$$+ \left(\lambda_{s+1}\, a_{m,s+1} - \lambda_{s+1}^* a_{x,s+1}^*\right)\tilde{p}_{a_m}\left(t_s, a_{m,s}, a_{x,s}^*\right)$$

$$a_{x,s}^*\left(\tilde{p}\left(t_{s-1}, a_{m,s-1}, a_{x,s-1}^*\right) - \tilde{p}*\left(t_s, a_{m,s}, a_{x,s}^*\right)\right) = -\lambda_x^* \tilde{p}*\left(t_{s-1}, a_{m,s-1}, a_{x,s-1}^*\right)$$

$$+ \left(\lambda_{s+1}\, a_{m,s+1} - \lambda_{s+1}^*\, a_{x,s+1}^*\right)\tilde{p}_{a_\infty}^*\left(t_s, a_{m,s}, a_{x,s}^*\right)$$

The left-hand side in each equation represents the difference between the beliefs of workers regarding the price of Good 1 and the world price of Good 1. When the left hand is positive, workers value Good 1 at a greater value than its value on world markets. Therefore, workers will put too much value on being in Sector 1. The right-hand side in each equation is the effect of an additional worker on the labor mobility constraint.

In cases where there is a tendency for too much movement of workers to Sector 1 at home (i.e., the right-hand side is negative), then trade policy should be used to reduce worker's beliefs about the domestic price of Good 1 below its world price. In the foreign country, on the other hand, too much movement will result in an incentive to have the price of Good 1 in the foreign market decline over time. In contrast to the case with distortions in the cost of moving, the adjustment in this case will take more than one period.

References

Bond, E. W. Forthcoming. 'Compensation, Gradualism, and Safeguards.' In *The WTO and Economic Development*, edited by Benjamin Zissimos.

Dix-Carneiro, R. 2014. 'Trade Liberalization and Labor Market Dynamics.' *Econometrica* 82(3): 825–85.

Furusawa, T. and E. Lai. 1997. 'Adjustment Costs and Gradual Trade Liberalization.' *Journal of International Economics* 49: 333–61.

Jones, R. W. 1971. 'A Three Factor Model in Theory, Trade, and History.' In *Trade, the Balance of Payments, and Growth*, edited by J. Bhagwati, R.W. Jones, R. A. Mundell, and J. Vanek. Amsterdam: North Holland Publishing.

Karp, L. and T. Paul. 1994. 'Phasing in and Phasing out Protectionism with Costly Adjustment.' *Economic Journal* 104: 1379–92.

Lapan, H. E. 1978. 'International Trade, Factor Market Distortions, and the Optimal Dynamic Subsidy.' *American Economic Review* 66: 335–46.

Maggi, G. and A. Rodriguez-Clare. 2007. 'A Political Economy Theory of Trade Agreements.' *American Economic Review* 97: 1374–406.

Mussa, M. 1978. 'Dynamic Adjustment in the Heckscher-Ohlin Samuelson Model.' *Journal of Political Economy* 86(5): 775–91.

————. 1982. 'Government Policy and the Adjustment Process.' In *Import Competition and Response*, edited by J. Bhagwati. Chicago: University of Chicago Press.

3

Farsightedly Stable FTA Structures

The Roles of Preexisting Tariff Rates

Noritsugu Nakanishi[1]

Introduction

Since the late 1980s, preferential (or regional) trade agreements such as customs unions (CUs) and free trade agreements (FTAs) have been growing rapidly in number and are becoming more prevalent in the international trade scene. Well-known examples of such preferential trade agreements include the European Union (EU), the North American Free Trade Agreement (NAFTA), the South American Common Markets (MERCOSUR), and the Association of South-East Asian Nations (ASEAN). Even Japan, which has for long been advocating for a multilateral approach to trade liberalization under the GATT/WTO regime, has already concluded a number of bilateral FTAs, which are sometimes referred to as the Economic Partnership Agreements (EPAs), with Singapore, Mexico, Malaysia, the Philippines, Chile, and other countries.[2]

[1] This is a substantially extended version of the paper formerly entitled 'Stable FTA Structure—An Application of the von Neumann-Morgenstern Stable Set to International Trade.' The author is grateful to Professors Eric Bond, Ngo Van Long, Yasukazu Ichino, Toru Kikuchi, Sugata Marjit, Saibal Kar, Biswajit Mandal, and the participants of the conferences held in the Tokyo Institute of Technology (28 February–2 March, 2011) and in the Centre for Studies in Social Sciences in Calcutta (17–18 November, 2015) for their valuable comments and suggestions. He also acknowledges the financial support of the Japan Society for the Promotion of Science [Grant-in-Aid for Scientific Research (A) No.~22243024 and No.~16H02016].

[2] WTO has reported in its website (as of 6 July 2016) that 'Regional trade agreements (RTAs) have become increasingly prevalent since the early 1990s. As of 1 February 2016, some 625 notifications of RTAs (counting goods, services, and accessions separately) had been received by the GATT/WTO. Of these, 419 were in force. These WTO figures correspond to 454 physical RTAs (counting goods, services, and accessions together), of which 267 are currently in force.'

Bhagwati (1991, 1993) has argued that this trend of regionalism/bilateralism is harmful to the accomplishment of *global free trade* under the auspices of the GATT/WTO regime, which has been traditionally considered to be *efficient* and/or *welfare enhancing* from the point of view of the world as a whole. Further, he has raised questions as to whether preferential trading blocs (CUs and/or FTAs) reduce or increase the welfare of the world and whether the prevalence of bilateralism/ regionalism can eventually lead to a situation where the welfare of the world is maximized. In other words, he raises a question as to whether preferential trading blocs can be a 'building block' for or a 'stumbling block' against the achievement of global free trade. The former can be traced back to the question raised by Viner (1950) whether preferential trading blocs could be trade-creating or trade diverting. The latter is now known as the 'dynamic time-path' question.[3]

To answer these questions raised by Bhagwati (1991, 1993), a considerable number of theoretical as well as empirical literature has emerged. Recent theoretical studies (on the 'dynamic time-path' question) can be split into the following two interesting approaches: one approach is based on the coalition/network formation games, and the other approach is based on some 'dynamic' games.[4]

For example, Yi (1996, 2000), Das and Ghosh (2006), and Saggi and Yildiz (2010) have followed the line of coalition formation game approach. Yi (1996) has constructed a model with *ex ante* symmetric countries, in which countries intend to form CUs of certain sizes. In his model, global free trade is *efficient* (in the sense that the welfare of the world is maximized), formation of CUs exhibits *negative externalities* on the welfare of the outsider countries, and international income transfers are not allowed. He has shown that global free trade is the unique Nash equilibrium outcome of the simultaneous move, open regionalism game. He has also shown that although global free trade is the only *symmetric* outcome of the subgame perfect Nash equilibrium (SPNE) of the sequential move, in open regionalism game, a typical SPNE outcome is *asymmetric* such that it contains the largest customs union that is unique as well as some other smaller CUs.[5] Das and Ghosh (2006) have considered a four-country model of coalition formation. They have assumed asymmetry among countries in terms of income levels generated by the difference in human capital content, with two of these countries being high-income

---

[3] In this chapter, we mainly focus on the latter dynamic time–path question.

[4] Because there is a vast amount of literature concerning the dynamic time–path question, we only consider those studies that are the most relevant.

[5] Yi (2000) has considered a similar model in which regional trade agreements take the form of FTAs instead of CUs. There is an important difference between the cases of CUs and FTAs in his model, which are as follows: formation of CUs exhibits 'negative' externalities on the welfare of the outsider countries, whereas formation of FTAs exhibits 'positive' externalities.

North countries, and the other two countries being low-income South countries. Adopting the coalition-proof Nash equilibrium (CPNE) as the solution concept, they have shown that when the market size difference (the difference in income levels) is sufficiently high, only the North–North pair and the South–South pair form FTAs (i.e., polarization). They also noted that no North–South pair is realized in the CPNE; in case if it happens to be otherwise, global free trade is realized in the CPNE. Saggi and Yildiz (2010) have constructed a three-country model, as well as investigated both bilateralism and multilateralism games. Assuming *ex ante* symmetry among countries, they have shown that global free trade is the only CPNE outcome in both games.

On the other hand, Furusawa and Konishi (2005, 2007) and Goyal and Joshi (2006) have formulated the situation within the framework of network formation games as developed by Jackson and Wolinsky (1996). They have examined the incentives for countries when either forming or dissolving bilateral FTAs. Thereafter, adopting the notion of *pairwise stability* as the solution concept, they have shown (simultaneously, but independently) that the complete network of FTAs, which corresponds to *efficient* global free trade, is pairwise stable. At the same time, they have also shown that some other *inefficient* configurations of FTA networks, in which one country is isolated and all the other countries form as many bilateral FTAs as possible, can be pairwise stable.

In their coalition/network formation approach, we find two common features embedded in their models. One is concerned with the *myopia* of the countries. In the coalition formation models, countries are considered to play the Nash equilibrium strategies in one-shot games. Although the concepts of SPNE and CPNE take account of the *farsightedness* on the side of the countries to some extent, these are myopic concepts and, therefore, fail to capture the farsightedness of the countries satisfactorily. Considering the network formation models, the pairwise stability requires for a particular network to be pairwise stable, such that each country has no incentive to abandon an existing FTA and any pair of countries with no FTA between them has no incentive to form a new FTA. In the definition of pairwise stability, countries are supposed only to consider the immediate consequence of their actions of forming an FTA or abandoning an existing FTA; however, the countries could ignore possible subsequent reactions by other countries. The notion of pairwise stability fails to deal with the farsightedness of the countries as well.

The other common feature among the models is concerned with the ability of the models to predict the realization of the equilibrium outcomes. The solution concepts adopted in the coalition/network formation approach only tell us that *once an equilibrium FTA structure has been reached*, then no country wants to change it. These solution concepts together with the construction of the models, however, are totally silent regarding *whether and how an equilibrium FTA structure can be reached* from nonequilibrium FTA structures. In particular, these models, at the very outset, ignore the possibility that some interim FTAs might be formed en route to the final outcome.

The models based on the 'dynamic' game approach have taken explicit account of the possibility of forming interim FTAs. Aghion, Antras, and Helpman (2007) have considered a transferable utility, extensive form, as well as bargaining game among three countries. In their model, one country is assumed to be the agenda setter, and the others are assumed to be followers. The agenda setter decides whether to consider sequential bilateral bargaining with other countries or to consider simultaneous multilateral bargaining with all countries at once. In addition, the agenda setter also decides endogenously how much income transfers should be made. They have shown that if global free trade is efficient—if the *grand-coalition superadditivity* in the terminology of Aghion *et al.* (2007) is satisfied—and if the formation of bilateral FTAs imposes *negative externalities* on the outsider countries, then the agenda setter prefers sequential bargaining and, thereby, a grand coalition is formed. In other words, some interim FTA between the agenda setter and a follower country is formed on the SPNE path, and eventually, global free trade is reached.

Macho-Stadler and Xue (2007) have considered a transferable utility, partition function form, as well as infinite horizon game among three countries. In their model, unlike in the model presented by Aghion *et al.* (2007), countries are assumed to be *ex ante* symmetric, and they move successively according to a predetermined order. Further, they assume that the surplus accruing from the formation of a trading bloc (CU) is divided through income transfers among the concerned countries according to a fixed sharing rule. Similar to as suggested by Aghion *et al.* (2007), their model exhibits the grand-coalition superadditivity and the negative externality on the outsider countries. Thereafter, they have shown that in the Markov Perfect Equilibrium (MPE) of the game, first, some trading bloc is formed, and eventually, a worldwide trading bloc is formed. Seidmann (2009) has, in a sense, further extended the model of Macho-Stadler and Xue (2007) by allowing countries to form not only CUs but also FTAs. He has shed new light on the motive for forming a trading bloc, which he called the 'strategic positioning'. He suggested that countries form a trading bloc in order to shift the status quo in a direction that is more favorable for member countries than the initial position.[6]

---

[6] Zhang, Xue, and Yin (2011) have examined the possibility of achieving global free trade within the framework of a sequential-move non-cooperative network formation game; they have shown that there exists a stationary subgame perfect equilibrium that supports paths of sequential formations of (interim) FTAs toward global free trade. Lake (2016) has constructed a three-country dynamic network formation game and examined the roles of discount factor and asymmetry among countries.

In the models of Aghion *et al.* (2007) and Macho-Stadler and Xue (2007), the grand-coalition superadditivity and the negative externality due to the formation of trading blocs imposed on the outsider countries play important roles in achieving global free trade. The intuition behind this is explained in the forthcoming sentences. If two or more countries form a trading bloc, the outsider countries become worse off by the negative externalities; this gives the outsider countries higher incentives to form new trading blocs or to join the existing ones. Furthermore, the grand-coalition superadditivity guarantees (or, at least, makes it possible) that every country will be made better-off after global free trade is achieved. This explanation, however, relies on the fact that the existing trading blocs will never be dissolved as assumed (implicitly or explicitly) by Aghion *et al.* (2007), Macho-Stadler and Xue (2007), and Seidmann (2009). If countries can dissolve some of the existing trading blocs, even the 'positive' externality can serve as a device that enhances the incentives of the countries to move toward global free trade.[7] The point is not whether the externality is positive or negative, but that countries can change their positions strategically, thereby altering the incentive structure of the countries involved, as was pointed out by Seidmann (2009).

In this chapter, as in Furusawa and Konishi (2005, 2007) and Goyal and Joshi (2006), we address the 'dynamic time–path' question within the framework of the network formation games. Our approach, however, is different from theirs in that we take full account of the *farsightedness* on the side of the countries (players), and that we adopt the *von Neumann-Morgenstern (vNM) stable set*—the set of outcomes that satisfy both internal and external stabilities—as the solution concept.[8] With the notion of the vNM stable set, we can incorporate the farsightedness of the countries appropriately into the model. Further, the vNM stability (in particular, external stability) consistently explains whether and how some stable networks can be realized through the behavior of the farsighted players from other unstable networks; in other words, it takes account of the possibility of forming interim trading blocs as mentioned in Aghion *et al.* (2007), Macho-Stadler and Xue (2007), and Seidmann (2009). To highlight the roles of farsightedness and the notion of vNM stability, we also consider cases in which countries are myopic; thereafter, we compare the vNM stable set with another well-known solution concept, that is, the core.

---

[7] The result of the referendum in the United Kingdom (23 June 2016) was earthshaking—the UK people chose, though by a narrow margin, to leave the European Union, which is one of the largest trading blocs in the world. The UK referendum is a shocking example of unilateral dissolution of (or withdrawal from) a trading bloc.

[8] The notion of the vNM stable set was originally introduced by von Neumann and Morgenstern (1944) as a solution concept for games in characteristic function form. Greenberg's (1990) theory of social situations has paved the way for its application to the games in other forms.

To make the model tractable, we adopt the same background trade model as Goyal and Joshi (2006) and Macho-Stadler and Xue (2007). We assume that there are *ex ante* symmetric countries; each country has one oligopolistic firm who sells a homogeneous good in both the domestic market and the foreign market. Firms compete in the Cournot fashion. The markets are separated. Our model exhibits the grand-coalition superadditivity and the negative externality. Further, unlike Aghion *et al.* (2007), Macho-Stadler and Xue (2007), and Seidmann (2009), we assume away international income transfers (even within the member countries of a trading bloc).

Trading blocs in our model take the form of FTAs rather than that of CUs. It is noted that when a pair of countries forms a bilateral FTA, they eliminate tariffs on mutual trade, but they do not coordinate the tariff rates on the imports from outsider countries. A pair of countries can form a new FTA without consent from the member countries of the existing FTAs; in addition, each single country can unilaterally annul the existing FTAs, as many as it wants.

We assume that the pre-agreement tariff rates are given *exogenously*.[9] Then, we consider two extreme cases: one in which the pre-agreement tariffs are very (prohibitively) high and the other in which they are very low (almost zero). When the pre-agreement tariffs are very high, we show that (i) if the countries are myopic, there exists a unique nonempty myopic core consisting not only of the complete FTA network, which corresponds to global free trade, but also of FTA networks in each of which all countries except for one form a complete FTA network (i.e., a free-trade club) and the remaining one country is isolated—the myopic core in this case coincides with the set of all pairwise stable FTA networks; and that (ii) if the countries are farsighted, there exists a unique farsighted vNM stable set consisting only of the complete FTA network, which coincides with the farsighted core. On the other hand, when the pre-agreement tariffs are very low, we show that (iii) if the countries are myopic, there exists a unique nonempty myopic core consisting only of the complete FTA network; and that (iv) if the countries are farsighted, the farsighted core is empty, but (v) there exists a unique farsighted vNM stable set consisting of FTA networks in each of which all countries except for one form a free-trade club.

In the case of high pre-agreement tariffs, the farsighted vNM stable set, refining the myopic core and the set of pairwise stable networks, supports only global free trade. The external stability of the farsighted vNM stable set explains whether and how global free trade is achieved from other situations through the successive formation (and/or possible dissolutions) of bilateral FTAs. In this case, we can

---

[9] This assumption conforms Article XXIV of the GATT, which requires the members of a preferential trade agreement (FTA in this case) not to raise tariffs on nonmembers.

say that bilateral FTAs can be *building blocks* toward global free trade. On the other hand, in the case of low pre-agreement tariffs, the farsighted vNM stable set predicts that global free trade cannot be achieved; instead, it supports some other *inefficient* FTA networks. In this case, bilateral FTAs can be said to be *stumbling blocks* against global free trade.

Based on the same background trade model of Goyal and Joshi (2006) as the current chapter, Zhang, Xue, and Zu (2013) have examined an FTA network formation game incorporating the farsightedness of the countries. To capture the farsightedness, they have adopted the notion of *pairwise farsightedly stable set* developed by Herings, Mauleon, and Vannetelbosch (2009), which is closely related to (but, different from) our farsighted vNM stable set. The farsighted vNM stability requires both internal and external stabilities. On the other hand, the pairwise farsighted stability requires deterrence of external deviations, minimality, and external stability. Zhang *et al.* (2013) have assumed, unlike our model, that the countries impose optimal tariffs on non-FTA countries. Their model admits a multiplicity of the pairwise farsightedly stable sets, with one of them supporting global free trade as a stable outcome, while the others do not. In contrast to this, the farsighted vNM stable set in our model is determined uniquely. The differences between their results and ours are attributable to the differences in the solution concepts; this aspect will be discussed after we have presented our main results.

The rest of the chapter is organized as follows. In the second section, we introduce the background trade model and show how to represent FTA network configurations by using some graph–theoretical concepts. In the third section, we explicitly formulate the FTA network formation game and introduce the solution concepts of the vNM stable set and the core. In the fourth and the fifth section, we examine the high pre-agreement tariff case and the low pre-agreement tariff case, respectively, and show our main results. The sixth section contains some remarks.

To facilitate the discussion, all the proofs of Lemmas and Theorems are relegated to the Appendices. Although we describe the model and state the lemmas and theorems based on the general *n*-country model as far as possible, some of the lemmas and theorems (in particular, Theorem 2 and Theorem 5) can be proved rigorously only by a four-country model. If the restriction on the number of the countries is necessary, we state it explicitly.

Basic Model

In each country, there is one oligopolistic firm that can sell in the domestic market and the foreign market. The markets are segmented. If two countries have agreed on a bilateral FTA, then each country allows the other country's firm to enter its own market without imposing an import tariff. Otherwise, each country imposes a nonzero tariff on the imports from the other. For a firm of Country k (i.e., Firm k), the competitiveness and/or the profitability in Country j's market depends not only on whether Country k has established an FTA with Country j but also on whether Country j has established FTAs with other countries. This implies that the welfare of a country (which is the sum of the consumers' surplus, the profit of its firm, and the tariff revenue) depends on the whole structure of FTA configurations.

Demand, Production, and Welfare

Let $N = \{1, 2, \ldots, n\}$ be the set of symmetric countries (as mentioned in the Introduction, we describe the model and state the lemmas and theorems in terms of the general n-country model as far as possible. When we intend to be more specific, we make use of the four-country model). In Country j, there is a single firm (Firm j) producing a homogeneous good with constant marginal cost technology; we assume that the marginal costs are zero. Let Q_j^k be the output of Firm k in Country j. Then, the total output supplied to Country j's market is $Q_j \equiv \Sigma_{k \in N} Q_j^k$. Let p_j be the price of the good in Country j. The inverse demand function of Country j is given by $p_j = \alpha - Q_j$, where $\alpha > 0$.

The unit tariff rate faced by Firm k in Country j is denoted by t_k^j. The profit of Firm k obtained from operating in Country j is as follows:

$$\pi_j^k \equiv \left[\alpha - \sum_{i \in N} Q_j^i - t_k^j \right] Q_j^k \tag{1}$$

Thereby, the total profit of Firm k is $\Sigma_{j \in N} \pi_j^k$. Firms compete in a Cournot fashion in each market. Because we assumed zero marginal costs, we can consider each country's market separately. The first-order condition for profit maximization of Firm k in Country j is

$$\alpha - \sum_{i \in N} Q_j^i - t_k^j - Q_j^k = 0 \tag{2}$$

By symmetry, we obtain the following result:

$$Q_j^k = \frac{\alpha - (n+1) t_k^j + \Sigma_{i \in N} t_i^j}{n+1} \tag{3}$$

Then, the profit of Firm k obtained from operation in Country j can be expressed as follows:

$$\pi_j^k \equiv \left[\frac{\alpha - (n+1) t_k^j + \Sigma_{i \in N} t_i^j}{n+1} \right]^2 \tag{4}$$

On the other hand, the consumers' surplus CS^k of Country k depends on the total supply in Country k as is seen in the following equation:

$$CS^k = \frac{1}{2}\left[\frac{n\alpha - \sum_{i \in N} t_i^k}{n+1}\right]^2 \tag{5}$$

The tariff revenue R_j^k that Country k can collect from Firm j operating in Country k's market is

$$R_j^k = t_j^k Q_k^j = \frac{\alpha t_j^k - (n+1)\left(t_j^k\right)^2 + \left(\sum_{i \in N} t_j^k\right)t_j^k}{n+1} \tag{6}$$

Let N_k be the set of Country k itself and the countries with which Country k has FTAs; let n_k be the number of those countries, that is, $n_k = |N_k|$. If Country k and Country j form an FTA, then eliminate their tariffs: $t_j^k = t_k^j = 0$. On the other hand, if Country k has no FTA with Country j, it sets its tariff rate at $t_j^k > 0$.

Further, we assume that Country k's tariff imposed on the imports from non-FTA countries are the same: $t_j^k = t^k > 0$ for all $j \in N \setminus N_k$. This reflects the Most-Favored Nations principle in the GATT/WTO.

The social welfare W^k of Country k is measured by the sum of the consumer's surplus, the total tariff revenue, and the total profit of Firm k:

$$W^k = CS^k + \sum_{j \in N} R_j^k + \sum_{j \in N} \pi_j^k$$

$$= \frac{1}{2}\left[\frac{n\alpha - (n - n_k)t^k}{n+1}\right]^2 + \frac{t^k(n-n_k)\{\alpha - (1+n_k)t^k\}}{n+1}$$

$$+ \sum_{j \in N_k}\left[\frac{\alpha + (n-n_j)t^j}{n+1}\right]^2 + \sum_{j \in N \setminus N_k}\left[\frac{\alpha - (1+n_j)t^j}{n+1}\right]^2 \tag{7}$$

In general, the welfare of Country k depends upon (i) the tariff rates of all countries (i.e., $t^1, t^2, ..., t^n$); (ii) the number of FTAs that Country k forms (i.e., n_k); (iii) the number of FTAs that Country k's partners have (i.e., n_j for $j \in N_k$); and (iv) the number of FTAs that non-partners have (i.e., n_j for $j \in N \setminus N_k$).

As is easily seen from Eq.(7), an increase in the tariff rate of a partner country (t^j for $j \in N_k$) raises the welfare of Country k, while an increase in the tariff rate of a non-partner country (t^j for $j \in N \setminus N_k$) reduces the welfare of Country k. Further, if a partner country or a non-partner country forms a new FTA, which increase the number of FTAs (n_j for $j \neq k$), then the welfare of Country k deteriorates. In this sense, formation of an FTA in our model imposes 'negative externalities' on the outsider countries.

Some Graph–Theoretical Concepts

To describe FTA networks in a formal way, we need to introduce some graph–theoretical concepts.[10] A graph g is a pair of the following two sets: $g = (V(g); E(g))$, where $V(g)$ is the set of **vertices** in g, and $E(g)$ is the set of unordered pairs of distinct vertices (called **edges**) in $V(g)$.[11] We denote the number of edges of g as $e(g) \equiv |E(g)|$. For $v, w \in V(g)$, unordered pair $(v; w)$ is simply denoted by vw. If $vw \in E(g)$, v and w are said to be adjacent to each other in g. If the context is clear, we simply denote $vw \in g$ instead of writing $vw \in E(g)$. The **degree** of a vertex $v \in V(g)$, denoted by $d_g(v)$, is the number of vertices adjacent to v in g. A vertex of degree zero is said to be **isolated**. An **empty graph** is a graph in which every vertex is isolated. A **complete graph** is a graph such that for every pair $\{v.w\}$ of distinct vertices, there is an edge joining them.[12]

A path from v_0 to v_l (i.e., a $v_0 - v_l$ path) in a graph g is an alternating sequence of vertices and edges $W = v_0, v_0 v_1, v_1, v_1 v_2, ..., v_{l-1} v_l, v_l$, where $v_{k-1} v_k \in E(g)$ for $k = 1, 2, ..., \ell$ and all vertices are distinct. A graph is connected if for every pair $\{v, w\}$ of distinct vertices, there is a v-w path. A graph (V_1, E_1) is a subgraph of another graph (V_2, E_2) if $V_1 \subset V_2$ and $E_1 \subset E_2$. A maximal connected subgraph of a graph g is a **component** of g.[13] Two graphs (V_1, E_1) and (V_2, E_2) are isomorphic if there exists a bijection $\varphi : V_1 \to V_2$ such that $vw \in E_1$ if and only if $\varphi(v)\varphi(w) \in E_2$. Intuitively speaking, two isomorphic graphs are of the *same shape*.

Given a graph $g = (V(g), E(g))$, we can obtain new graphs from g by deleting or adding some edges. If $vw \in E(g)$, then $g - vw$ denotes the graph obtained by deleting the edge vw from g, that is, $g - vw = (V(g), E(g) \setminus \{(v, w)\})$. Similarly, if $vw \notin E(g)$, then $g + vw$ denotes the graph obtained by adding the edge vw to g, that is, $g + vw = (V(g), E(g) \cup \{v, w\})$.

---

[10] Most of the definitions of the graph–theoretical concepts introduced here are borrowed from the works of Bollobas (1979).

[11] The vertex set $V(g)$ is always assumed to be nonempty, but the edge set $E(g)$ may be empty.

[12] Note that some authors adopt a slightly different definition of a graph, in which two or more distinct edges that join v and w (i.e., parallels), as well as an edge that joins a vertex to itself (i.e., a loop), are allowed. In our definition, no parallels and loops are allowed.

[13] Here, 'maximal' is taken with respect to the set inclusion.

Representation of FTA Networks

An FTA network is a description of how the countries form bilateral FTAs with other countries. An FTA network is represented by a graph g such that $V(g) = N$ and $(i, j) \in E(g)$ if and only if Country i and Country j have a bilateral FTA between them. Let G be the set of all graphs with their vertex sets being identified with the set N of all countries. Then, G represents all possible FTA networks. The empty graph, denoted by $g^\emptyset$, corresponds to the situation where no FTA exists. On the other hand, the complete graph, denoted by g^N, corresponds to the situation where every pair of countries forms a bilateral FTA—global free trade.

Let $N_k(g) \equiv \{k\} \cup \{j \in N | (k, j) \in E(g)\}$ be the set of Country k itself and all countries with which Country k has FTAs in the FTA network g. Further, let $n_k(g) \equiv |N_k(g)|$ be the cardinality of $N_k(g)$. By definition, we have $n_k(g) = d_g(k) + 1 \geq 1$ for all $k \in N$ and for all $g \in G$. By substituting $n_k(g)$ and $n_j(g)$ into Eq. (7), we can write the welfare of Country k as a function of g, that is, $W^k(g)$ for all $g \in G$.

Examples of FTA networks in the benchmark model with four countries are illustrated in Figure 3.1. Small circles (i.e., a, b, c, and d) represent possible 'addresses' at which countries are located (one address for one country) in a graph. The numbers in small circles represent the countries located at the corresponding addresses. A bold solid line between a pair of addresses means that a bilateral FTA is formed by the countries located at these addresses. On the other hand, a thin broken line between a pair of addresses means that there is no FTA between these respective countries.

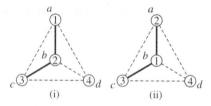

Figure 3.1 Examples of FTA networks

Let g and g' be the graphs that correspond to panel (i) and panel (ii) of Figure 3.1, respectively. Both g and g' represent a situation where Countries 1, 2, and 3 form a 'hub-and-spoke' system of FTAs, and the remaining Country 4 is excluded from the hub-and-spoke system. Although the same three countries participate in the hub-and-spoke systems in both g and g', the welfare of each country obtained in g can be different from that in g'. Take Country 1 for example. Country 1 is a spoke in g, but it is the hub in g'. We have $n_1(g) = 2$, $n_2(g) = 3$, $n_3(g) = 2$, and $n_4(g) = 1$ for g, while we have $n_1(g') = 3$, $n_2(g') = 2$, $n_3(g') = 3$, and $n_4(g') = 1$ for g'.

By substituting these results into Eq. (7), we can verify that $W^1(g) < W^1(g')$.[14] In general, the welfare of a country depends upon the current graph; more specifically, it depends both on the *shape* of the current graph (i.e., the isomorphic class to which the graph belongs) and on the *address* at which the country is located in the graph.

In the benchmark model with four countries, we have eleven different shapes for the graphs. In other words, the set G of all possible graphs is partitioned into the following eleven isomorphic classes: $G_1, G_2, G_3, G_4, G_5, G_6, G_7, G_8, G_9, G_{10}$, and G_{11}. The partitioning is done such that $G = \cup_{r=1}^{11} G_r$ and $G_r \cap G_s = \emptyset$ if $r \neq s$. The shape of a (representative) graph in each isomorphic class G_r is illustrated in panel (r) of Figure 3.2 ($r = 1, 2, \ldots, 11$).

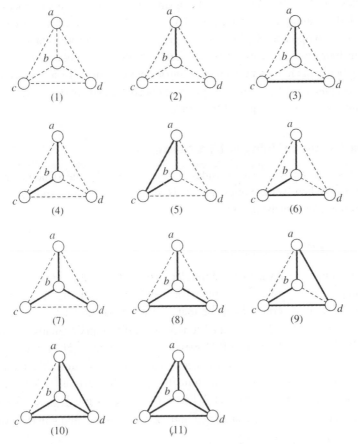

Figure 3.2 Possible shapes (isomorphic classes) of FTA networks

---

[14] See also Table 3.1.

Let us examine some of the isomorphic classes. The isomorphic class G_1 contains only one graph, that is, the empty graph g^ϕ. The empty graph g^ϕ means that there is no FTA in the world. The isomorphic class G_3, which contains six graphs, corresponds to a situation wherein the world is divided into two small trading blocs of equal size. For example, let us consider a graph $g \in G_3$ such that $E(g) = \{(1, 2),$ $(3, 4)\}$(i.e., $a = 1, b = 2, c = 3, d = 4$). This describes the situation where Countries 1 and 2 form a bilateral FTA and Countries 3 and 4 form another bilateral FTA. It needs to be noted that there are no other bilateral FTAs. The isomorphic class G_4 corresponds to a three-country hub-and-spoke system (exclusive of one isolated country). The isomorphic class G_5 contains four graphs. Let us consider a graph g' $\in G_5$ such that $E(g') = \{(1, 2), (2, 3), (3, 1)\}$. This describes the situation where three countries, that is, Countries 1, 2, and 3, form a free-trade club among themselves, but exclude Country 4 from the club. FTAs among Countries 1, 2, and 3 constitute a complete component of g' (a 3-cycle graph). The isomorphic class G_7, which contains four graphs, corresponds to a worldwide hub-and-spoke system with one country being the hub and the other countries being spokes. Last, let us consider the isomorphic class G_{11}. This is a singleton consisting only of the complete graph g^N, which corresponds to global free trade.

Formation and Stability of FTA Networks

In the last section, we have considered how to describe the structure of FTA networks and their welfare implications. Here, we consider how an FTA network is formed and/or dissolved.

Inducement Correspondence

Let g be a current FTA network. First, let us consider what a single country can do. A single country, of course, cannot form an FTA by itself, but it can annul the existing FTAs unilaterally. Suppose that Country k has an FTA with Country j $\left(j \in N_k(g) \setminus \{k\}\right)$ in the current FTA network g. If Country k annuls the existing FTA with Country j, the current FTA network g changes to $g - kj$. Further, Country k can choose some (possibly all) partner countries in g and cancel the FTAs with those countries simultaneously. Technically, from the current FTA network g, Country k can *induce* another FTA network $g' = g - \sum_{j \in T} kj$ for some $T \subset N_k(g) \setminus \{k\}$.[15] When a single Country k can induce g' and g in this way, we write $g \xrightarrow{\{k\}} g'$ or $g \xrightarrow{k} g'$.

---

[15] When $T = \{j_1, j_2, ..., j_R\}$, the expression $g - \sum_{j \in T} k\, j$ means $g - k\, j_1 - k\, j_2 - ... - k\, j_R$.

Next, let $S = \{k, j\}$ be a coalition of two Countries k and j and let us consider what S can do. If Countries k and j have no FTA between them in g (i.e., $kj \notin g$) and if they negotiate and agree on a bilateral FTA, then a new FTA kj is added to the current network g, and accordingly, a new FTA network $g + kj$ is established. More generally, when Countries k and j form a new FTA, Country k, at the same time, can annul some of its FTAs with other countries unilaterally; the same is true for Country j. In this case, from the current g, a two-country coalition S can induce $g' = g + k\,j - \sum_{i \in T_k} ki - \sum_{i \in T_j} ji$ for some $T_k \subset N_k(g) \setminus \{k\}$ and $T_j \subset N_j(g) \setminus \{j\}$. If Countries k and j have a bilateral FTA in g (i.e., $k\,j \in g$), Countries k and j can annul some of the existing FTAs (possibly, including the FTA $k\,j$ itself) at the same time. Therefore, in this case, S can induce $g' = g - \sum_{i \in T_k} ki - \sum_{i \in T_j} ji$ for some $T_k \subset N_k(g) \setminus \{k\}$ and $T_j \subset N_j(g) \setminus \{j\}$.

In this way, any coalition S of two countries can *induce* a new FTA network g' from a current FTA network g. When a coalition $S = \{k, j\}$ of Countries k and j can induce g' and g, we write $g \xrightarrow{\;\;S\;\;} g'$ or $g \xrightarrow{\;\{k,\,j\}\;} g'$.[16]

When there is a single country or a pair of countries that can induce g' from g. we simple write $g \rightarrow g'$. Following the terminology of the theory of social situations (Greenberg, 1990), we call the binary relation $\{\rightarrow\}$ defined on the set G of all graphs as the inducement correspondence. The inducement correspondence only describes how countries *can* change the current FTA network to another network. It should be noted that neither $g \xrightarrow{\;\{k,\,j\}\;} g'$ nor $g \xrightarrow{\;\{k\}\;} g'$ implies that g' is better than g for the countries concerned.

Domination Relations

Let g be a current FTA network and consider a coalition $S = \{k, j\}$ of two countries. Suppose that $g \xrightarrow{\;\;S\;\;} g'$ in such a context, the coalition S has some power to change the current FTA network g to another network g'. However, whether the coalition S actually exercises this power depends on the welfare consequence and also on the *perspectives* of the countries in S as to how the other countries react to their initial actions. If the countries anticipate that exercising the power to induce g' from g eventually leads to a situation in which they are made worse off

---

[16] A similar argument can also be applied to any nonempty coalition with an arbitrary number of countries.

than the current situation, then they will not do so. On the other hand, if the countries anticipate that exercising the power eventually leads to a situation in which they are made better-off, then they do exercise their power.[17]

Taking different levels of the countries' perspectives into account, we define two domination relations on the set G of all possible FTA networks. The first one reflects the *myopia* of the countries.

Definition 1: (Direct domination relation). For two FTA networks g and g', if there exists a nonempty coalition S of countries with $1 \leq |S| \leq 2$ such that $g \xrightarrow{S} g'$ and $W^i(g) < W^i(g')$ for all $i \in S$, then we say that "g' directly dominates g through S" and we write $g \prec_S g'$. Further, when $g \prec_S g'$ for some nonempty $S \subset N$, we simply say that "g' directly dominates g" and write $g \prec g'$.

Consider a coalition S that *can* induce g' from g $\left(\text{i.e., } g \xrightarrow{S} g'\right)$. If all the countries in S believe that they will be made better-off in g' than in g and also believe that g' will remain in the status quo after being induced (i.e., S believes that the other countries do not react in g' at all), the countries actually exercise their power to induce g' and g. Thus, the direct domination relation $g \prec_S g'$ is realized if the countries in S ignore the possibility that g' will be replaced with another network g'' through subsequent (re)actions by other countries. In this sense, the direct domination relation reflects the *myopia* of the countries in S. When $g \prec_S g'$, we say that the countries in S have *myopic incentives* to move from g to g'.

The indirect domination relation defined below reflects the *farsightedness* of the countries.

Definition 2: (Indirect domination relation). For two FTA networks g and g'. If there exist a sequence of FTA networks $\{g_r\}_{r=0}^{R}$ and a corresponding sequence of coalitions of countries $\{S_r\}_{r=1}^{R}$ that satisfy the following conditions:

(i) $g_0 = g$ and $g_R = g'$,

(ii) $g_{r-1} \xrightarrow{S_r} = g_r$ and $1 \leq |S_r| \leq 2$ for all $r = 1, 2, ..., R$, and

(iii) $W^i(g_{r-1}) < W^i(g')$ *for all* $i \in S_r$ and for all $r = 1, 2, ..., R$, then we say

that "g' indirectly dominates g" and we write $g \ll g'$.

The second requirement that the number of deviating countries in each step of the indirect domination should not exceed two reflects the *bilateralism* in our

---

[17] The same explanation also applies to a single country.

model. If we relax this requirement and allow the simultaneous deviation by more than three (possible, by all) countries we can define another indirect domination relation that reflects the *multilateralism*. After showing our main results, we will discuss how the multilateralism works in our model.

Let us consider a coalition S_r that appears in the definition of the indirect domination relation. When S_r induces g_r, Country k in S_r compares the current welfare level $W^k(g_{r-1})$ with the welfare level $W^k(g')$ that can be obtained in the 'final' FTA network g', but not with the welfare level $W^k(g_r)$ that can be obtained in the FTA network g_r realized immediately after g_{r-1}. Therefore, it may be the case that S_r *does* exercise the power to change g_{r-1} to g_r even if some countries in S_r are made worse-off in g_r immediately after g_{r-1}, anticipating that subsequent inducements by other countries will eventually lead to g' in which all the countries in S_r are made better-off than in g_{r-1}. In this sense, the indirect domination relation reflects the *farsightedness* of the countries.[18]

The definition of indirect domination relation is akin to that of a *farsighted improving path* introduced by Herings *et al.* (2009) in order to define their solution concept of the pairwise farsightedly stable set. In each step of farsighted improving path, only one link (edge) can be formed or severed. On the other hand, in each step of a sequence realizing indirect domination, only one link (edge) can be formed, but, at the same time, some of the existing links can be severed (if a country or a pair of countries concerned wants to do so). In a sense, the indirect domination relation allows the countries a higher degree of freedom to deviate from a current FTA network than the farsighted improving path. This fact plays an important role in establishing our main results.[19]

Solution Concepts

In general, an **abstract system** is a pair $(X, \angle)$ of a nonempty set X and a domination relation $\angle$ defined on X: for $x, y \in X$, we say that y dominates x if $x \angle y$. Based on the domination relations defined in the previous subsection, we have two particular abstract system $(G, \prec)$ and $(G, \prec\prec)$, which we call the myopic system and the farsighted system, respectively. Let us define the solution concepts for $(X, \angle)$,

Definition 3 (Core): The core of an abstract system $(X, \angle)$, denoted by $C(X, \angle)$, is a subset of X consisting of all outcomes that are not dominated. That is,

---

[18] Note that $g \prec\prec g'$.

[19] The proof of Theorem 5, for example, heavily relies upon the fact that a pair of two countries can form an FTA between then and, at the same time, abandon some of the existing FTAs. See the discussion after Theorem 5.

$$C(X, \angle) \equiv \left\{ x \in X \middle| \text{there is no } y \in X \text{ such that } x \angle y \right\} \qquad (8)$$

The core of $(X, \angle)$ always exists and is unique, but it can be an empy set. Once an outcome in the core has been reached, it will never be replaced with any other outcome according to the domination relation $\angle$. Therefore, we can say that in a sense, outcomes in the core are 'stable'. The concept of the core, however, fails to explain whether and how outcomes in it can be reached from (unstable) outcomes outside of the core.

Definition 4 (von Neumann-Morgenstern stable set): The vNM stable set is a subset K of X that satisfies the following conditions:

  (i) for all $x \in K$, there does not exist $y \in K$ such that $x \angle y$ (internal stability);
  (ii) for all $x \in X \backslash K$, there exists $y \subset K$ such that $x \angle y$ (external stability).

The set of all vNM stable sets for $(X, \angle)$ is denoted by $K(X, \angle)$

Let K be a vNM stable set for $(X, \angle)$. Internal stability means that any stable outcome, in the sense that it is included in K, will not be replaced with any other stable outcome according to $\angle$. On the other hand, external stability means that any unstable outcome, in the sense that it is excluded from K, will be replaced with some stable outcome according to $\angle$. In this manner, the concept of the vNM stable set (in particular, its external stability) consistently explains what the concept of the core fails to do.

We call the core and vNM stable set for the myopic system $(G, \prec)$ as the myopic core and a myopic vNM stable set, respectively; similarly, we call those for the farsighted system $(G, <<)$ as the farsighted core and a farsighted vNM stable set, respectively. Although the definitions are slightly different, the myopic core in our model coincides with the set of all *pairwise stable* networks as defined by Jackson and Wolinsky (1996).

Based on the notion of farsighted improving path, Herings *et al.* (2009) have defined the *von Neumann-Morgensten (vNM) pairwise farsightedly stable set* and examined its relation to the pairwise farsightedly stable set. They have shown, in particular that a vNM pairwise farsightedly stable set is a pairwise farsightedly stable set. The difference in the definitions of the farsighted improving path and the indirect dominations relation renders our farsighted vNM stable set different from the vNM pairwise farsightedly stable set. The farsighted vNM stable set is not necessarily a pairwise farsightedly stable set; therefore, the prediction by the farsighted vNM stable set and by the vNM pairwise farsightedly stable set can be different.

High Pre-agreement Tariff Case

We first consider the case in which the pre-agreement tariff rates are very high. More specifically, we assume, as in Goyal and Joshi (2006), that each country levies prohibitive tariffs on the imports from countries with whom the country does not have bilateral FTAs. In this case, international trade occurs only between those countries who have bilateral FTAs; isolated countries (in a graph–theoretical sense) actually adopt isolationist policies (i.e., they are in autarky). Therefore, no country earns tariffs revenue. Then, the welfare of Country k in an FTA network g can be expressed as the sum of the consumers' surplus and the profits obtained in the markets of Country k's partners. Accordingly, Eq. (7) is reduced to

$$W^k(g) = \frac{1}{2}\left[\frac{\alpha n_k(g)}{n_k(g)+1}\right]^2 + \sum_{j \in N_k(g)}\left[\frac{\alpha}{n_j(g)+1}\right]^2 \tag{9}$$

Note that the negative externality on the welfare of Country k in this case only comes from an increase in the number of FTAs in Country k's partners (i.e., the number of partners' partners). The reason for this is quite simple. If Country k's partner (say, Country j) forms a new FTA with a third country (say, Country i), then the market in Country j becomes more competitive due to the entry of Firm i after the formation of the FTA (j, i). Because Firm k has no access to Country i's market, it only suffers from a decrease in its profit obtained in Country j's market. This makes Country k worse off. On the other hand, even if countries separated from Country k and its partners form some new FTAs, the markets in which Firm k is operating are not affected by the formation of these new FTAs. Firm k experiences no loss (gain) in its profit, and therefore, the welfare of Country k is kept unchanged.

Because Eq. (9) contains only one exogenous parameter, we can easily calculate the value of $W^k(g)$ for every $g \in G$. As mentioned earlier, Country k's welfare depends both on the isomorphic class to which g belongs and on the address at which Country k is located in g. Table 3.1 summarizes the values of $W^k(g)$ in the four-country case. The table also provides information regarding world welfare, which is defined as the sum of the welfare of all countries. As can be seen from Table 3.1, a single country can attain the highest welfare when it becomes the hub of a worldwide hub-and-spoke system (i.e., when it is located at b in a graph $g \in G_7$), whereas world welfare is maximized when global free trade is achieved (i.e., $g^N \in G_{11}$). In our model, the complete network g^N is *efficient*, and therefore, satisfies the *grand-coalition superadditivity*.[20]

---

[20] The fact that the complete network g^N is efficient in a general n-country model has been proved by Goyal and Joshi (2006).

Table 3.1 **Welfare levels when the pre-agreement tariffs are high**

	Addresses in each isomorphic class				
	a	b	c	d	*World welfare*
G_1	3/8	3/8	3/8	3/8	3/2
	(0.375)	(0.375)	(0.375)	(0.375)	(1.5)
G_2	4/9	4/9	3/8	3/8	59/36
	(0.444)	(0.444)	(0.375)	(0.375)	(1.638)
G_3	4/9	4/9	4/9	4/9	16/9
	(0.444)	(0.444)	(0.444)	(0.444)	(0.777)
G_4	19/48	*163/288	19/48	3/8	499/288
	(0.395)	(*0.565)	(0.395)	(0.375)	(1.732)
G_5	15/32	15/32	15/32	3/8	57/32
	(0.468)	(0.468)	(0.468)	(0.375)	(1.781)
G_6	19/48	*149/288	*149/288	19/48	263/144
	(0.395)	(*0.517)	(*0.517)	(0.395)	(1.826)
G_7	28/75	*52/75	28/75	28/75	136/75
	(0.373)	(*0.693)	(0.373)	(0.373)	(1.813)
G_8	28/75	*1073/1800	357/800	357/800	6703/3600
	(0.373)	(*0.596)	(0.446)	(0.446)	(1.861)
G_9	15/32	15/32	15/32	15/32	15/8
	(0.468)	(0.468)	(0.468)	(0.468)	(1.875)
G_{10}	21/40	*339/800	21/40	*339/800	759/400
	(0.423)	(*0.525)	(0.423)	(*0.525)	(1.8975)
G_{11}	12/25	12/25	12/25	12/25	48/25
	(0.480)	(0.480)	(0.480)	(0.480)	(1.920)

Note: (i) The fractions are the exact numbers while the decimals in parentheses are approximate numbers; (ii) To obtain $W^k(g)$, the values in the table must be multiplied by α^2. (iii) The values with an asterisk (*) are higher than the corresponding values obtained in the complete graph; (iv) World welfare is the sum of the welfare of four countries.

Concerning the incentives of a country to form FTAs, Goyal and Joshi (2006) have shown the following results.

Observation 1 (Goyal and Joshi, 2006).

(i) *If a country is involved in one or more FTAs, it has an incentive to form an additional FTA.*

(ii) *If $n \geq 4$, in an FTA network in which one country is isolated and the other $n - 1$ countries constitute a complete component FTA network, the isolated country has no incentive to form an additional FTA.*

Based on the aforementioned observations, Goyal and Joshi (2006) have shown that (i) the complete network (i.e., global free trade) is pairwise stable, (ii) if $n \geq$ 4, an FTA in which one country is isolated and the other $n-1$ countries constitute a complete component FTA network (i.e., a free-trade club with $n-1$ countries) is pairwise stable, and (iii) there is no other type of pairwise stable networks. In the four-country model, we can rephrase their results as follows:

Theorem 1. *In the case of high pre-agreement tariffs with four countries, the myopic core $C(G, \prec)$ is nonempty and is characterized by*

$$C(G, \prec) = G_5 \cup G_{11} \tag{10}$$

The formal proof is omitted; instead, we give an illustration. Bold black arrows in Figure 3.3 represent the direct domination relation when the pre-agreement tariffs are high.[21] For example, the arrow from panel (2) to panel (3) means that for any FTA network $g \in G_2$, there exists an FTA network $g' \in G_3$ that directly dominates g. Other bold black arrows in the figure carry similar information about the direct domination relation. It should be noted that any FTA network in some isomorphic class cannot directly dominate other FTA networks in the same isomorphic class. As illustrated in Figure 3.3, there is no bold black arrow that begins from panel (5) or from panel (11), meaning that any FTA network in G_5 or G_{11} cannot be directly dominated by other FTA networks. This proves Theorem 1.

When the countries are myopic and the pre-agreement tariffs are very high, global free trade is *not* the only stable outcome. Once a free club with $n-1$ countries (exclusive of one country) has been formed, the world is trapped in an inefficient situation. Although each member of the free-trade club has an incentive to form a new FTA with the isolated country, the isolated country has no *myopic incentive* to do so.

Let us consider, in the four country model, an FTA network $g \in G_5$ where there exist a three-country free-trade club and an isolated country. Suppose that Countries 1, 2, and 3 form a free-trade club and Country 4 is isolated in g. Because Country 4 is located at d in g, it receives $W^4(g) = 3\alpha^2/8$. On the other hand, a member of the free-trade club (say, Country 3) receives $W^3(g) = 15\alpha^2/32$ in g. If global free trade g^N is achieved, both Countries 3 and 4 will receive $W^3(g^N) = W^4(g^N) = 12\alpha^2/25$ (no matter where they are located in g^N), which is higher than $W^3(g)$ and $W^4(g)$. Therefore, if all countries are farsighted enough to understand the consequences of not only the immediate outcome of their own action but the final outcome that will be realized through the chain reactions of other countries, then, anticipating that global free trade will be realized eventually, Countries 3 and 4 may form a new FTA between them (even though Country 4 becomes worse-off in the immediate FTA network). In the following, we show that this is indeed the case.

---

[21] For the moment, ignore other symbols such as thin arrows with heads, double circles, and asterisks.

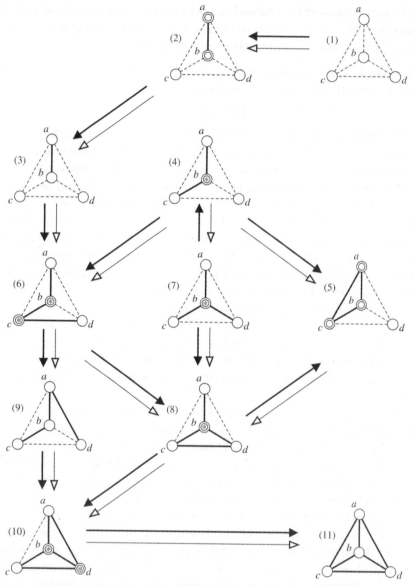

Figure 3.3 Direct domination relation among FTA networks

Note: (i) Bold black arrows indicate the direct domination relation when the pre-agreement tariffs are high; (ii) Thin arrows with white heads indicate the direct domination relation when the pre-agreement tariffs are low; (iii) Asterisks mean that the welfare of countries located at these addresses is higher than the welfare under global free trade in the case of high pre-agreement tariffs; (iv) Double circles mean that the welfare of countries located at these addresses is higher than the welfare under global free trade in the low pre-agreement tariffs.

Lemma 1. *In the case of high pre-agreement tariffs with four countries,*
  (i) no FTA network can indirectly dominate the complete network g^N;
  (ii) the complete network g^N indirectly dominates any other FTA network.

With the above results, we can establish the following theorem.

Theorem 2. *In the case of high pre-agreement tariffs with four countries, there exists a unique farsighted stable set K_H that is characterized by*

$$K_H = G_{11} \equiv \left\{ g^N \right\} \tag{11}$$

Further, K_H coincides with the farsighted core $C(G, \ll)$ of the farsighted system.[22]

Comparing Theorem 1 and Theorem 2, we find that FTA networks in the isomorphic class G_5, which are included in the myopic core, fail to be stable when the countries are farsighted. To see how FTA networks in G_5 are 'destabalized' through the behavior of farsighted countries, let us consider the following example. Take an FTA network $g \in G_5$ such that $E(g) = \left\{ (1, 2), (2, 3), (3, 1) \right\}$ and Country 4 is isolated. Consider the coalitions $\{1, 4\}, \{2, 4\}, \{3, 4\} \subset N$; correspondingly, let us define the networks such that $g_1 = g + (1, 4)$, $g_2 = g_1 + (2, 4)$, and $g_3 = g_2 + (3, 4)$. By definition and from Table 3.1, we obtain the following results:

$$g \xrightarrow{\{1, 4\}} g_1 \in G_8 \text{ and } W^i(g) < W^i\left(g^N\right) \text{ for } i = 1, 4,$$

$$g_1 \xrightarrow{\{2, 4\}} g_2 \in G_{10} \text{ and } W^i(g_1) < W^i\left(g^N\right) \text{ for } i = 2, 4,$$

$$g_2 \xrightarrow{\{3, 4\}} g_3 \in G_{11} \text{ and } W^i(g_2) < W^i\left(g^N\right) \text{ for } i = 3, 4$$

Therefore, the sequence $g \xrightarrow{\{1, 4\}} g_1 \xrightarrow{\{2, 4\}} g_2 \xrightarrow{\{3, 4\}} g_3 = g^N$

realizes $g \ll g^N$. The key is the behavior of Country 4 in the first step in this sequence: Country 4 together with Country 1 induces g_1 from g. In the first step, Country 4 itself becomes worse-off. At the same time, due to the negative externality, Countries 2 and 3 become worse-off; therefore, they have higher incentives to move from g_1 toward global free trade g^N. This makes it possible to realize global free trade.

---

[22] Applying the notion of the (myopic) vNM stable set to Krugman (1993)'s monopolistically competitive FTA formation model, Oladi and Beladi (2008) have shown that there exist a unique myopic vNM stable set suppporting global free trade. Although it can be easily shown that there exists a unique mypic vNM stable set for our model, it contains not only global free trade but also some other inefficient FTA networks. We omit the proof of existence and the characterization of the myopic vNM stable set for our model, because it is of less analytical interest.

Theorem 2 implies that if the pre-agreement tariffs are very high, global free trade is the only final outcome that emerges from the chains of bilateral FTA negotiations among the countries. Even under the prevalence of bilateralism (as embedded in the definition of our inducement correspondence), global free trade can be achieved through the formation of bilateral FTAs by farsighted countries. In this case, we can say that bilateral FTAs are *building blocks* toward global free trade.

Low Pre-agreement Tariff Case

In this section, we consider a scenario in which the pre-agreement tariff rates are very low. In such a situation, even an isolated country (in a graph–theoretical sense) engages in international trade with all other countries. In other words, even if Country k does not have FTAs with some (possibly, all) countries in the current situation, Firm k is operating in the markets of those countries. The welfare of Country k is represented by Eq. (7), which contains many exogenous parameters such as t^k, t^j, and α. To compare the welfare levels at different addresses in different graphs effectively, we assume that $t^k = t^j = t$ for all $k, j \in N$ in Eq. (7) and that t is positive but sufficiently close to zero.

The following lemma characterizes the differences in the welfare of a single country and the world welfare across different FTA networks.

Lemma 2. *In the case of low pre-agreement tariffs, we have for all $k \in N$ and for all $g', g \in G$,*

(i) $W^k(g') > W^k(g)$ *if and only if*

$$\Delta \equiv n_k(g') - n_k(g) - \frac{4}{2n+1}\{e(g') - e(g)\} > 0 \text{ and} \tag{12}$$

(ii) $\Sigma_{k \in N} W^k(g') > \Sigma_{k \in N} W^k(g)$ *if and only if*

$$e(g') - e(g) > 0 \tag{13}$$

The difference in the welfare of a single country (say, Country k) in different FTA networks depends both on the number of FTAs that Country k has and on the number of existing FTAs in the world. On the other hand, the difference in the world welfare in different FTA networks depends only on the number of existing FTAs in the world. As the number of FTAs increases, the world welfare increases. The following results are immediate from Lemma 2.

Observation 2.

(i) *If FTAs not involving Country k are formed, the welfare of Country k decreases.*

(ii) *If FTAs involving Country k and no other FTAs are formed, the welfare of Country k increases.*

(iii) *Global free trade is efficient.*

Observation 2-(i) implies the *negative externality* due to the formation of FTAs. In the high pre-agreement tariff case, the negative externality on Country k only comes from the formation of FTAs by the countries with whom Country k has already formed FTAs. In the low pre-agreement tariff case on the other hand, even the formation of FTAs by the countries that are separated from Country k in the current situation can negatively affect the welfare of Country k. In this sense, we can say that the negative externality is stronger in the low pre-agreement tariff case than in the high pre-agreement tariff case.

Observation 2-(ii) contrasts with Observation 1-(ii). In the low pre-agreement tariff case, every country always has a *myopic incentive* to form as many new FTAs as possible. This observation leads us to the following result.

Theorem 3. In the case of low pre-agreement tariffs, the myopic core $C(G, \prec)$ is nonempty and it is characterized by

$$C(G, \prec) = \left\{ g^N \right\}. \tag{14}$$

Note that the complete graph constitutes the myopic core in a general n-country model and that the complete graph is the only pairwise stable FTA network in this case. In Figure 3.3, the direct domination relation in the four country model is illustrated by thin arrows with white heads. For example, the arrow pointing from G_5 to G_8 implies that for any $g \in G_5$, there exists an FTA network in G_8 that directly dominates g. As illustrated in the figure, G_{11} is the only isomorphic class that has no originating arrow.[23]

If the countries are myopic and the pre-agreement tariffs are sufficiently low, global free trade g^N is the only stable outcome in the sense that it is included in the myopic core. From a single country's viewpoint, because global free trade contains as many FTAs as possible, the negative externality is maximized in g^N. Therefore, if the countries are farsighted, some of them may want to abandon some existing FTAs anticipating the eventual realization of an FTA network in which they can be made better-off. The following lemma clearly shows this point.

Lemma 3. *In the case of low pre-agreement tariffs with four countries, global free trade g^N is indirectly dominated by an FTA network in G_5.*

---

[23] Differences between the direct domination relation in the low pre-agreement tariff case and that in the high pre-agreement tariff case only appear in the relations between G_4 and G_7 and between G_5 and G_7.

The proof is omitted; see the discussion after Theorem 5. This lemma together with Observation 2-(ii) implies the following results.

Theorem 4. In the case of low pre-agreement tariffs with four countries, the farsighted core $C(G, \ll)$ is empty.

The proof is omitted, because it follows directly from Theorem 3 and Lemma 3. When the countries are farsighted and the pre-agreement tariffs are sufficiently low, the notion of the core predicts nothing.

Myopic countries, only taking account of the immediate effects of their own FTA formation, do not want to leave global free trade. On the other hand, in order to avoid strong negative externalities, farsighted countries have incentives to leave global free trade and to induce other FTA configurations with less FTAs in the world. The tension between the incentives of a country to enlarge FTAs (Observation 2 (ii)) and to avoid the negative externality due to the formation of FTAs by other countries determines the stability of FTA networks.

Theorem 5. In the case of low pre-agreement tariffs with four countries, there exists a unique farsighted stable set K_L that is characterized by

$$K_L = G_5:$$
(15)

To show how global free trade g^N is 'destabilized' and how an FTA network g' in K_L is realized, we give an example of a sequence that realizes the indirect domination $g^N \ll g'$. Let us consider the following set of FTA networks:

$$g_1 \in G_{10} : E(g_1) = \{(1,2),(1,3),(2,3),(2,4),(3,4)\}, \quad e(g_1) = 5,$$

$$g_2 \in G_8 : E(g_2) = \{(1,2),(2,3),(2,4),(3,4)\}, \quad e(g_2) = 4,$$

$$g_3 \in G_6 : E(g_3) = \{(1,2),(2,4),(3,4)\}, \quad e(g_2) = 3,$$

$$g_4 \in G_9 : E(g_4) = \{(1,2),(1,3)(2,4),(3,4)\}, \quad e(g_4) = 4,$$

$$g' \in G_5 : E(g') = \{(1,2),(1,3),(2,3)\}, \quad e(g') = 3.$$

In g', Countries 1, 2, and 3 form a free-trade club, but Country 4 is excluded. As compared to global free trade g^N, each member of the free-trade club loses only one FTA in g', while the number of FTAs in the world is reduced by three. Each member experiences less negative externalities in g' than in g^N. Country 1 can induce g_1 and g^N unilaterally by abandoning the FTA with Country 4. Further, because $n_1(g') - n_1(g^N) = -1$ and $e(g') - e(g^N) = -3$, we have $W^k(g') > W^1(g^N)$ by Lemma 2. That is,

$$g^N \xrightarrow{\{1\}} g_1 \text{ and } W^1(g^N) < W^1(g')$$

Similarly, we can show that

$$g_1 \xrightarrow{\{1\}} g_2 \text{ and } W^1(g_1) < W^1(g'),$$

$$g_2 \xrightarrow{\{3\}} g_3 \text{ and } W^3(g_2) < W^3(g')$$

$$g_3 \xrightarrow{\{1,3\}} g_4 \text{ and } W^i(g_3) < W^i(g') \text{ for } i = 1, 3$$

$$g_4 \xrightarrow{\{2,3\}} g' \text{ and } W^i(g_4) < W^i(g') \text{ for } i = 2, 3.$$

In the second step, Country 1 cancels the FTA with Country 3 unilaterally. (We can compress the first and second steps by assuming that Country 1 annuls the FTAs with Countries 3 and 4 simultaneously.) Thereafter, Country 2 comes to occupy a hub-like position in g_2. In the third step, Country 3 cancels the FTA with Country 2. Thereafter, Countries 1 and 3 form an FTA in the fourth step. In the last step, Countries 2 and 3 form an FTA between them and, at the same time, abandon the FTAs with Country 4 simultaneously. Thereby, we obtain $g^N \ll g'$.[24]

It is worth noting that in the aforementioned sequence realizing $g^N \ll g'$, the FTA between Countries 1 and 3 is abandoned once (by Country 1 unilaterally) and is reorganized by them bilaterally. A similar argument would also apply to the FTA between Countries 2 and 3. In this way, by forming and dissolving FTAs, countries can change their relative addresses in FTA networks strategically. This can be seen as a reflection of the *strategic positioning* as indicated by Seidmann (2009).

Our Theorem 5 is in sharp contrast to the results obtained by Aghion *et al.* (2007) and Macho-Stadler and Xue (2007). Although their models and our model share several important properties such as the grand-coalition superadditivity, negative externality, and farsightedness of the countries, their models predict the realization of global free trade, whereas our model predicts the realization of other inefficient FTA structures. The possibility of dissolving the existing FTAs and the strength of the negative externality are the differences between their models and ours. In their models, it is assumed that if FTAs have been formed, they will never be dissolved. On the other hand, in our model, it is assumed that countries can form and/or dissolve FTAs; as such, countries can make the most of their *strategic positioning* to avoid the strong negative externality accruing from the formation of FTAs by other countries. If we assume away the possibility of dissolving the existing FTAs from our model, we can realize global free trade, but we cannot exclude the inefficient FTA networks from the farsighted vNM stable set.[25]

---

[24] This proves Lemma 3.

[25] The inducement correspondence can be modified easily not to allow the possibility of dissolving the existing FTAs. Further, it is easy to show the existence of the farsighted vNM stable set, which includes global free trade and other inefficient FTA networks, under the modified inducement correspondence.

Thus far, we have assumed that only a single country or a pair of two countries can induce one FTA network from another FTA network; in other words, we have only considered the role of *bilateralism*. Here, let us briefly discuss the role of *multilateralism*. By dropping the requirement of $|S_r| \leq 2$ in the definition of the indirect domination relation $\ll$, we can define a new indirect domination relation under multilateralism. Is global free trade secured by the farsighted vNM stable set under the new indirect domination relation? Unfortunately, the answer is no. Even though the grand-coalition superadditivity is satisfied, a coalition with three countries has a strong incentive to deviate from global free trade g^N to an FTA network in the isomorphic class G_5, and actually, it can do so in only one step. Global free trade is 'destabilized' much easily under multilateralism than under bilateralism when the pre-agreement tariffs are sufficiently low.[26]

Remarks

We have shown that when the pre-agreement tariffs are very high, the farsighted vNM stable set only supports global free trade, and that when the pre-agreement tariffs are sufficiently low, the farsighted vNM stable set does not support global free trade and instead supports some inefficient FTA networks. In the former case, we can say that bilateral FTAs are the *building blocks* for achieving global free trade, and in the latter case, to the contrary, they are the *stumbling blocks* against achieving global free trade. These results make a somewhat ironic impression: the closer the world economy is to global free trade (in the sense that the pre-agreement tariffs are very low), the harder it is to realizing the same.

Of course, our results depend upon the details and strong assumptions of our model. In particular, we have assumed that the tariff rates on non-FTA countries are exogenously determined. As Yi (2000) and Bond *et al.* (2004) have reported, if the tariff rates on non-FTA countries are determined *endogenously* to maximize the social welfare of each country, the tariff rates after the formation of an FTA decrease. This *tariff–complementarity* effect makes non-FTA countries better-off and, thereby, generates *positive externalities* on them.[27] In such a scenario, the

---

[26] This conclusion depends on the nonavailability of international transfers in our model. If we allow international transfers and coalitional moves by more than three countries, the isolated country in a stable FTA network in G_5 becomes able to bribe all the other countries to move toward global free trade g^N. In this case, it may be possible (though not proved) that G_5 is destabilized and global free trade is established as the stable outcome through the behavior of farsighted countries.

[27] The fact that the optimal tariff rate after the formation of an FTA is lower than before has been reported by several other authors. The term 'tariff–complementarity' is attributable to Bagwell and Staiger (1998).

mechanisms supporting our results and the roles of bilateralism and multilateralism can be reversed. Hence, it may be the case that global free trade is supported by the farsighted vNM stable set. To investigate this possibility is a subject of future research.

Appendix: Proofs

A.1 Proof of Lemma 1

Part (i)

Suppose, in negation, that there exists g' that indirectly dominates g^N and that the following sequence of FTA networks $\{g_r\}_{r=1}^R$ and corresponding coalitions $\{S_r\}_{r=1}^R$ realizes $g^N \ll g'$:

$$g^N \xrightarrow{S_1} g_1 \xrightarrow{S_2} g_2 \xrightarrow{S_3} \dots \xrightarrow{S_R} g_R = g' . \tag{16}$$

Note that because no pair of two countries can form a new FTA in g^N, the first coalitions S_1 must dissolve one or some of the existing FTAs in g^N. Because the situation in g^N is symmetric for all countries, we can assume $S_1 = \{1\}$ or $S_1 = \{1, 2\}$. Further, without loss of generality, we can concentrate on the welfare of Country 1. If g^N were to be indirectly dominated by g', we must have $W^1\left(g^N\right) < W^1\left(g'\right)$. From Table 3.1, we can show that $W^1\left(g^N\right) < W^1\left(g'\right)$ holds true only in the following five cases: (i) $g' \in G_4$ and Country 1 is located at b; (ii) $g' \in G_6$ and Country 1 is located at b or at c; (iii) $g' \in G_7$ and Country 1 is located at b; (iv) $g' \in G_8$ and Country 1 is located at is b; and (v) $g' \in G_{10}$ and Country 1 is located at b or at d. Figure 3.3 illustrates the situation: vertices with asterisks (*) means that countries located at these addresses receive higher welfare than when they are in g^N.

We prove only case (i), because essentially the same proof applies to the other cases as well. Because Country 1 has three FTAs in g^N, it can annul one or two or three FTAs unilaterally. Therefore, we have three subcases: (i-1) $g_1 \in G_5$ (when Country 1 annuls all three FTAs), (i-2) $g_1 \in G_8$ (when Country 1 annuls two of the three FTAs), and (i-3) $g_1 \in G_{10}$ (when Country 1 annuls one of its FTAs).

Let us consider subcase (i-1). In g', because Country 1 is located at b, each of the other three countries must be located at a or c or d. Then, from Table 3.1, we have $W^i\left(g'\right) = 19\alpha^2 / 48$ or $W^i\left(g'\right) = 3\alpha^2 / 8$ for $i = 2, 3, 4$. Hence, we have $W^i\left(g_1\right) > W^i\left(g'\right)$ for $i = 2, 3, 4$. This implies that Countries 2, 3, and 4 will not be members of S_2 in sequence (16). Therefore, S_2 must be a singleton consisting only of Country 1. Because Country 1 is isolated in g_1. It cannot induce any other

FTA network form g_1 unilaterally–a contradiction. Hence, subcase (i-1) is not possible.

Next, let us consider subcase (i-2). Country 1 is locate at a and the other countries are located at b, c, or d in g_1. Similar to subcase (i-1), we have $W^i(g_1) > W^i(g')$ for $i = 2, 3, 4$. Then, Countries 2, 3, and 4 will not be members of S_2. The only possibility is $S_2 = \{1\}$ and g_2 must be in G_5. Once an FTA network in G_5 has been reached, the same argument as subcase (i-1) applies. Hence, subcase (i-2) is not possible either.

Lastly, let us consider subcase (i-3). Country 1 is located at a or c in g_1. Similar to subcases (i-1) and (i-2), we must have $S_2 = \{1\}$ and $g_2 \in G_5 \cup G_8$. Once an FTA network in either G_5 or G_8 has been reached, the situation becomes parallel to subcases (i-1) or (i-2). Hence, subcase (i-3) is not possible either. This completes the proof of part (i).

Part (ii)

Take the empty graph $g^{\emptyset} \in G_1$. We now show that $g^{\emptyset}$ is indirectly dominated by the complete network g^N. By definition, we have $E(g^{\emptyset}) = \emptyset$ and $E(g^N) = \{(1, 2), (2, 3), (3, 4), (4, 1), (2, 4), (1, 3)\}$. To be specific, let us consider a sequence of FTA networks $\{g_r\}_{r=1}^5$ whose edge sets are given as follows:

$$E(g_1) = \{(1, 2)\},$$
$$E(g_2) = \{(1, 2), (3, 4)\},$$
$$E(g_3) = \{(1, 2), (2, 3), (3, 4)\},$$
$$E(g_4) = \{(1, 2), (2, 3), (3, 4), (4, 1)\},$$
$$E(g_5) = \{(1, 2), (2, 3), (3, 4), (4, 1), (2, 4)\}.$$

By construction and from Table 3.1, we have

$$g^{\emptyset} \xrightarrow{\{1, 2\}} g_1 \in G_2 \text{ and } W^i(g^{\emptyset}) < W^i(g^N) \text{ for } i = 1, 2,$$

$$g_1 \xrightarrow{\{3, 4\}} g_2 \in G_3 \text{ and } W^i(g_1) < W^i(g^N) \text{ for } i = 3, 4,$$

$$g_2 \xrightarrow{\{2, 3\}} g_3 \in G_6 \text{ and } W^i(g_2) < W^i(g^N) \text{ for } i = 2, 3,$$

$$g_3 \xrightarrow{\{4, 1\}} g_4 \in G_9 \text{ and } W^i(g_3) < W^i(g^N) \text{ for } i = 1, 4,$$

$$g_4 \xrightarrow{\{2, 4\}} g_5 \in G_{10} \text{ and } W^i(g_4) < W^i(g^N) \text{ for } i = 2, 4,$$

$g_5 \xrightarrow{\{1,3\}} g^N \in G_{11}$ and $W^i(g_5) < W^i(g^N)$ for $i = 1, 3$.

Hence, $g^\emptyset \ll g^N$. Similarly, for all $g \in G_1 \cup G_2 \cup G_3 \cup G_6 \cup G_9 \cup G_{10}$, we can show that $g \ll g^N$.

Next, take an FTA network $g_0' \in G_7$. Again, we have that g_0' is indirectly dominated by g^N. To be specific, let us consider a sequence of FTA networks $\{g_r'\}_{r=0}^4$ whose edge sets are given as follows:

$E(g_0') = \{(1, 2), (2, 3), (2, 4)\},$

$E(g_1') = \{(2, 3), (2, 4)\},$

$E(g_2') = \{(2, 3), (3, 4), (4, 2)\},$

$E(g_3') = \{(1, 2), (2, 3), (3, 4), (4, 2)\},$

$E(g_4') = \{(1, 2), (2, 3), (3, 4), (4, 2), (1, 4)\},$

By construction and from Table 3.1, we have

$g_0' \xrightarrow{\{1\}} g_1' \in G_4$ and $W^1(g_0') < W^1(g^N)$,

$g_1' \xrightarrow{\{3,4\}} g_2' \in G_5$ and $W^i(g_1') < W^i(g^N)$ for $i = 3, 4$,

$g_2' \xrightarrow{\{1,2\}} g_3' \in G_8$ and $W^i(g_2') < W^i(g^N)$ for $i = 1, 2$,

$g_3' \xrightarrow{\{1,4\}} g_4' \in G_{10}$ and $W^i(g_3') < W^i(g^N)$ for $i = 1, 4$,

$g_4' \xrightarrow{\{1,3\}} g^N \in G_{11}$ and $W^i(g_4') < W^i(g^N)$ for $i = 1, 3$.

Hence, $g_0' \ll g^N$. Similarly, for all $g' \in G_4 \cup G_5 \cup G_7 \cup G_8$, we can show that $g' \ll g^N$. This completes the proof of part (ii).

A.2. Proof of Theorem 2

First, we show that K_H coincides with the farsighted core. Lemma 1 implies that the complete network is included in the farsighted core. On the other hand, Lemma 1 implies that no FTA network other that g^N can be included in the farsighted core. Thus, $\{g^N\}$ is the farsighted core.

Next, we show that $\{g^N\}$ is a farsighted vNM stable set. Because K_H is a singleton, its internal stability is trivial. External stability directly follows from Lemma 1. Thus, K_H is a farsighted vNM stable set. Uniqueness directly follows from the coincidence of the farsighted core and the farsighted vNM stable set.

A.3. Proof of Lemma 2

Before proceeding, we show some elementary fasts. It is well known in graph theory that $\sum_{v \in V(g)} d_g(v) = 2e(g)$ holds true for any graph $g = \left(V(g), E(g)\right)$. In our context, since $n_i(g) = d_g(i) + 1$ for any $g \in G$ and for any $i \in N$ by definition, then we obtain

$$\sum_{i \in N} n_i(g) = n + 2e(g) \tag{17}$$

Next, given an arbitrary country (say, Country k) and arbitrary graphs $g', g \in G$, let us define the following subsets A, B, C, D of N.

$A \equiv N_k(g') \cap N_k(g)$: the subset of countries that have FTAs with Country k in both g' and g.

$B \equiv N \setminus \left[N_k(g') \cup N_k(g) \right]$: the subset of countries that do not have FTAs with Country k in both g' and g.

$C \equiv N_k(g') \cap \left[N \setminus N_k(g) \right]$: the subset of countries that have FTAs in g', but do not in g.

$D \equiv N_k(g) \cap \left[N \setminus N_k(g') \right]$: the subset of countries that have FTAs in g, but do not in g.

Because $n_k(g') = |A \cup C| = |A| + |C|$ and $n_k(g) = |A \cup D| = |A| + |D|$, then we have $n_k(g') - n_k(g) = |C| - |D|$. We make use of the above facts in the following calculation.

Country k's welfare depends not only on the graph, but also on the common pre-agreement tariff rate t. Then, the difference $W^k(g') - W^k(g)$ multiplied by a positive constant $(n+1)^2$ can be considered a function of the common pre-agreement tariff rate t. Using Eq.(7), we obtain the following expression:

$$f(t) \equiv (n+1)^2 \left[W^k(g') - W^k(g) \right]$$

$$
= \frac{1}{2}\Big[n\alpha - \big(n - n_k(g')\big)t \Big]^2 - \frac{1}{2}\Big[n\alpha - \big(n - n_k(g)\big)t \Big]^2
$$

$$
+ (n+1)\big(n - n_k(g')\big)\big[\alpha - \big(1 + n_k(g')\big)t\big]t
$$

$$
- (n+1)\big(n - n_k(g)\big)\big[\alpha - \big(1 + n_k(g)\big)t\big]t
$$

$$
+ \sum_{i \in A}\Big[\big\{\alpha + \big(n - n_i(g')\big)t\big\}^2 - \big\{\alpha + \big(n - n_i(g)\big)t\big\}^2 \Big]
$$

$$
+ \sum_{i \in B}\Big[\big\{\alpha - \big(1 + n_i(g')\big)t\big\}^2 - \big\{\alpha - \big(1 + n_i(g)\big)t\big\}^2 \Big]
$$

$$
+ \sum_{i \in C}\Big[\big\{\alpha + \big(n - n_i(g')\big)t\big\}^2 - \big\{\alpha - \big(1 + n_i(g)\big)t\big\}^2 \Big]
$$

$$
+ \sum_{i \in D}\Big[\big\{\alpha - \big(1 + n_i(g')\big)t\big\}^2 - \big\{\alpha + \big(1 + n_i(g)\big)t\big\}^2 \Big]
$$

It is easy to verify that $f(0) = 0$. Therefore, by making use of the Taylor expansion of f around zero (up to the first order), we obtain $f(t) \doteq f'(0) \times t$. Consequently, for a sufficiently small positive t, we have $f(t) > 0$ if and only if $f'(t) > 0$. Simply calculating $f'(t)$, we obtain

$$
f'(t) = -\big\{n - n_k(g')\big\}\big[n\alpha - \big\{n - n_k(g')\big\}t \big] + \big\{n - n_k(g)\big\}\big[n\alpha - \big\{n - n_k(g)\big\}t \big]
$$

$$
+ (n+1)\big\{n - n_k(g')\big\}\big[\alpha - \big\{1 + n_k(g')\big\}t\big] - (n+1)\big\{n - n_k(g')\big\}\big\{1 + n_k(g')\big\}t
$$

$$
- (n+1)\big\{n - n_k(g)\big\}\big[\alpha - \big\{1 + n_k(g)\big\}t\big] + (n+1)\big\{n - n_k(g)\big\}\big\{1 + n_k(g)\big\}t
$$

$$
+ 2\sum_{i \in A}\Big\langle \big\{n - n_i(g')\big\}\big[\alpha - \big\{n - n_i(g')\big\}t\big] - \big\{n - n_i(g)\big\}\big[\alpha + \big\{n - n_i(g)\big\}t\big] \Big\rangle
$$

$$
+ 2\sum_{i \in B}\Big\langle -\big\{1 + n_i(g')\big\}\big[\alpha - \big\{1 + n_i(g')\big\}t\big] + \big\{1 + n_i(g)\big\}\big[\alpha - \big\{1 + n_i(g)\big\}t\big] \Big\rangle
$$

$$
+ 2\sum_{i \in C}\Big\langle \big\{n - n_i(g')\big\}\big[\alpha + \big\{n - n_i(g')\big\}t\big] + \big\{1 + n_i(g)\big\}\big[\alpha - \big\{1 + n_i(g)\big\}t\big] \Big\rangle
$$

$$
+ 2\sum_{i \in D}\Big\langle -\big\{1 + n_i(g')\big\}\big[\alpha - \big\{1 + n_i(g')\big\}t\big] - \big\{n - n_i(g)\big\}\big[\alpha + \big\{n - n_i(g)\big\}t\big] \Big\rangle
$$

By substituting $t = 0$ into $f'(t)$, we obtain

$$
f'(0) = -\big\{n - n_k(g')\big\}n\alpha + \big\{n - n_k(g)\big\}n\alpha
$$

$$
+ \big\{n - n_k(g')\big\}(n+1)\alpha - \big\{n - n_k(g)\big\}(n+1)\alpha
$$

$$
+ 2\alpha\sum_{i \in A}\big\{n - n_i(g') - n + n_i(g)\big\} + 2\alpha\sum_{i \in B}\big\{-1 - n_i(g') + 1 + n_i(g)\big\}
$$

$$
+ 2\alpha\sum_{i \in C}\big\{n - n_i(g') + 1 + n_i(g)\big\} + 2\alpha\sum_{i \in D}\big\{-1 - n_i(g') - n + n_i(g)\big\}
$$

$$= \alpha\{n - n_k(g')\}(-n + n + 1) + \alpha\{n - n_k(g)\}(n - n - 1)$$
$$+ 2\alpha \sum_{i \in A} \{n_i(g') - n_i(g)\} + 2\alpha \sum_{i \in B} \{n_i(g) - n_i(g')\}$$
$$+ 2\alpha \sum_{i \in C} \{n + 1 + n_i(g) - n_i(g')\} + 2\alpha \sum_{i \in D} \{n(g) - n_i(g') - (n + 1)\}$$

$$= \alpha\{n - n_k(g')\} - \alpha\{n - n_k(g)\}$$
$$+ 2\alpha \left\{ \begin{array}{l} \sum_{i \in A} n_i(g) - \sum_{i \in A} n_i(g') + \sum_{i \in B} n_i(g) - \sum_{i \in B} n(g') \\ + \sum_{i \in C} (n + 1) + \sum_{i \in C} n_i(g) - \sum_{i \in C} n_i(g') \\ - \sum_{i \in D} (n + 1) + \sum_{i \in D} n_i(g) - \sum_{i \in D} n_i(g') \end{array} \right\}$$

$$= \alpha\{n_k(g) - n_k(g')\} + 2\alpha \left\{ \sum_{i \in N} n_i(g) - \sum_{i \in N} (g') + (n + 1)\{|C| - |D|\} \right\}$$

$$= -\alpha\{n_k(g') - n_k(g)\} + 2\alpha \left\{ \sum_{i \in N} n_i(g) - \sum_{i \in N} n_i(g') + (n + 1)\{n_k(g') - n_k(g)\} \right\}$$

$$= \alpha\{2(n + 1) - 1\}\{n_k(g') - n_k(g)\} + 2\alpha \left\{ \sum_{i \in N} n_i(g) - \sum_{i \in N} n_i(g') \right\}$$

$$= \alpha(2n + 1)\{n_k(g') - n_k(g)\} + 2\alpha \left\{ \sum_{i \in N} n_i(g) - \sum_{i \in N} n_i(g') \right\}$$

$$= \alpha(2n + 1)\{n_k(g') - n_k(g)\} + 2\alpha\{n + 2e(g) - n - 2e(g')\}$$

$$= \alpha(2n + 1)\{n_k(g') - n_k(g)\} - 4\alpha\{e(g') - e(g)\}$$

$$= \alpha(2n + 1)\left\{n_k(g') - n_k(g) - \frac{4}{2n + 1}\{e(g') - e(g)\}\right\}$$

$$= \alpha(2n + 1)\Delta$$

Therefore, we have $f'(0) > 0$ if and only if $\Delta > 0$. This proves Lemma 2-(i). To prove Lemma 2-(ii), it suffices to show that $\sum_{k \in N} W^k(g') - \sum_{k \in N} W^k(g) > 0$ if and only if $\sum_{k \in N} \Delta > 0$.

$$\sum_{k \in N} \Delta = \sum_{k \in N} \left\{ \{n_k(g') - n_k(g)\} - \frac{4}{2n + 1}\{e(g') - e(g)\} \right\}$$

$$= \sum_{k \in N} n_k(g') - \sum_{k \in N} n_k(g) - \sum_{k \in N} \frac{4}{2n + 1}\{e(g') - e(g)\}$$

$$= \{n + 2e(g')\} - \{n + 2e(g)\} - \frac{4n}{2n + 1}\{e(g') - e(g)\}$$

$$= 2\{e(g') - e(g)\} - \frac{4n}{2n + 1}\{e(g') - e(g)\}$$

$$= \left(2 - \frac{4n}{2n+1}\right)\{e(g') - e(g)\}$$

$$= \frac{2}{2n+1}\{e(g') - e(g)\}.$$

This completes the proof.

A.4. Proof of Observation 2

Part (i)

If Country k forms new FTAs and if no other FTAs are formed, we have $n_k(g') - n_k(g) = e(g') - e(g) > 0$. By substituting this into Eq. (12), we obtain

$$\Delta = \left(1 - \frac{4}{2n+1}\right)\{n_k(g') - n_k(g)\} = \frac{2n-3}{2n+1}\{n_k(g') - n_k(g)\} \qquad (18)$$

Because $n \geq 2$, we have $\Delta > 0$.

Part (ii)

If the number of FTAs not involving Country k increases, we have $n_k(g') - n_k(g)$ $= 0$ and $e(g') - e(g) > 0$. By substituting this into Eq. (12), we obtain

$$\Delta = -\frac{4}{2n+1}\{e(g') - e(g)\} < 0 \qquad (19)$$

Part (iii)

For any g other than the complete network g^N, we have $e\left(g^N\right) > e(g)$. Then, Lemma 2 implies $\sum_{k \in N} W^k\left(g^N\right) > \sum_{k \in N} W^k(g)$

A.5. Proof of Theorem 3

Let g be a current network in which a pair of countries do not have a bilateral FTA between them. Then, by Observation 2-(ii), they have myopic incentives to form a new FTA between them. In other words, g can be directly dominated by another graph.

Let us consider the complete network g^N. Then, no pair of countries can form a bilateral FTA; moreover, by Obseration 2 again, no country has an incentive to abandon the existing FTAs. The complete network is not directly dominated.

A.6. Proof of Theorem 5

As mentioned in the text, any graph cannot indirectly dominate other graphs in the same isomorphic class. Therefore, internal stability is achieved.

Let us turn to external stability. As show in the proof of Lemma 3, any graph $G_6 \cup G_8 \cup G_9 \cup G_{10} \cup G_{11}$ is indirectly dominated by a graph in $K_L = G_5$. It remains to be shown that for any $g \in G_1 \cup G_2 \cup G_3 \cup G_4 \cup G_7$, there exists a graph $g' \in K_L$ that indirectly dominates g.

Take the empty graph $g^\emptyset \in G_1$ and consider the following sequence of graphs:

$$g_1 \in G_2 : E(g_1) = \{(1,2)\}, \qquad\qquad e(g_1) = 1,$$
$$g_2 \in G_4 : E(g_2) = \{(1,2),(2,3)\}, \qquad e(g_2) = 2,$$
$$g' \in G_5 : E(g') = \{(1,2),(1,3),(2,3)\}, \qquad e(g') = 3.$$

Similar to the proof of Lemma 3, we can show that

$$g^\emptyset \xrightarrow{\{1,2\}} g_1 \text{ and } W^i(g^\emptyset) < W^i(g') \text{ for } i = 1,2,$$
$$g_1 \xrightarrow{\{2,3\}} g_2 \text{ and } W^i(g_1) < W^i(g') \text{ for } i = 2,3,$$
$$g_2 \xrightarrow{\{1,3\}} g' \text{ and } W^i(g_2) < W^i(g') \text{ for } i = 1,3.$$

Hence, $g^\emptyset$ is indirectly dominated by $g' \in K_L$. The above argument can be modified to show that any graph in $g \in G_1 \cup G_2 \cup G_4$ is indirectly dominated by a graph in K_L.

Next, let us consider $J_0 \in G_7$ and a sequence of graphs such that

$$J_0 \in G_7 : E(J_0) = \{(1,3),(2,3),(4,3)\}, \qquad e(J_0) = 3,$$
$$J_1 \in G_3 : E(J_1) = \{(1,2),(3,4)\}, \qquad e(J_1) = 2,$$
$$J_2 \in G_4 : E(J_2) = \{(1,2),(2,3)\}, \qquad e(J_2) = 2,$$
$$g' \in G_5 : E(g') = \{(1,2),(1,3),(2,3)\}, \qquad e(g') = 3.$$

Again, similar to the proof of Lemma 3, we have show that

$$J_0 \xrightarrow{\{1,2\}} J_1 \text{ and } W^i(J_0) < W^i(g') \text{ for } i = 1,2,$$
$$J_1 \xrightarrow{\{2,3\}} J_2 \text{ and } W^i(J_1) < W^i(g') \text{ for } i = 2,3,$$
$$J_2 \xrightarrow{\{1,3\}} g' \text{ and } W^i(J_2) < W^i(g') \text{ for } i = 1,3.$$

Hence, J_0 is indirectly dominated by $g' \in K_L$. The above arguments also implies that any graph in $G_3 \cup G_7$ is indirectly dominated by a graph in K_L.

Consequently, any graph not in G_5 is indirectly dominated by a graph in G_5. External stability is achieved.

References

Aghion, P., P. Antras, and E. Helpman. 2007. 'Negotiating free trade.' *Journal of International Economics*. 73: 1–30.

Bagwell, K. and R. W. Staiger. 1998. 'Regionalism and multilateral tariff cooperation.' In *International Trade Policy and the Pacific Rim,* edited by J. Piggott and A. Woodland. London: Macmillan.

Bhagwati, J. N. 1991. *The World Trading System at Risk*. Princeton: Princeton University Press.

_____. 1993. 'Regionalism and multilateralism: an overview.' In *New Dimensions in Regional Integration*, edited by J. de Melo and A. Panagariya. Cambridge: Cambridge University Press.

Bollobas, B. 1979. *Graph Theory: An Introductory Course*. Berlin: Springer-Verlag.

Bond, E., R. Riezman, and C. Syropoulos. 2004. 'A strategic and welfare theoretic analysis of free trade areas.' *Journal of International Economics* 64: 1–27.

Das, S. P. and S. Ghosh. 2006. 'Endogenous trading bloc formation in a North-South global economy.' *Canadian Journal of Economics* 39: 809–30.

Furusawa, T. and H. Konishi. 2005. 'Free trade networks with transfers.' *Japanese Economic Review* 56: 144–64.

_____. 2007. 'Free trade networks.' *Journal of International Economics* 72: 310–35.

Goyal, S. and S. Joshi. 2006. 'Bilateralism and free trade.' *International Economic Review* 47: 749–78.

Greenberg, J. 1990. *The Theory of Social Situations: An Alternative Game-Theoretic Approach*. Cambridge: Cambridge University Press.

Herings, P. J-J., A. Mauleon, and V. Vannetelbosch. 2009. 'Farsightedly stable networks.' *Games and Economic Behavior* 67: 526–41.

Jackson, M. and A. Wolinsky. 1996. 'A strategic model of social and economic networks.' *Journal of Economic Theory* 71: 44–74.

Krugman, P. 1993. 'Regionalism versus multilateralism: analytical notes.' In *New Dimensions in Regional Integration,* edited by J. de Melo and A. Panagariya. Cambridge: Cambridge University Press.

Lake, J. 2016. 'Free trade agreements as dynamic farsighted networks.' *Economic Inquiry,* 30 May. Online version. DOI: 10.1111/ecin.12360

Macho-Stadler, I. and L. Xue. 2007. 'Winners and losers from the gradual formation of trading blocs.' *Economica* 74: 664–81.

Oladi, R. and H. Beladi. 2008. 'Is regionalism viable? A case for global free trade.' *Review of International Economics* 16: 293–300.

Seidmann, D. J. 2009. 'Preferential trading arrangements as strategic positioning.' *Journal of International Economics* 79: 143–59.

Saggi, K. 2006. 'Preferential trade agreements and multilateral tariff cooperation.' *International Economic Review* 47: 29–57.

Saggi, K. and H. M. Yildiz. 2010. 'Bilateralism, multilateralism, and the quest for global free trade.' *Journal of International Economics* 81: 26–37.

Viner, J. 1950. *The Customs Union Issue*. New York: Carnegie Endowment for International Peace.

von Neumann, J. and O. Morgenstern. 1944. *Theory of Games and Economic Behavior* (2nd edition, 1947; 3rd edition: 1953). Princeton: Princeton University Press.

WTO (World Trade Organisation). 2010. 'Regional Trade Agreements.' http://www.wto.org/english/tratop_e/region_e/region_e.htm (as of October 15, 2010).

Yi, S. S. 1996. 'Endogenous formation of customs unions under imperfect competition: open regionalism is good.' *Journal of International Economics* 41: 153–77.

Yi, S. S. 2000. 'Free-trade areas and welfare: an equilibrium analysis.' *Review of International Economics* 8: 336–47.

Zhang, J., L. Xue, and X. Yin. 2011. 'Forming efficient free-trade networks: A sequential mechanism.' *Review of International Economics* 19(2): 402–17.

Zhang, J., L. Xue, and L. Zu. 2013. 'Farsighted free trade networks.' *International Journal of Game Theory* 42: 375–98.

4

Skilled–Unskilled Wage Inequality and Dynamic Skill Accumulation

A Theoretical Analysis

Priya Brata Dutta

Introduction

The increasing wage income inequality throughout the world is a widely discussed topic in Development Economics. The conventional belief is that globalization brings a welfare improvement, both from aggregative and distributive perspectives. However, with regard to its distributive effect, many empirical researchers show that income inequality has surged in different countries because income and employment of unskilled labor have declined in a significant manner comparatively to those of skilled labor. This growing income inequality was experienced in the United States between the 1960s and the 1970s.[1] A similar phenomenon was observed in European countries between 1978 and 1988.[2] A similar picture is also noticed in many developing countries. This is primarily because wage inequality has increased in many Latin American and South Asian countries since the mid-1980s.[3] However, the experience by the East Asian countries between the 1960s and the 1970s upholds the conventional theory that a greater openness to international trade tends to reduce the skilled–unskilled wage gap.[4] Various studies provide various explanations for this increase in income inequality. Trade liberalization and technological progress are the main two controversial reasons for this phenomenon.[5]

---

[1] See, for example, Bound and Johnson (1992), Leamer (2000), Marjit and Acharyya (2003), etc. Table 2.1 in page 10 in Marjit and Acharyya (2003) is important in this context.

[2] See, for example, Lawrence (1994), Katz *et al.* (1992), etc.

[3] See, for example, Wood (1997), Dev (2000), Borjas and Ramey (1993), Banga (2005), Beyer *et al.* (1999), etc.

[4] See, for example, Wood (1997).

[5] According to Wood (1998), Beyer *et al.* (1999), Green *et al.* (2000), Behrman *et al.* (2000), Isgut (2001), etc., trade liberalization is to be blamed for this growing wage inequality.

Many empirical studies point out other causes for this growing inequality, and these include international outsourcing[6], increase in the price of skill intensive good[7], entry of overpopulated low-income countries in the global market[8], etc.

Theoretical literature also deals with the problem of growing wage inequality and trade liberalization; a subset of this literature is based on the framework of static competitive general equilibrium models.[9] These models consider two different types of labor—skilled and unskilled. These models consider the ratio of the skilled wage rate to the unskilled wage rate as a measure of wage inequality. We can divide the existing theoretical literature into two groups. One group of models assumes exogenous supply of skilled labor, and this group includes the works of Gupta and Dutta (2011, 2010a), Chaudhuri (2008, 2004), Yabuuchi and Chaudhuri (2007), Chaudhuri and Yabuuchi (2008, 2007), Beladi *et al.* (2008), Marjit and Acharyya (2006, 2003), Marjit and Kar (2005), Marjit *et al.* (2004), etc. Hence, these models cannot analyze the role played by endogenous skill formation on the skilled–unskilled wage inequality. Another small group of models considers endogenous formation of skilled labor with static competitive general equilibrium models, and this group includes works of Gupta and Dutta (2010b), Yabuuchi and Chaudhuri (2009), Kar and Beladi (2004), and Marjit and Acharyya (2003). Endogenous formation of skilled labor means the transformation of unskilled labor into skilled labor. In the aforementioned static models, this transformation takes place instantaneously. However, skill formation takes place over time; and a dynamic model is more appropriate to deal with this issue. Dynamics of human capital accumulation are analyzed in endogenous growth models of Lucas (1988), Rebelo (1991), etc. However, none of these models were designed to explain the skilled–unskilled wage gap deals with dynamics of skill formation.

In this chapter, we consider the intertemporal accumulation of skilled labor. We first consider a static small open-economy model with three sectors and three

---

However, Wood (1997, 1998), Dev (2000) and Görg and Strobl (2002) are of the view that technological progress worsens wage inequality through an increase in the relative demand for skilled labor. Esquivel and López (2003) show that technological change aggravates, but trade liberalization lowers wage inequality in Mexico.

[6] See Feenstra and Hanson (1997) in this context.

[7] See Harrison and Hanson (1999), Hanson and Harrison (1999), and Beyer *et al.* (1999) in this context.

[8] See Wood (1997) in this context.

[9] A few works, for example, Gupta and Dutta (2011b), Acemoglu (1998, 1999, 2002a, 2002b), Kiley (1999), Sener (2001), Ranjan (2001), Fang *et al.* (2008), Wang *et al.* (2009), etc. analyze how technological change affects skilled–unskilled wage inequality in dynamic models. However, Anwar and Rice (2009), Anwar (2006, 2009), etc. show how trade liberalization affects wage inequality using static product variety models of imperfect competition.

factors—unskilled labor, skilled labor, and capital. Two of the three sectors produce final traded goods, of which one sector produces a manufacturing product using all three inputs. and another sector produces an agricultural product using unskilled labor and capital. The third sector, called education sector, produces additional skilled labor, using skilled labor and capital as inputs. This education sector is publicly owned and organizes production following a no-profit–no-loss objective, and its cost of production is financed by the tax revenue of the government. This additional skilled labor produced in this model is added to the existing stock of skilled labor at the next point of time. Therefore, the stock of skilled labor accumulates over time.

We derive interesting results from our model. An exogenous increase in skilled labor endowment and/or unskilled labor endowment always raises the skilled–unskilled relative wage, but an exogenous increase in capital endowment reduces this in the static model, where no factor endowment changes endogenously over time. An increase in capital (unskilled labor) endowment raises (lowers) the stock of skilled labor in the new long-run equilibrium of a dynamic model with endogenous accumulation of skilled labor. An exogenous increase in unskilled labor endowment always raises the skilled–unskilled relative wage, but an exogenous increase in capital endowment reduces it in the new long-run equilibrium of the dynamic model. We also consider Gini coefficient of wage income distribution as a measure of inequality, showing that, in the static part of the model, the effect of a change in capital stock on Gini coefficient of wage income distribution of the entire working population depends on the Gini coefficient of wage income distribution within skilled laborers and also on the average income of skilled laborers. However, in the dynamic part of the model where skilled labor accumulates over time, this effect on Gini coefficient of wage income distribution of the entire working population also depends on the effect on the rate of change in skilled labor, which involves ambiguities.

This chapter is organized into the following sections. The second section describes the static model model, and the dynamic analysis is given in the third section. Concluding remarks are made in the fourth section.

The Static Model

We consider a small open economy with three sectors and three factors—unskilled labor, skilled labor, and capital. Sector 1 produces a manufacturing product using all three inputs, and Sector 2 produces an agricultural product using unskilled labor and capital. Sectors 1 and 2 produce final and traded products, but the Sector S produces additional skilled labor using skilled labor and capital as inputs. This education sector is publicly owned and organizes production following a no-profit–no-loss objective. The cost of production in the education sector is financed by taxing the income; and the proportional income tax rate is exogenously given in this model. This additional skilled labor produced by Sector S is added to the existing stock of skilled labor at the next point of time. Thus the stock of skilled labor accumulates over time. Production function of each of the traded good sectors satisfies all standard neoclassical properties, including CRS. Production function of Sector S is of fixed coefficient type.[10] Factor endowments such as capital and unskilled labor in this static model are exogenously given because we rule out the possibility of capital accumulation and population growth. Capital is mobile among all these three sectors; however, skilled labor is mobile between Sector 1 and Sector S. However, unskilled labor is mobile between Sector 1 and Sector 2. Factor prices in each of these three sectors are perfectly flexible, except for skilled wage rate in Sector 1. This flexibility ensures full employment of all factors. Wage rate of skilled labor is fixed in Sector 1, and this fixed wage rate is always higher than the flexible wage rate in the education sector (Sector S). So skilled laborers are always willing to work in the manufacturing sector. If a part of the skilled labor force cannot be absorbed in the manufacturing sector due to fixed wage rate, they then move to the low-wage education sector. All markets are competitive. The representative firm maximizes profit, and the representative consumer maximizes utility subject to the budget constraint.

We use the following notations.

a_{Ki} = Capital output ratio in ith sector for $i = 1, 2, S$.

a_{Si} = Skilled labor output ratio in ith sector for $i = 1, S$.

a_{Li} = Labor–output ratio in ith sector for $i = 1,2$.

P_i = Price of ith commodity for $i = 1,2$.

P_S = Price (average cost of production) of the educational service.

W_S^* = Fixed wage rate of skilled labor in Sector 1.

W_S = Flexible wage rate of skilled labor in Sector S.

W_U = Wage rate of unskilled labor.

W_S^A = Average skilled wage rate.

r = Common rate of return to capital in all the sectors.

τ = Rate of proportional income tax.

Y = Total factor income.

X_i = Level of output of ith sector for $i = 1,2,S$.

S = Endowment of skilled labor.

L = Exogenously given total unskilled labor endowment.

K = Exogenously given capital endowment.

---

[10] This is a simplifying assumption.

θ_{ji} = Distributive share of jth input in ith sector for $j = S, K, L$ and $i = 1,2,S$.

λ_{ji} = Proportion of jth input employed in ith sector for $j = S, K, L$ and $i = 1,2,S$.

$\hat{x}$ = $\dfrac{dx}{x}$ = Relative change in x.

The following equations describe the model:

$$(1 - \tau)P_1 = a_{S1}W_S^* + a_{L1}W_U + a_{K1}r \tag{1}$$

$$(1 - \tau)P_2 = a_{L2}W_U + a_{K2}r \tag{2}$$

$$P_S = a_{SS}W_S + a_{KS}r \tag{3}$$

$$P_S X_S = \tau Y \tag{4}$$

$$Y = W_S^A S + W_U L + rK \tag{5}$$

$$W_S^A = \lambda_{S1}W_S^* + \lambda_{SS}W_S \tag{6}$$

$$a_{S1}X_1 + a_{SS}X_S = S \tag{7}$$

$$a_{L1}X_1 + a_{L2}X_2 = L \tag{8}$$

and $$a_{K1}X_1 + a_{K2}X_2 + a_{KS}X_S = K \tag{9}$$

Here equations (1) and (2) represent profit maximizing conditions of competitive firms in Sectors 1 and 2. Equation (3) defines the average cost of production of educational service. Equation (4) implies that the budget of the government to run the educational sector is balanced. Equation (5) represents total factor income (national income at factor cost in the absence of taxes and subsidies on factor income). Equation (6) represents average skilled wage rate, and equations (7), (8), and (9) stand for equilibrium conditions in factor markets.

In this model, P_1 and P_2 are internationally given. There are nine unknowns in the model, which are as follows: W_S, W_U, W_S^A, r, P_S, X_1, X_2, X_S, and Y. Parameters of this system are as follows: L, S, K, P_1, P_2, and τ. There are nine independent equations with nine unknowns. As the wage rate of skilled labor in the manufacturing sector is fixed, so sector 1 and sector 2 form a Heckscher–Ohlin subsystem and has the decomposition property because wage rate of unskilled labor and rental rate on capital can be determined independent of factor endowments.

The working of the general equilibrium model is described as follows. Two input prices W_U and r are determined from equations (1) and (2) simultaneously. Thereafter, from equation (3), we obtain W_S as a function of P_S. Now, from equations (7), (8), and (9), we can simultaneously solve for X_1, X_2, and X_S given L, S, and K. From equation (6), we obtain W_S^A as a function of P_S. Thereafter, from equation (5), we can find Y as function of P_S. Finally, from equation (4), we can solve for P_S.

Using equations (1), (2), (3), (5), (7), (8), and (9), it can be easily shown that

$$Y = P_1 X_1 + P_2 X_2,$$

which is the aggregate sales revenue (national income at the product price in the absence of commodity taxes and subsidies).

Differentiating equation (3) and using profit maximizing conditions, we obtain

$$\widehat{W}_S = \frac{\widehat{P}_S}{\theta_{SS}} \tag{10}$$

As the sector S is of fixed coefficient type, therefore, with given P_1, P_2, and τ, and using equations (7), (8), and (9), we obtain following equations.

$$\lambda_{S1}\widehat{X}_1 + \lambda_{SS}\widehat{X}_S = \widehat{S} \tag{11}$$

$$\lambda_{L1}\widehat{X}_1 + \lambda_{L2}\widehat{X}_2 = \widehat{L} \tag{12}$$

and $\quad \lambda_{K1}\widehat{X}_1 + \lambda_{K2}\widehat{X}_2 + \lambda_{KS}\widehat{X}_S = \widehat{K} \tag{13}$

Using equations (11), (12), and (13), we obtain

$$\widehat{X}_1 = \frac{\lambda_{L1}\lambda_{KS}\widehat{S}_1 + \lambda_{SS}\lambda_{K2}\widehat{L} - \lambda_{SS}\lambda_{L2}\widehat{K}}{|d|} \tag{14}$$

and $\quad \widehat{X}_S = \dfrac{(\lambda_{L1}\lambda_{K2} - \lambda_{K1}\lambda_{L2})}{|d|}\widehat{S} - \dfrac{\lambda_{S1}\lambda_{K2}}{|d|}\widehat{L} + \dfrac{\lambda_{S1}\lambda_{L2}}{|d|}\widehat{K} \tag{15}$

where $|d| = \lambda_{L2}(\lambda_{S1}\lambda_{KS} - \lambda_{SS}\lambda_{K1}) + \lambda_{SS}\lambda_{L1}\lambda_{k2}$.

We assume that education sector (Sector S) is more capital intensive than the manufacturing sector (Sector 1). So we have $\lambda_{S1}\lambda_{KS} > \lambda_{SS}\lambda_{K1}$ and $|d| > 0$. In addition, we assume that Sector 1 is more capital intensive than the agricultural sector (Sector 2), that is, $\lambda_{K1}\lambda_{L2} > \lambda_{L1}\lambda_{K2}$.

From equations (4), (5), (6), (10), (14), and (15), we obtain[11]

$$\widehat{W}_S = \frac{1}{(1-\tau)\theta_{SS}}\left[\frac{1}{|d|Y}\left\{a_{S1}X_1 W_S^* \lambda_{L2}\lambda_{KS} + (Y - a_{SS}X_S W_S)(\lambda_{K1}\lambda_{L2} - \lambda_{L1}\lambda_{K2})\right\}\widehat{S}\right.;$$

$$+\left\{\frac{1}{|d|Y}(a_{S1}X_1 W_S^* \lambda_{SS}\lambda_{K2} + (Y - a_{SS}X_S W_S)\lambda_{S1}\lambda_{K2}) + \frac{W_U L}{Y}\right\}\widehat{L};$$

$$-\left.\left\{\frac{1}{|d|Y}(a_{S1}X_1 W_S^* \lambda_{SS}\lambda_{L2} + (Y - a_{SS}X_S W_S)\lambda_{S1}\lambda_{L2}) - \frac{rK}{Y}\right\}\widehat{K}\right] \tag{16}$$

---

[11] Detailed derivation is given in the Appendix.

Here, $\dfrac{1}{(1-\tau)\theta_{SS}}\dfrac{1}{|d|Y}\left\{a_{S1}X_1W_S^*\lambda_{L2}\lambda_{KS} + (Y - a_{SS}X_SW_S)(\lambda_{K1}\lambda_{L2} - \lambda_{L1}\lambda_{K2})\right\}$,

$\dfrac{1}{(1-\tau)\theta_{SS}}\left\{\dfrac{1}{|d|Y}\left(a_{S1}X_1W_S^*\lambda_{SS}\lambda_{K2} + (Y - a_{SS}X_SW_S)\lambda_{S1}\lambda_{K2}\right) + \dfrac{W_UL}{Y}\right\}$,

and $\dfrac{1}{(1-\tau)\theta_{SS}}\left\{\dfrac{1}{|d|Y}\left(a_{S1}X_1W_S^*\lambda_{SS}\lambda_{L2} + (Y - a_{SS}X_SW_S)\lambda_{S1}\lambda_{L2}\right) - \dfrac{rK}{Y}\right\}$ are the

elasticities of W_S with respect to S, L, and K, respectively. Here, $|d|$ and $\lambda_{K1}\lambda_{L2} - \lambda_{L1}\lambda_{K2}$ are assumed to have positive signs. In addition, $(Y - a_{SS}X_SW_S) > 0$. Therefore, all three elasticities are positive[12]. Hence from equation (16), it is clear that an increase in skilled labor endowment and/or unskilled labor endowment raises skilled wage rate in the education sector, but an increase in capital stock lowers this skilled wage rate.

There exists a positive degree of wage inequality in the skilled labor market itself, and it is measured by $\left(\dfrac{W_S^*}{W_S}\right)$. Here, an increase in skilled/unskilled labor endowment lowers this degree of inequality within the skilled labor sector, but an increase in capital stock aggravates this problem.

From equation (14), we have $\dfrac{\widehat{X}_1}{\widehat{S}} = \dfrac{\lambda_{L2}\lambda_{KS}}{|d|}$ with $\widehat{L} = \widehat{K} = 0$.

Now, $\dfrac{\lambda_{L2}\lambda_{KS}}{|d|} > 1$, because by assumption, $|d| > 0$ and $\lambda_{K1}\lambda_{L2} > \lambda_{L1}\lambda_{K2}$.

Therefore, a change in S causes X_1 to move in the same direction and at a higher rate. Hence, the change in S causes λ_{S1} to change in the same direction.

Due to change in the skilled labor endowment, λ_{S1} is changed in the same direction, and hence, λ_{SS} must change in the opposite direction. As $W_S^* > W_S$, equation (6) shows that W_S^A and W_S always move in the same direction. The same mechanism works when there is a change in unskilled labor endowment or in capital endowment. Therefore, the change in any factor endowment causes the average skilled wage rate as well as the flexible skilled wage rate in the education sector to move in the same direction.

The skilled–unskilled wage ratio, which is a measure of wage inequality, is defined as

$$R = \frac{W_S^A}{W_U}.$$

---

[12] The sign of rate of change in skilled wage rate due to change in capital inflow is explained in the Appendix.

The unskilled wage rate, W_U, is independent of changes in factor endowments in this model. Therefore, the effect of a change in any factor endowment on the skilled–unskilled wage inequality, R, works through its effect on the average skilled wage rate, W_S^A.

Consequently, we can establish the following proposition.

PROPOSITION 1: *An exogenous increase in skilled labor endowment and/or unskilled labor endowment always raises the skilled–unskilled relative wage, but an exogenous increase in capital endowment reduces this in the static model where no factor endowment changes endogenously over time.*

An exogenous increase in the endowment of skilled labor lowers the level of output of the educational sector (Sector S) and raises that of manufacturing sector (Sector 1) at given W_S, because Sector S is more capital intensive than Sector 1. This increase in skilled labor endowment raises the total factor income at the given skilled wage rate in the education sector. Hence, the total budget allotted for producing the educational service is increased. Therefore, an excess demand for skilled labor is created in the education sector, and this raises the skilled wage rate in the education sector in the new equilibrium. This, in turn, raises the average wage rate of skilled labor in the economy. This is followed by an increase in the degree of skilled–unskilled wage ratio, because the unskilled wage rate is independent of changes in factor endowments.

An exogenous increase in unskilled labor endowment also lowers the level of output of Sector S and raises that of Sector 1 at given W_S. This increase in unskilled labor endowment raises the total factor income at given W_S, as well as the tax revenue. Therefore, the demand for skilled labor goes up in the education sector. This raises the wage rate of skilled labor in that sector and consequently the skilled–unskilled wage ratio.

An exogenous increase in capital endowment raises the level of output of Sector S at given W_S, because Sector S is the most capital-intensive sector. This also raises the total factor income and tax revenue, as well as the demand for skilled labor in the education sector at given W_S. However, an increase in the skilled labor allocation to Sector S also takes place at given W_S. This increase in supply outweighs the increase in demand. Therefore, skilled wage rate falls in the education sector in the new equilibrium; and thus skilled–unskilled wage ratio is reduced.

We consider the Gini coefficient of wage income distribution as a measure of wage income inequality of the working population; and this Gini coefficient, denoted by G, is obtained as follows[13]:

---

[13] Derivation of equations (17) and (18) are given in the Appendix.

$$G = \frac{\left(1 - \dfrac{W_U}{W_S^A}\right)L + G^S(S - 1)}{(S + L - 1)\left(1 + \dfrac{LW_U}{SW_S^A}\right)} \tag{17}$$

where
$$G^S = \frac{S}{(S - 1)}\frac{\lambda_{SS}\lambda_{S1}\left(W_S^* - W_S\right)}{W_S^A} \tag{18}$$

Here, G^S is the Gini coefficient of wage income distribution within skilled workers. From equation (17), it is clear that Gini coefficient of wage income distribution of the entire working population depends on the Gini coefficient of wage income distribution within skilled laborers and on the average income of skilled laborers. Given, G^S direct effect of an increase in the average wage rate of skilled labor raises G. In addition, G rises with increase in G^S, which, in turn, varies inversely with W_S^A; therefore, this is the indirect effect.

Now, we analyze the effect of a change in K only and ignore[14] the effects of change in L and S. From Proposition 1, we find that a rise in capital endowment reduces the average wage rate of skilled laborers. However, from equation (18), we find that a change in capital endowment raises G^S if λ_{SS} is very small. Therefore, the final effect of a change in K on G is indeterminate.

The Dynamic Analysis

In this section, we assume that the level of output of the education sector (Sector S), which represents the additional supply of skilled labor, adds to the existing stock of skilled labor and a constant fraction of existing stock depreciates. Let η be the constant rate of depreciation of the stock of skilled labor. We thus introduce the following equation of motion:

$$\dot{S} = X_S - \eta S \tag{19}$$

For the sake of technical simplicity, we rule out the possibility of accumulation of capital stock. In the long-run equilibrium, $\dot{S} = 0$. Hence, the long-run equilibrium value of S is given by

$$S^* = \frac{X_S}{\eta}. \tag{20}$$

---

[14] These two effects are highly complicated because changes in L and S affect all frequencies of wage income distribution.

Equations (15) and (19) show that $\dot{S}$ is a negative function of S, because Sector 1 is more capital intensive than Sector 2. Therefore, the long-run equilibrium is stable. If the economy initially starts with a higher (lower) stock of skilled labor, then that stock falls (rises) over time, and the system converges to its long-run equilibrium value.

In the long-run equilibrium, we find, from equation (19), that

$$dS = -\frac{\dfrac{\partial X_S}{\partial K}}{\left(\dfrac{\partial X_S}{\partial S} - \eta\right)} dK - \frac{\dfrac{\partial X_S}{\partial L}}{\left(\dfrac{\partial X_S}{\partial S} - \eta\right)} dL \qquad (21)$$

Using equation (15), we find that

$$-\frac{\dfrac{\partial X_S}{\partial K}}{\left(\dfrac{\partial X_S}{\partial S} - \eta\right)} > 0 \text{ and } \frac{\dfrac{\partial X_S}{\partial L}}{\left(\dfrac{\partial X_S}{\partial S} - \eta\right)} < 0.$$

Therefore, we have $\dfrac{dS}{dK} > 0$ and $\dfrac{dS}{dL} < 0$. Hence, we can establish the following proposition.

PROPOSITION 2: *An increase in capital (unskilled labor) endowment raises (lowers) the stock of skilled labor in the new long-run equilibrium.*

Using equations (5), (15), (16), (20), and (21), we obtain the following[15]:

$$\widehat{W}_S = \frac{1}{(1-\tau)\theta_{SS}} \left[\left\{ \frac{\lambda_{S1}\lambda_{K2}\left(Y - SW_S^A\right)}{Y\left\{\left(\lambda_{K1}\lambda_{L2} - \lambda_{L1}\lambda_{K2}\right) + |d|\right\}} + \frac{W_U L}{Y} \right\} \widehat{L} \right.$$

$$\left. - \frac{1}{Y}\left(\frac{\lambda_{L2}\left(W_U L + rK\right)}{\left(\lambda_{L2}\left(1 - \lambda_{K2}\right) - \lambda_{L1}\lambda_{K2}\right)} - rK\right)\widehat{K} \right] \qquad (22)$$

Here, $\dfrac{\lambda_{L2}}{\lambda_{L2}\left(1 - \lambda_{K2}\right) - \lambda_{L1}\lambda_{K2}} > 1$

and $\lambda_{L2}\left(1 - \lambda_{K2}\right) - \lambda_{L1}\lambda_{K2} = \left\{\left(\lambda_{K1}\lambda_{L2} - \lambda_{L1}\lambda_{K2}\right) + |d|\right\} > 0.$

Hence, $\left(\dfrac{\lambda_{L2}\left(W_U L + rK\right)}{\lambda_{L2}\left(1 - \lambda_{K2}\right) - \lambda_{L1}\lambda_{K2}} - rK\right) > 0.$

Therefore, with $\widehat{L} = 0$, a change in K causes W_S to move in the same direction. Since $Y > SW_S^A$, W_S varies positively with L, given K.

---

[15] Detailed derivation is given in Appendix.

Therefore, an increase in unskilled labor endowment raises the skilled wage rate in the education sector in the new long-run equilibrium; conversely, an increase in capital endowment lowers it.

Using long-run equilibrium value of S in the expression of average skilled wage rate given by equation (6), we obtain

$$W_S^A = W_S^* - a_{SS}\eta\left(W_S^* - W_S\right) \tag{23}$$

Here, a_{SS} and η are constants. Therefore, equation (23) clearly shows that W_S and W_S^A are directly related. The unskilled wage rate, W_U, is also independent of change in any factor endowment. Therefore, the skilled–unskilled wage rate $\left(\dfrac{W_S^A}{W_U}\right)$ varies positively with W_S even in the long-run equilibrium. Hence, we can establish the following proposition:

PROPOSITION 3: *In a dynamic model with endogenous accumulation of skilled labor, an exogenous increase in unskilled labor endowment always raises the skilled–unskilled relative wage, but an exogenous increase in capital endowment reduces it in the new long-run equilibrium.*

Again, here we consider the Gini coefficient of wage income distribution. In this dynamic model where skilled labor accumulates over time, Gini coefficient of wage income distribution is also affected by the rate of change in skilled labor, as the stock of skilled labor is changed due to capital accumulation. This is an additional effect compared to previous effects obtained in the static model.

Using equation (17), we obtain[16]

$$\hat{G} = \frac{G^S(S-1)}{G(S+L-1)\left(1+\dfrac{LW_U}{SW_S^A}\right)}\widehat{G^S} + \frac{LW_U}{SW_S^A\left(1+\dfrac{LW_U}{SW_S^A}\right)}\left\{1+\frac{S}{G(S+L-1)}\right\}\widehat{W_S^A}$$

$$+\frac{S}{G(S+L-1)}\left\{-1+\frac{1}{\left(1+\dfrac{LW_U}{SW_S^A}\right)}\left(\frac{S+L-1}{1}\frac{LW_U}{SW_S^A}+\frac{G^S}{G}\right)\hat{S}\right\} \tag{24}$$

From equation (24), we find that the coefficients with $\widehat{G^S}$ and $\widehat{W_S^A}$ are positive, but the sign of coefficient with $\hat{S}$ is indeterminate. In addition, due to a change in

---

[16] Derivation of equation (24) is given in the Appendix.

capital endowment, G^S changes in the same direction if λ_{SS} is very small. However, W_S^A and S change in the opposite direction. All these results create ambiguities in the final affect of capital accumulation on G in this dynamic model.

Conclusion

The model developed in this chapter is a three-sector small open-economy model focusing on the dynamics of human capital accumulation. Two of the three sectors produce final traded goods, but the third sector, called the education sector, produces additional skilled labor using skilled labor and capital as inputs. This additional skilled labor produced in this model is added to the existing stock of skilled labor at the next point of time. Thus, the stock of skilled labor accumulates over time. None of the competitive general equilibrium models of small-open economies available in the literature consider intertemporal skill formation.

We derive some interesting results from this model. An exogenous increase in skilled labor endowment and/or unskilled labor endowment always raises the skilled–unskilled relative wage. However, an exogenous increase in capital endowment reduces this in the static model, in which no factor endowment changes endogenously over time. An increase in capital (unskilled labor) endowment raises (lowers) the stock of skilled labor in the new long-run equilibrium in the dynamic model with endogenous accumulation of skilled labor. An exogenous increase in unskilled labor endowment always raises the skilled–unskilled relative wage. However, an exogenous increase in capital endowment reduces it in the new long-run equilibrium.

However, our model is abstract and does not introduce many important aspects of reality. The problem of imperfection of markets is ignored here. We do not analyze the role of sector-specific capital and the role of backward institutions on unskilled labor using sectors. We also rule out the possibility of unemployment and of induced migration caused by interregional or rural–urban wage gap. We do not consider the role of any non-traded final good or intermediate good. We plan to remove these problems in future works.

Appendix

Derivation of equation (16):
Using equations (5) and (6), we obtain
$$Y = a_{S1}X_1W_S^* + a_{SS}X_SW_S + W_UL + rK \qquad (A.1)$$

Using equations (4) and (A.1), we obtain

$$\frac{P_S X_S}{\tau} = a_{S1} X_1 W_S^* + a_{SS} X_S W_S + W_U L + rK \qquad (A.2)$$

Differentiating both sides of (A.2), we have

$$\widehat{P}_S + \widehat{X}_S - \hat{\tau} = \frac{a_{S1} X_1 W_S^*}{Y} \widehat{X}_1 + \frac{a_{SS} X_S W_S}{Y} \widehat{W}_S + \frac{a_{SS} X_S W_S}{Y} \widehat{X}_S + \frac{W_U L}{Y} \hat{L} + \frac{rK}{Y} \widehat{K}$$

$$(A.3)$$

Using equations (10) and (A.3), we have

$$(1 - \tau)\theta_{SS} \widehat{W}_S = \frac{a_{S1} X_1 W_S^*}{Y} \widehat{X}_1 - \left(1 - \frac{a_{SS} X_S W_S}{Y}\right) \widehat{X}_S + \frac{W_U L}{Y} \hat{L} + \frac{rK}{Y} \widehat{K} \qquad (A.4)$$

Using equations (14), (15) and (A.4), we have

$$\widehat{W}_S = \frac{1}{(1 - \tau)\theta_{SS}} \left[\frac{a_{S1} X_1 W_S^*}{Y} \left\{ \frac{\lambda_{L2}\lambda_{KS} \widehat{S} + \lambda_{SS}\lambda_{K2} \hat{L} - \lambda_{SS}\lambda_{L2} \widehat{K}}{|d|} \right\} - \hat{L} \right.$$

$$\left(1 - \frac{a_{SS} X_S W_S}{Y}\right) \left\{ \frac{\lambda_{L1}\lambda_{K2} - \lambda_{K1}\lambda_{L2}}{|d|} \widehat{S} - \frac{\lambda_{S1}\lambda_{K2}}{|d|} \hat{L} + \frac{\lambda_{S1}\lambda_{L2}}{|d|} \widehat{K} \right\} + \frac{W_U L}{Y} \hat{L} + \frac{rK}{Y} \widehat{K} \right]$$

$$\Rightarrow \widehat{W}_S = \frac{1}{(1 - \tau)\theta_{SS}} \left[\frac{1}{|d|Y} \left\{ a_{S1} X_1 W_S^* \lambda_{L2}\lambda_{KS} + (Y - a_{SS} X_S W_S)(\lambda_{K1}\lambda_{L2} - \lambda_{L1}\lambda_{K2}) \right\} \widehat{S} \right.$$

$$+ \left\{ \frac{1}{|d|Y} a_{S1} X_1 W_S^* \lambda_{SS}\lambda_{K2} + (Y - a_{SS} X_S W_S) \lambda_{S1}\lambda_{K2} + \frac{W_U L}{Y} \right\} \hat{L}$$

$$- \left\{ \frac{1}{|d|Y} \left(a_{S1} X_1 W_S^* \lambda_{SS}\lambda_{L2} + (Y - a_{SS} X_S W_S) \lambda_{S1}\lambda_{L2} \right) - \frac{rK}{Y} \right\} \widehat{K} \right] \qquad (A.5).$$

Equation (A.5) is same as equation (16) in the body of the chapter.

Relationship between skilled wage rate and the capital endowment:

From equation (16) we show that the expression with $\widehat{K}$ is as follows:

$$\frac{1}{|d|Y} \left(a_{S1} X_1 W_S^* \lambda_{SS}\lambda_{L2} + (Y - a_{SS} X_S W_S) \lambda_{S1}\lambda_{L2} \right) - \frac{rK}{Y}$$

$$= \frac{1}{Y} \left[\frac{1}{|d|} \left\{ a_{S1} X_1 W_S^* (1 - \lambda_{S1})\lambda_{L2} + (Y - a_{SS} X_S W_S) \lambda_{S1}\lambda_{L2} \right\} - rK \right]$$

$$= \frac{1}{Y|d|} \left[a_{S1} X_1 W_S^* \lambda_{L2} + \lambda_{S1}\lambda_{L2} \left\{ (Y - a_{S1} X_1 W_S^* - a_{SS} X_S W_S) - \frac{rK|d|}{\lambda_{S1}\lambda_{L2}} \right\} \right]$$

$$= \frac{1}{Y|d|} \left[a_{S1} X_1 W_S^* \lambda_{L2} + \lambda_{S1}\lambda_{L2} \left\{ Y - SW_S^A - \frac{rK|d|}{\lambda_{S1}\lambda_{L2}} \right\} \right]$$

Here, $\dfrac{|d|}{\lambda_{S1}\lambda_{L2}} < 1$. Hence, using equation (5), we have

$$Y - SW_S^A - \frac{rK|d|}{\lambda_{S1}\lambda_{L2}} > YSW_S^A - rK > 0.$$

So $\dfrac{1}{Y|d|}\left[a_{S1}X_1 W_S^* \lambda_{L2} + \lambda_{S1}\lambda_{L2}\left\{ Y - SW_S^A - \frac{rK|d|}{\lambda_{S1}\lambda_{L2}} \right\} > 0 \right].$

Therefore, an increase in capital inflow lowers the skilled wage rate.
Derivation of equations (17) and (18):

$$G = \frac{\bar{\Delta}}{2\mu} \tag{A.6}$$

where $\bar{\Delta} = \dfrac{1}{n(n-1)} \sum\limits_{i=1}^{n} \sum\limits_{j=1}^{n} |x_i - x_j|$ and μ = Mean Income.

Here, $\sum\limits_{i=1}^{n} \sum\limits_{j=1}^{n} |x_i - x_j|$

$$= 2\left[\left(W_S^* - W_U \right)a_{S1}X_1 L + \left(W_S^* - W_S \right)a_{S1}X_1 a_{SS}X_S + \left(W_S^* - W_U \right)a_{SS}X_S S \right]$$

and $\mu = \dfrac{a_{SS}X_S W_S + a_{S1}X_1 W_S^* + W_U L}{(S + L)} \tag{A.7}$

Using equations (A.6) and (A.7), we have

$$G = \frac{\left[\left(W_S^* - W_U \right)a_{S1}X_1 L + \left(W_S^* - W_S \right)a_{S1}X_1 a_{SS}X_S + \left(W_S^* - W_U \right)a_{SS}X_S S \right]}{(S + L - 1)\left(a_{SS}X_S W_S + a_{S1}X_1 W_S^* + W_U L \right)}$$

$$\tag{A.8}$$

Using equations (6) and (A.8), we have

$$G = \frac{\left[\left(W_S^* - W_U \right)a_{S1}X_1 L + \left(W_S^* - W_S \right)a_{S1}X_1 a_{SS}X_S + \left(W_S^* - W_U \right)a_{SS}X_S S \right]}{(S + L - 1)\left(SW_S^A + W_U L \right)}$$

$$\tag{A.9}$$

Similarly considering Gini coefficient of wage income distribution of skilled labors, we have

$$G^S = \frac{\left(W_S^* - W_S \right)a_{S1}X_1 a_{SS}X_S}{(S - 1)\left(a_{SS}X_S W_S + a_{S1}X_1 W_S^* \right)} \tag{A.10}$$

Using equations (6) and (A.10), we have

$$G^S = \frac{S}{(S-1)} \frac{\lambda_{SS}\lambda_{S1}\left(W_S^* - W_S\right)}{W_S^A} \tag{A.11}$$

Using equations (A.8) and (A.11), we obtain

$$G = \frac{\left[\left(W_S^* - W_U\right)a_{S1}X_1L + \left(W_S^* - W_U\right)a_{SS}X_SS\right]}{(S+L-1)\left(SW_S^A + W_UL\right)} \frac{G^S(S-1)}{(S+L-1)\left(1+\dfrac{LW_U}{SW_S^A}\right)} \tag{A.12}$$

Using equations (6), (7) and (A.12), we obtain

$$G = \frac{\left(1 - \dfrac{W_U}{W_S^A}\right)L + G^S(S-1)}{(S+L-1)\left(1+\dfrac{LW_U}{SW_S^A}\right)} \tag{A.13}$$

Equation (A.13) and equation (A.11) are same as equation (17) and equation (18) respectively in the body of the chapter.

Derivation of equation (22)

Using equations (15) and (21), we obtain

$$\hat{S} = -\frac{\lambda_{S1}\lambda_{L2}}{\left(\lambda_{L1}\lambda_{K2} - \lambda_{K1}\lambda_{L2}\right) - \dfrac{h|d|S}{X_S}}\hat{K} + \frac{\lambda_{S1}\lambda_{K2}}{\left(\lambda_{L1}\lambda_{K2} - \lambda_{K1}\lambda_{L2}\right) - \dfrac{h|d|S}{X_S}}\hat{L} \tag{A.14}$$

Using equations (16) and (A.6), we obtain

$$\widehat{W}_S = \frac{1}{(1-\tau)\theta_{SS}}\left[\frac{1}{|d|Y}\left\{a_{S1}X_1W_S^*\lambda_{L2}\lambda_{KS} + \left(Y - a_{SS}X_SW_S\right)\left(\lambda_{K1}\lambda_{L2} - \lambda_{L1}\lambda_{K2}\right)\right\}\right.$$

$$\left(-\frac{\lambda_{S1}\lambda_{L2}}{\left(\lambda_{K1}\lambda_{L2} - \lambda_{L1}\lambda_{K2}\right) + |d|}\widehat{K} + \frac{\lambda_{S1}\lambda_{K2}}{\left(\lambda_{K1}\lambda_{L2} - \lambda_{L1}\lambda_{K2}\right) + |d|}\hat{L}\right) +$$

$$\left\{\frac{1}{Y|d|}\left(a_{S1}X_1W_S^*\lambda_{SS}\lambda_{K2} + \left(Y - a_{SS}X_SW_S\right)\lambda_{S1}\lambda_{K2}\right) + \frac{W_UL}{Y}\right\}\hat{L} -$$

$$\left\{\frac{1}{|d|Y}\left(a_{S1}X_1W_S^*\lambda_{SS}\lambda_{L2} + \left(Y - a_{SS}X_SW_S\right)\lambda_{S1}\lambda_{L2}\right) - \frac{rK}{Y}\widehat{K}\right\}\right] \tag{A.15}$$

Using equations (20) and (A.15), we obtain

$$\widehat{W}_S = \frac{1}{(1-\tau)\theta_{SS}}\left[\frac{1}{|d|Y}\left\{a_{S1}X_1W_S^*\lambda_{L2}\lambda_{KS} + \left(Y - a_{SS}X_SW_S\right)\left(\lambda_{K1}\lambda_{L2} - \lambda_{L1}\lambda_{K2}\right)\right\}\right.$$

$$\left(\frac{\lambda_{S1}\lambda_{L2}}{(\lambda_{L1}\lambda_{K2}-\lambda_{K1}\lambda_{L2})-\dfrac{\eta|d|S}{X_S}}\widehat{K}-\frac{\lambda_{S1}\lambda_{K2}}{(\lambda_{L1}\lambda_{K2}-\lambda_{K1}\lambda_{L2})-\dfrac{\eta|d|S}{X_S}}\widehat{L}\right)$$

$$+\left\{\frac{1}{Y|d|}\left(a_{S1}X_1W_S^*\lambda_{SS}\lambda_{K2}+(Y-a_{SS}X_SW_S)\lambda_{S1}\lambda_{K2}\right)+\frac{W_UL}{Y}\right\}\widehat{L}-$$

$$\left.\left\{\frac{1}{|d|Y}\left(a_{S1}X_1W_S^*\lambda_{SS}\lambda_{L2}+(Y-a_{SS}X_SW_S)\lambda_{S1}\lambda_{L2}\right)-\frac{rK}{Y}\right\}\widehat{K}\right]$$

$$\Rightarrow\widehat{W}_S=\frac{1}{(1-\tau)\theta_{SS}}\left[\frac{1}{|d|Y}\left\{-\left(a_{S1}X_1W_S^*\lambda_{L2}\lambda_{KS}+(Y-a_{SS}X_SW_S)\right.\right.\right.$$

$$\left(\lambda_{K1}\lambda_{L2}-\lambda_{L1}\lambda_{K2}\right))\frac{\lambda_{S1}\lambda_{K2}}{(\lambda_{K1}\lambda_{L2}-\lambda_{L1}\lambda_{K2})+|d|}+a_{S1}X_1W_S^*\lambda_{SS}\lambda_{K2}$$

$$\left.+(Y-a_{SS}X_SW_S)\lambda_{S1}\lambda_{K2}\right\}+\frac{W_UL}{Y}\right\}\widehat{L}-\left\{\frac{1}{Y|d|}\right.$$

$$\left\{\left(a_{S1}X_1W_S^*\lambda_{L2}\lambda_{KS}+(Y-a_{SS}X_SW_S)(\lambda_{K1}\lambda_{L2}-\lambda_{L1}\lambda_{K2})\right)\frac{\lambda_{S1}\lambda_{L2}}{(\lambda_{K1}\lambda_{L2}-\lambda_{L1}\lambda_{K2})+|d|}\right.$$

$$\left.\left.+a_{S1}X_1W_S^*\lambda_{SS}\lambda_{L2}+(Y-a_{SS}X_SW_S)\lambda_{S1}\lambda_{L2}\right\}-\frac{rK}{Y}\right\}\widehat{K}\right]$$

$$\Rightarrow\widehat{W}_S=\frac{1}{(1-\tau)\theta_{SS}}\left[\left\{\frac{1}{|d|Y}\left\{-a_{S1}X_1W_S^*\lambda_{S1}\lambda_{K2}\frac{|d|}{(\lambda_{K1}\lambda_{L2}-\lambda_{L1}\lambda_{K2})+|d|}\right.\right.\right.$$

$$\left.\left.+(Y-a_{SS}X_SW_S)\lambda_{S1}\lambda_{K2}\frac{|d|}{(\lambda_{K1}\lambda_{L2}-\lambda_{L1}\lambda_{K2})+|d|}\right\}+\frac{W_UL}{Y}\right\}\widehat{L}-$$

$$\left\{\frac{1}{|d|Y}\left\{-a_{S1}X_1W_S^*\lambda_{S1}\lambda_{L2}\frac{|d|}{(\lambda_{K1}\lambda_{L2}-\lambda_{L1}\lambda_{K2})+|d|}+(Y-a_{SS}X_SW_S)\lambda_{S1}\lambda_{L2}\right.\right.$$

$$\left.\left.\frac{|d|}{(\lambda_{K1}\lambda_{L2}-\lambda_{L1}\lambda_{K2})+|d|}\right\}-\frac{rK}{Y}\right\}\widehat{K}\right]$$

$$\widehat{W}_S=\frac{1}{(1-\tau)\theta_{SS}}\left[\left\{\frac{\lambda_{S1}\lambda_{K2}\left(Y-SW_S^A\right)}{Y\left\{(\lambda_{K1}\lambda_{L2}-\lambda_{L1}\lambda_{K2})+|d|\right\}}+\frac{W_UL}{Y}\right\}\widehat{L}\right.$$

$$\left.-\left(\frac{\lambda_{S1}\lambda_{L2}\left(Y-SW_S^A\right)}{Y\left\{(\lambda_{K1}\lambda_{L2}-\lambda_{L1}\lambda_{K2})+|d|\right\}}-\frac{rK}{Y}\right)\widehat{K}\right] \qquad \text{(A.16)}$$

Using equations (5) and (A.8), we have

$$
\widehat{W}_S = \frac{1}{(1-\tau)\theta_{SS}}\left[\left\{\frac{\lambda_{S1}\lambda_{K2}\left(Y - SW_S^A\right)}{Y\left\{(\lambda_{K1}\lambda_{L2} - \lambda_{L1}\lambda_{K2}) + |d|\right\}} + \frac{W_U L}{Y}\right\}\hat{L}\right.
$$

$$
\left.- \frac{1}{Y}\left(\frac{\lambda_{L2}\left(W_U L + rK\right)}{\lambda_{L2}\left(1 - \lambda_{K2}\right) - \lambda_{L1}\lambda_{K2}} - rK\right)\widehat{K}\right] \quad (A.17)
$$

Equation (A.17) is same as equation (22) in the body of the chapter.

Derivation of equation (24):

Differentiating equation (17), we have

$$
\hat{G} + \frac{S}{(S+L-1)}\hat{S} - \frac{LW_U}{SW_S^A\left(1 + \dfrac{LW_U}{SW_S^A}\right)}\left(\hat{S} + \widehat{W_S^A}\right)
$$

$$
= \frac{\left(1 - \dfrac{W_U}{W_S^A}\right)L}{G(S+L-1)\left(1 + \dfrac{LW_U}{SW_S^A}\right)W_S^A\left(1 - \dfrac{W_U}{W_S^A}\right)} \cdot \frac{W_U}{W_S^A}\widehat{W_S^A}
$$

$$
+ \frac{G^S\left(S-1\right)}{G(S+L-1)\left(1 + \dfrac{LW_U}{SW_S^A}\right)}\left(\widehat{G^S} + \frac{S}{(S-1)}\hat{S}\right)
$$

$$
\hat{G} = \frac{G^S\left(S-1\right)}{G(S+L-1)\left(1 + \dfrac{LW_U}{SW_S^A}\right)}\widehat{G^S} + \frac{LW_U}{SW_S^A\left(1 + \dfrac{LW_U}{SW_S^A}\right)}\left\{1 + \frac{S}{G(S+L-1)}\right\}\widehat{W_S^A}
$$

$$
+ \frac{S}{(S+L-1)}\left\{-1 + \frac{1}{\left(1 + \dfrac{LW_U}{SW_S^A}\right)}\left(\frac{S+L-1}{S}\frac{LW_U}{SW_S^A} + \frac{G^S}{G}\right)\hat{S}\right\} \quad (A.18)
$$

Equation (A.18) is same as equation (24) in the body of the chapter.

References

Acemoglu, D. 1999. 'Changes in Unemployment and Wage Inequalty: An Alternative Theory and Some Evidence.' *American Economic Review* 89: 1258–78.

———. 2002b. 'Directed Technical Change.' *Review of Economic Studies* 69: 781–809.

———. 2002a. 'Technical Change, Inequality, and the Labor Market.' *Journal of Economic Literature* 40: 7–72.

Acemoglu, D. 1998. 'Why Do New Tecchnologies Complement Skills? Directed Technical Change and Wage Inequality.' *Quarterly Journal of Economics* 113: 1055–89.

Anwar, S. 2006. 'Factor Mobilty and Wage Inequality in the Presence of Specialistion-Based External Economics.' *Economics Letters* 93(1): 88–93.

Anwar, S. 2009. 'Wage inequality, welfare and downsizing.' *Economics Letters* 103: 75–77.

Anwar, S. and J. Rice. 2009. 'Labour Mobility and Wage Inequality in The Presence of Endogenous Foreign Investment.' *Economic Modelling* 26(6): 1135–39.

Banga, R. 2005. 'Liberalisation and Wage Inequality in India.' ICRIER Working Paper 156.

Behrman, J. R., N. Birdsall, and M. Szekely. 2000. 'Economic Reform and Wage Differentials in Latin America.' BID Working Paper 435.

Beyer, H., P. Rojas, and R. Vergara. 1999. 'Trade Liberalization and Wage Inequality.' *Journal of Development Economics* 59: 103–23.

Borjas, G. and V. A. Ramey. 1993. 'Foreign Competition, Market Power and Wage Inequality: Theory and Evidence.' NBER Working Paper 4556.

Bound, J. and G. Johnson. 1992. 'Changes in the Structure of Wages in the 1980s: An Evaluation of Alternative Explanations.' *American Economic Review* 82: 371–92.

Chaudhuri, S. 2004. 'International Migration of Skilled and Unskilled Labour, Welfare and Skilled-Unskilled Wage Inequality: A simple Model.' *Journal of Economic Integration* 19(4): 726–41.

Chaudhuri, S. 2008. 'Wage Inequality in a Dual Economy and International Mobility of Factors: Do Factor Intensities Always Matter?' *Economic Modelling* 25: 1155–64.

Chaudhuri, S. and S. Yabuuchi. 2007. 'Economic Liberalization and Wage Inequality in the Presence of Labour Market Imperfection.' *International Review of Economics and Finance* 16: 592–603.

————. 2008. 'Foreign Capital and Skilled- Unskilled Wage Inequality in a Developing Economy with Non-traded Goods.' In *Contemporary and Emerging Issues in Trade Theory and Policy,* edited by S. Marjit and E. Yu. UK, North America, Japan, Malaysia, China: Elsevier Science and Technology Books.

Dev, M. 2000. 'Economic Liberalization and Employment in South Asia.' *Economic and Political Weekly* 40–51.

Esquivel, G. and J. A. Lopez. 2003. 'Technology, Trade and Wage Inequality in Mexico Before and After Nafta.' *Journal of Development Economics* 72: 543–65.

Fang, C., L. Huang, and M. Wang. 2008. 'Technology spillover and wage inequality.' *Economic Modelling* 25: 137–47.

Feenstra, R. C. and G. H. Hanson. 1997. 'Foreign Direct Investment and Relative Wages: Evidence from Mexico's Maquiladoras.' *Journal of Inrenational Economics* 42: 371–94.

Gorg, H. and E. Strobl. 2002. 'Relative Wages, Openness and Skill-Baised Technological Change.' IZA Discussion Paper Series 596.

Green, F., A. Dickerson, and J. Arbache. 2001. 'A Picture of Wage Inequality and the allocation of Labour Through a Period of Trade Liberalization: The Case of Brazil.' *World Development* 29(11): 1923–39.

Gupta, M. R., and P. B. Dutta. 2011. 'Skilled-Unskilled Wage Inequality and Unemployment: A General Equilibrium Analysis.' *Economic Modelling* 28(4): 1977–83.

————. 2010a. 'Skilled–unskilled wage inequality, nontraded good and endogenous supply of skilled labour: A theoretical analysis.' *Economic Modelling* 27: 923–34.

_____. 2010b. 'Skilled–unskilled wage inequality: A general equilibrium analysis.' *Research in Economics* 64: 247–63.

Hanson, G. and A. Harisson. 1999. 'Trade Liberalization and Wage Inequality in Mexico.' *Industrial and Labor Economics Review* 52: 271–88.

Harrison, A. and Hanson, G. 1999. 'Who Gains from Trade Reform? Some Remmaning Puzzles.' *Journal of Development Economics* 59: 125–54.

Isgut, A. E. 2001. 'What's Different about Exporters? Evidence from Colombian Manufacturing.' *Journal of Development Studies* 37: 57–82.

Kar, S. and H. Beladi. 2004. 'Skill Formation and International Migration: Welfare Perspective of Developing Countries.' *Japan and the World Economy* 16: 33–54.

Katz, L., G. W. Loveman, and D. G. Blanchflower. 1992. 'A comparison of Changes in the structure of Wages in Four OECD Countries.' NBER Working Paper 4297.

Kiley, M. T. 1999. 'The Supply of Skilled Labor and Skilled-baised Technological Progress.' *Economic Journal* 109: 708–24.

Lawrence, R. Z. 1994. 'Trade, Multinationals and Labour.' NBER Working Paper 4836.

Leamer, E. 2000. 'What's the Use of Factor Contents?' *Journal of International Economics* 50: 51–71.

Lucas, R. E. 1988. 'On the Mechanics of Economic Development.' *Journal of Monetary Economics* 22(1): 3–42.

Marjit, S. and R. Acharyya. 2003. *International Trade, Wage Inequality and the Developing Economy- A General Equilibrium Approach.* Berlin: Springer-Verlag.

_____. 2006. 'Trade Liberalization, Skill-linked Intermediate Production and the Two-sided Wage Gap.' *The Journal of Policy Reform* 9: 203–17.

Marjit, S. and S. Kar. 2005. 'Emigration and Wage Inequality.' Economics Letters 88: 141–145.

Marjit, S., H. Beladi, and A. Chakrabarti. 2004. 'Trade and Wage Inequality in Developing Countries.' *Economic Inquiry* 42(2): 295–303.

Ranjan, P. 2001. 'Dynamic Evaluation of Income Distribution and Credit Constrained Human Development Investment in Open Economies.' *Journal of International Economics* 55: 329–58.

Rebelo, S. 1991. 'Long-Run Policy Analysis and Long-Run Growth.' *Journal of Political Economy* 99(3): 500–21.

Sener, F. 2001. 'Schumpeterian Unemployment, Trade and Wages.' *Journal of International Economics* 54: 119–48.

Wang, M., C. Fang, and L. Huang. 2009. 'International knowledge spillovers and wage inequality in developing countries.' *Economic Modelling* 26(6): 1208–14.

Wood, A. 1998. 'Globalisation and the Rise in Labor Market Inequalities.' *The Economic Journal* 108: 1463–82.

_____. 1997. 'Openness and Wage Inequality in Developing Countries- The Latin American Challenge to East Asian Conventional Wisdom.' *World Bank Research Observer* 33–57.

Yabuuchi, S. and S. Chaudhuri. 2007. 'International Migration of Labour and Skilled-unskilled Wage Inequality in a Developing Economy.' *Economic Modelling* 24(1): 128–37.

_____. 2009. 'Skill Formation, Capital Adjustment Cost and Wage Inequality.' *Review of Urban and Regional Development Studies* 21(1): 2–13.

5

FDI in Education *vs* FDI in Commodity Production

A Theoretical Model

Rashmi Ahuja

Introduction

For the past few decades, many developing economies are integrating rapidly into the world market. This rapid integration has led to a heavy influx of foreign capital in the form of foreign direct investment into these economies. Foreign direct investment (FDI) has been sought by many developing economies as a means to augment their endowment of domestic capital, source of advanced technology, better managerial practices, efficiency gains, and access to new foreign markets. Hence, most of the developing economies are seeking to enhance the level of foreign direct investment in their economies.

However, the distributional consequences of increasing foreign capital inflows are also widely debated in the literature. The studies in the empirical literature has put forward different contending theoretical perspectives on the impact of FDI on host countries (see Tsai, 2005; Figini and Gorg, 1999; Meschi and Vivarelli, 2007, etc.). A theoretical perspective supporting modernization theory implies that foreign capital inflows lead to a decrease in income inequality, whereas those supporting dependency theory imply that foreign direct investment leads to an increase in income inequality. Another perspective based on the Aghion and Howitt (1998) model implies that FDI follows non-linear relationship with income inequality.

A vast theoretical literature has developed based on general equilibrium models, which points out the impact of foreign capital inflows on wage inequality. There are two kinds of studies in this literature. One set of studies examines the impact of foreign capital inflows on wage inequality with supply of skilled labor to be fixed and given. Banerjee and Narayan (2011), Marjit and Kar (2011), Gilbert and Beladi (2011), Beladi, Chaudhuri, and Yabuuchhi (2008), Chaudhuri and Yabuuchi

(2007), and Chaudhuri(2008) found that the impact of foreign capital inflows on skilled–unskilled wage inequality depends on factor intensity condition of the sectors. Besides this, the impact is also found to be dependent on other factors such as type of good (i.e., intermediate or final good) produced in the non-traded sector (Chaudhuri and Yabucchi, 2008), efficiency function of skilled working class (Chaudhuri, 2011; Chaudhuri and Banerjee, 2010), and importance of environment quality (Pan and Zhou, 2013).

Another set of studies examines the impact of foreign capital inflows on wage inequality with supply of skilled labor to be endogenous. Yabuuchi and Chaudhuri (2009), Kar and Guha-Khasnobis (2006), and Gupta and Dutta (2010) considered a skill formation sector into their models and assumed the supply of skilled labor to be determined within the model. Both Yabuuchi and Chaudhuri (2009) and Gupta and Dutta (2010) found that the impact of foreign capital inflows on skilled–unskilled wage inequality depends on relative factor intensity condition. Gupta and Dutta (2010) with further inclusion of non-traded goods in their model also found that, apart from factor intensity condition, this impact also depends on relative strength of marginal effect on demand of the non-traded good over the corresponding effect on its supply. Kar and Guha-Khasnobis (2006) found that a tariff cut in the import-competing sector unambiguously promotes skill formation and reduces skilled–unskilled wage inequality. However, increase in incentives for foreign capital inflows reduces the rate of skill formation, lowers the rate of foreign capital inflow, and also lowers the skilled–unskilled wage gap under a reasonable factor intensity condition.

Although FDI is an integral part of economic integration and development, benefits of FDI do not accrue evenly across sectors within the developing economies. For instance, technology spillovers from FDI may vary in accordance with different economic sectors. Besides that, it is also observed that the increasing foreign capital inflows are not evenly distributed across the different economic sectors within an economy. Hence, the different distribution of foreign capital inflows in the economic sectors may have different impacts on skilled–unskilled wage inequality and skill formation. With increasing foreign capital inflows, the developing economies also face the challenge of managing and directing the foreign capital inflows into the appropriate sectors. This chapter has attempted to deal with this question faced by policymakers in the developing economies, as these economies integrate far more with the world economy. It specifically discusses about what happens to skill formation and skilled–unskilled wage inequality if there is foreign capital inflow into the education sector or foreign capital inflow into the commodity production sector.

Both commodity production sector and education sector are considered to be attractive sectors for foreign investment in developing economies. On the one hand, education sector is considered to be an integral part of economic development in developing economies in this era of increasing integration. The provision of right kind of skills to the youth of a country can help it in achieving higher overall progress and economic development. The education sector in developing economies is continuously evolving and has emerged as one of the high-potential markets for investments, especially for those such as India, which is experiencing service-led growth with an advantage of demographic dividend.[1] Therefore, the spread of education and skill formation have been given high priority in developing economies, and FDI in education is considered one of the ways of providing funds, expertise, and technology in the education and training sector in the developing economies. For instance, the Government of India has allowed 100 percent foreign direct investment in education through automatic route. China is also looking up to open service sectors such as education for foreign direct investment.[2]

The literature examining the impact of foreign capital inflows has also given due importance to the process of skill formation in developing economies. Yabuuchi and Chaudhuri (2009), Kar and Guha-Khasnobis (2006), Gupta and Dutta (2010), Chaudhuri (2008), Kar and Beladi (2004), Marjit (2006), and Beladi, Marjit and Broll (2011) have considered a skill formation or education sector in which the skilled labor is being produced. Yabuuchi and Chaudhuri (2009), Chaudhuri (2008), Kar and Beladi (2004), Marjit (2006), and Kar and Guha-Khasnobis (2006) have assumed that one unit of unskilled labor and some amount of capital are required in the skill formation sector to produce skilled labor in a developing economy. However, Gupta and Dutta (2010) have explained that the education or skill formation sector cannot run without skilled labor. They assumed that education sector uses skilled labor and capital as inputs to instantaneously transform unskilled labor into skilled labor. Beladi, Marjit, and Broll (2011) have used three types of labor—unskilled, mid-skilled, and high-skilled—with the possibility of unskilled being transformed into mid-skilled and mid-skilled being transformed into high-skilled using some amount of educational capital in the skill formation sector.

On the other hand, commodity production[3], which involves the production of commodities in both agriculture and industrial sectors, also forms an important

---

[1] Total amount of Foreign direct investments (FDI) inflow into the education sector in India stood at US$ 1,209.40 million from April 2000 to December 2016, according to data released by the Department of Industrial Policy and Promotion (DIPP).

[2] Press Trust of India wire (PTI), dated 18 March 2016.

[3] Commodity production includes agriculture, power, manufacturing, oil and gas, food and beverages, textile, etc.

backbone of any economy. Many developing economies have been giving various tax incentives and other benefits to attract more and more foreign investment in these sectors. For instance, the Government of India has allowed 100 percent FDI in some of the agriculture sectors such as the tea sector, floriculture, horticulture, and cultivation of vegetables and mushrooms. In India, around 30 percent of FDI was received by the manufacturing sector during the period 2000–2012.[4] With studies in literature pointing out the distributional consequences of increased FDI in developing economies, it becomes really important as well as interesting to examine how different sectoral compositions of foreign direct investment, specifically FDI in education and FDI in commodity production, impact the wage inequality in these economies.

This chapter examines the impact on skill formation and skilled–unskilled wage inequality due to FDI in education and FDI in commodity production. It builds a well-specified general equilibrium model based on Jones (1971) specific-factor model. A skill formation sector is introduced into the Jones (1971) two-sector three-factor specific-factor full employment model. This skill formation sector transforms unskilled labor into skilled labor using skilled labor[5] and educational capital. It is assumed that the commodity production sector involves production of both unskilled-intensive and skilled-intensive commodities. In this model, it is assumed that the commodity production and education sector both use specific capital, that is, commodity capital and education capital, respectively. In addition, our model does not assume any education subsidy or adjustment cost being given to the education sector unlike the model developed by Yabuuchi and Chaudhuri (2009).The studies available in the literature have not dealt with how the impact of FDI in education and FDI in commodity production may differ on skill formation and wage inequality. Hence, addressing this question in this chapter will provide us some scope for designing liberalization policies related to opening up of certain economic sectors for foreign direct investment.

The chapter is organized as follows. Following the introduction in the first section, the second section presents the model and discussion of results. In the final section, conclusions have been drawn.

Model and Results

There are three sectors in a perfectly competitive small open economy. These sectors are defined as follows: X, Y, and S. Sectors X and Y involve the production

---

[4] Based on the data provided in DIPP, SIA Newsletter, various issues.

[5] For instance, the education sector requires skilled labor, that is, teachers to transform unskilled labor into skilled labor.

of commodities, whereas Sector S is the education or skill formation sector. Sector X is the high-skilled commodity-producing sector, which uses skilled labor and commodity capital, whereas Sector Y is the low-skilled commodity-producing sector, which uses unskilled labor and commodity capital. Commodity capital is specific to the commodity-producing Sectors X and Y. Sector S transforms one unit of unskilled labor into skilled labor using skilled labor and educational capital. It is assumed that more than one unit of skilled labor is required to convert one unit of unskilled labor into skilled labor in the education sector.[6] Educational capital is specific to the education sector. The commodity capital as well as educational capital consists of both domestic as well as foreign stock of capital. The trade pattern is such that Good X is imported, whereas Good Y is exported. It is assumed that skilled wages are higher than unskilled wages, as there is a positive return to education. All the four factors are fully employed in our model.

To build the system of equations, following notations are used:

w: unskilled wages;

w_s: skilled wages;

r: return to commodity capital;

r_e: return to educational capital;

$(\overline{P_X}, \overline{P_Y})$: world prices of goods produced in Sectors X and Y, respectively;

t: tariff on imports of Good X;

$\wedge$: proportional change;

a_{ij} : per unit requirement of ith factor in j^{th} sector;

$i = $ L, S, K, E;

$j = $ X, Y, S;

L_S: Initial endowment of skilled labor in economy;

$(L_u, \overline{K}, \overline{E})$: given endowment of unskilled labor, commodity capital, and educational capital, respectively, in the economy;

(X, Y, S): Outputs of the Sectors X, Y, and S, respectively;

θ_{ij}'s: distributive share of ith input into the jth sector for $i = $ L, S, E, K and $j = $ X, Y, S;

λ_{ij}'s: proportion of ith input employed in the jth sector for $i = L_u$, $(L_s + S)$, E, K and $j = $ X, Y, S;

S_{ij}^k: degree of subsitution between the factors i and j in k^{th} sector, $i, j = $ L, S, E, K, and $k = $ X, Y, S. $S_{ij}^k > 0$ for $i \neq j$ and $S_{jj}^k < 0$.

The system follows standard neoclassical assumptions, that is, constant returns to scale and positive but diminishing marginal returns to factor. The general

---

[6] It means that $a_{SS} > 1$.

equilibrium structure is given by seven equations comprising the competitive price equations and the full employment equations, in that order.[7]

$$a_{SX}w_S + a_{KX}r = \overline{P_X}(1 + t) \tag{1}$$

$$a_{LY}w + a_{KY}r = \overline{P_Y} \tag{2}$$

$$a_{LS}w + a_{SS}w_S + a_{ES}r_e = w + a_{SS}w_S + a_{ES}r_e = w_s \tag{3}$$

$$a_{LY}Y + a_{LS}S = L_u \text{ or } a_{LY}Y = L_u - S \tag{4}$$

$$a_{SX}X + a_{SS}S = L_s + S \tag{5}$$

$$a_{KX}X + a_{KY}Y = \overline{K} = K_D + K_F \tag{6}$$

$$a_{ES}S = \overline{E} = E_D + E_F \tag{7}$$

The aforementioned seven equations can be used to solve for the seven unknowns in the model, that is, w, w_S, r, r_e, X, Y, and S. In addition, the model does not satisfy the decomposition property, because the four-factor prices cannot be determined from the commodity price equations alone independent of the full employment equations.[8]

Analysis

It is assumed that there is no change in trade policies, and hence, tariffs are given, which means that $\hat{t} = 0$. The comparative static equations (refer Appendix A.1) are obtained from the aforementioned system of equations, and skilled–unskilled wage inequality is given as:

$$\hat{w}_s - \hat{w} = \frac{1}{|\Delta|}\left[\left((\lambda_{SS} - \lambda_S)\lambda_{LY}\lambda_{KX} + \lambda_{LS}\lambda_{SX}\lambda_{KY}\right)\theta_{ES}\left(\theta_{KX}\theta_{LY} - \theta_{SX}\theta_{KY}\right)\right]\hat{\overline{E}}$$

$$+ \frac{\theta_{ES}\lambda_{SX}\lambda_{LY}\lambda_{ES}}{|\Delta|}\left[\theta_{KX}\theta_{LY} - \theta_{SX}\theta_{KY}\right]\hat{\overline{K}}$$

FDI in Education Sector

With inflow of foreign capital in education sector, that is, $\hat{\overline{E}} > 0$, the skilled–unskilled wage inequality[9] is as follows:

Increases, that is, $\hat{w}_s - \hat{w} > 0$ if $\theta_{KX}\theta_{LY} - \theta_{SX}\theta_{KY} > 0$, that is, $\dfrac{\theta_{KX}}{\theta_{SX}} > \dfrac{\theta_{KY}}{\theta_{LY}}$

---

[7] Note that $a_{LS} = 1$.

[8] Note that except a_{LS}, all input coefficients are variable and functions of factor returns.

[9] $\hat{w}_s - \hat{w} = \frac{1}{|\Delta|}\left[\left((\lambda_{SS} - \lambda_S)\lambda_{LY}\lambda_{KX} + \lambda_{LS}\lambda_{SX}\lambda_{KY}\right)\theta_{ES}\left(\theta_{KX}\theta_{LY} - \theta_{SX}\theta_{KY}\right)\right]\hat{\overline{E}}$

Decreases, that is, $\hat{w}_s - \hat{w} < 0$ if $\theta_{KX}\theta_{LY} - \theta_{SX}\theta_{KY} < 0$, that is, $\dfrac{\theta_{KX}}{\theta_{SX}} < \dfrac{\theta_{KY}}{\theta_{LY}}$

Hence, based on the aforementioned equations, the following proposition can be given:

Proposition 1: In a developing economy with the aforementioned setup, FDI in education sector

   (i) **Promotes skill formation if skilled labor-intensive sector is more capital intensive than the unskilled labor-intensive sector.**

  (ii) **Increases (decreases) wage inequality if skilled labor-intensive sector is more (less) capital intensive than the unskilled labor-intensive sector.**

It means that as long as skilled labor-intensive commodity-producing sector is more capital intensive than the unskilled labor-intensive sector, foreign capital inflow in the education sector promotes skill formation and increases wage inequality. This proposition can be explained in the following manner. Due to an inflow of foreign capital into the skill formation sector, the aggregate stock of educational capital increases. However, the education sector will expand only if skilled labor-intensive Sector X is more capital intensive than the unskilled labor-intensive Sector Y. This may be due to the fact that skilled labor is also required as one of the inputs in the education sector to transform unskilled labor into skilled labor. However, the Sector Y contracts, and unskilled labor from commodity production will move to the skill formation sector. Sector X can contract or expand. However, there is increase in both the skilled and unskilled wages. Hence, the impact of foreign capital inflow into the education sector on skilled–unskilled wage inequality will depend on which wages increase at a faster rate. The increase in skilled wages will be more if the skilled labor-intensive sector is more capital intensive than the unskilled labor-intensive sector, thereby increasing the wage inequality in that case. Conversely, the wage inequality decreases.

FDI in Commodity Production Sector

With inflow of foreign capital into the commodity production sector, the aggregate stock of commodity capital increases, that is, $\hat{K} > 0$, the skilled–unskilled wage inequality[10].

   (i) increases, that is, $\hat{w}_s - \hat{w} > 0$ if $\theta_{KX}\theta_{LY} - \theta_{SX}\theta_{KY} > 0$, that is,

---

10 $\dfrac{\hat{w}_s - \hat{w}}{\hat{K}} = \dfrac{\theta_{ES}\lambda_{SX}\lambda_{LY}\lambda_{ES}}{|\Delta|}\left[\theta_{KX}\theta_{LY} - \theta_{SX}\theta_{KY}\right]$

$$\frac{\theta_{KX}}{\theta_{SX}} > \frac{\theta_{KY}}{\theta_{LY}}$$

(ii) decreases, that is, $\hat{w}_s - \hat{w} < 0$ if $\theta_{KX}\theta_{LY} - \theta_{SX}\theta_{KY} < 0$, that is,

$$\frac{\theta_{KX}}{\theta_{SX}} < \frac{\theta_{KY}}{\theta_{LY}}$$

Hence, based on the aforementioned equations, the following proposition can be given:

Proposition 2: In a developing economy with the aforementioned setup, FDI in commodity production sector
   (i) Discourages skill formation.
   (ii) Increases (decreases) skilled–unskilled wage inequality if the skilled labor-intensive sector is more (less) capital intensive than the unskilled labor-intensive sector.

This proposition can be explained in the following manner. Due to an inflow of foreign capital into the commodity production, the aggregate stock of commodity capital increases, and it leads to expansion of Sector Y while there is a contraction of Sector S. The expansion of Sector Y will lead to more demand of the unskilled labor, and hence, higher wages for unskilled workers. Hence, the unskilled labor from the skill formation sector will move into Sector Y. The Sector X will expand if the skilled-intensive commodity-producing sector is more capital intensive than the unskilled-intensive commodity-producing sector. The demand for skilled labor in that case increases, and skilled wages increase. Due to contraction of the skill formation sector, the skilled labor will move from the skill formation sector to the skilled-intensive commodity-producing sector. There is increase in both the skilled and unskilled wages. In such a scenario, with the skilled–intensive sector being more capital intensive than the unskilled-intensive sector, the skilled wages will increase at a faster rate than unskilled wages leading to increase in skilled–unskilled wage inequality. Conversely, unskilled wages increase at a faster rate than skilled wages, and hence, the skilled–unskilled wage inequality decreases.

Conclusion

Increasing foreign capital inflows and International Trade have become an integral part of rapid globalization in developing economies. With increasing integration, concern has also been expressed regarding its distributional impacts in developing economies. It is also observed that benefits of these increasing foreign capital inflows do not accrue evenly to all the economic sectors. As these economies integrate far more with the world economy, they are faced with a question as to which sectors should be encouraged with foreign capital inflows taking into account the issue of skilled–unskilled wage inequality as well as skill formation in these economies. This chapter specifically discusses about the opening up of the education sector and commodity production sectors to foreign capital inflows in developing economies taking into account skilled–unskilled wage inequality and skill formation in these economies. Hence, it examines the impact on skill formation and skilled–unskilled wage inequality in the following two cases: (a) when FDI comes into the education sector and (b) when FDI comes into the commodity production sector.

A small open-developing economy consisting of a skill formation sector and commodity-producing sectors is considered. The commodity-producing sector consists of both unskilled labor-intensive and skilled labor-intensive sectors. The skill formation sector requires skilled labor and educational capital to transform unskilled labor into skilled labor. The unskilled-intensive commodity-producing sector uses unskilled labor and commodity capital to produce unskilled commodities, whereas the skilled-intensive commodity-producing sector uses skilled labor and commodity capital to produce skilled commodities. In such an economy, if there is foreign capital inflow into the education sector, then impact on skilled–unskilled wage inequality depends on the relative factor intensity of the two commodity-producing sectors. However, it will increase skill formation if the skilled-intensive commodity-producing sector is more capital intensive than the unskilled-intensive commodity-producing sector. However, if foreign capital inflows come into the commodity-producing sector, then it decreases skill formation unambiguously, while impact on skilled–unskilled wage inequality will again depend on the relative factor intensity ranking of the two commodity-producing sectors.

It is likely that the skilled-intensive sector is more capital intensive than the unskilled-intensive sector in a developing economy. In such a scenario, FDI in education will promote skill formation and increases skilled–unskilled wage inequality, whereas FDI in commodity production discourages skill formation and increases skilled–unskilled wage inequality. Although FDI in both the sectors increases inequality, it is still beneficial to promote FDI in the education sector in developing economies. This is because it will help in promoting skill formation. With increasing skill formation, as developing economies progress, it is likely that skilled labor will become more abundant and unskilled labor will become less abundant. In a skilled-intensive commodity-producing sector, capital will be replaced with skilled labor, as it becomes cheaper, which leads to a possible fall in capital intensity in a skill-intensive sector and a rise in capital intensity in unskilled-intensive commodity-producing sector. Hence, eventually, it can lead to decrease in skilled–unskilled wage inequality in such an economy.

Appendix

A.1. Comparative static equations

The comparative static equations obtained are as follows:-

$$\theta_{SX}\hat{w}_s + \theta_{KX}\hat{r} = T\hat{t}$$

$$\theta_{LY}\hat{w} + \theta_{KY}\hat{r} = 0$$

$$\theta_{LS}\hat{w} + \theta_{SS}\hat{w}_s + \theta_{ES}\hat{r}_e = \hat{w}_s$$

$$\lambda_{LY}\hat{Y} + \lambda_{LY}S_{LL}^Y\hat{w} + \lambda_{LY}S_{LK}^Y\hat{r} + \hat{S}\lambda_{LS} = 0$$

$$\lambda_{SX}S_{SK}^X\hat{r} + \lambda_{SX}\hat{X} + \left(\lambda_{SS} - \lambda_S\right)\hat{S} + \lambda_{SS}S_{SL}^S\hat{w} + B\hat{w}_s + \lambda_{SS}S_{SE}^S\hat{r}_e = 0$$

$$\lambda_{KX}\hat{X} + \lambda_{KX}S_{KS}^X\hat{w}_s + A\hat{r} + \lambda_{KY}\hat{Y} + \lambda_{KY}S_{KL}^Y\hat{w} = \widehat{K}$$

$$\lambda_{ES}\hat{S} + \lambda_{ES}S_{EL}^S\hat{w} + \lambda_{ES}S_{EE}^S\widehat{r_e} + \lambda_{ES}S_{ES}^S\hat{w}_s = \widehat{E}$$

where $T = \dfrac{t}{1+t}, \lambda_{LS} = \dfrac{a_{LS}S}{L_u} = \dfrac{S}{L_u}, B = \left(\lambda_{SS}S_{SS}^S + \lambda_{SX}S_{SS}^X\right),$

$A = \left(\lambda_{KX}S_{KK}^X + \lambda_{KY}S_{KK}^Y\right)$ and $\lambda_S = \dfrac{S}{L_S + S}$.

A.2. Expressions for change in skilled–unskilled wage inequality

The change in skilled–unskilled wage inequality w.r.t change in commodity capital is given by

$$\frac{\hat{w}_s - \hat{w}}{\widehat{K}} = \frac{\theta_{ES}\lambda_{SX}\lambda_{LY}\lambda_{ES}}{|\Delta|}\left[\theta_{KX}\theta_{LY} - \theta_{SX}\theta_{KY}\right]$$

The change in skilled–unskilled wage inequality w.r.t change in educational capital is given by

$$\frac{\hat{w}_s - \hat{w}}{\widehat{E}} = \frac{1}{|\Delta|}\left[\left(\left(\lambda_{SS} - \lambda_S\right)\lambda_{LY}\lambda_{KX} + \lambda_{LS}\lambda_{SX}\lambda_{KY}\right)\theta_{ES}\left(\theta_{KX}\theta_{LY} - \theta_{SX}\theta_{KY}\right)\right]$$

where $|\Delta| > 0$ if $a_{SS} > 1$, which is true as per our assumption.

References

Aghion, P. and P. Howitt. 1998. *Endogenous Growth Theory*. Cambridge, MA: MIT Press.

Beladi H., S. Marjit, and U. Broll. 2011. 'Capital mobility, skill formation and polarization.' *Economic Modelling* 28(4): 1902–06.

Beladi H., S. Chaudhuri, and S. Yabuuchi. 2008. 'Can international factor mobility reduce wage rate inequality in a dual economy?' *Review of International Economics* 16(5): 893–903.

Banerjee, R. and R. Narayan. 2011. 'Globalization, Labour Market Segmentation, Unemployment and Wage Inequality: A Theoretical Analysis.' *Journal of Economic Integration* 26(3): 578–99.

Chaudhuri, S. 2008a. 'International Factor Mobility, Skills Formation and Welfare.' Munich Personal RePEc Archive, University Library of Munich, Germany.

————. 2008b. 'Wage inequality in a dual economy and international mobility of factors: do factor intensities always matter?' *Economic Modelling* 25(6): 1155–64.

————. 2011. 'Fair Wage Hypothesis, Foreign Capital Inflow and Skilled-unskilled Wage Inequality in the Presence of Agricultural Dualism.' *Journal of International Economics* 2(2): 4.

Chaudhuri, S. and D. Banerjee. 2010. 'Foreign capital inflow, skilled–unskilled wage inequality and unemployment of unskilled labour in a fair wage model.' *Economic Modelling* 27(1): 477–86.

Chaudhuri, S. and S. Yabuuchi. 2007. 'Economic liberalization and wage inequality in the presence of labor market imperfection.' *International Review of Economics and Finance* 16(4): 592–603.

————. 2008. 'Foreign capital and skilled–unskilled wage inequality in a developing economy with non-traded goods.' In *Contemporary and Emerging Issues in Trade Theory and Policy*, edited by S. Marjit and E. Yu. UK, North America, Japan, Malaysia, China: Elsevier Science and Technology Books.

Figini, P. and H. Görg. 1999. 'Multinational Companies and Wage Inequality in the Host Country: The Case of Ireland.' *Review of World Economics* 135: 594–612.

Gilbert, J. and H. Beladi. 2011. 'Foreign Direct Investment, Non-Traded Goods and Real Wages.' *Pacific Economic Review* 16: 36–41.

Gupta, M. R. and P. B. Dutta. 2010. 'Skilled–unskilled wage inequality, nontraded good and endogenous supply of skilled labour: a theoretical analysis.' *Economic Modelling* 27(5): 923–34.

Kar, S. and B. Guha-Khasnobis. 2006. 'Economic reform, skill formation and foreign capital.' *World Economy* 29(1): 79–94.

Kar, S. and H. Beladi. 2004. 'Skill formation and international migration: Welfare perspective of developing countries.' *Japan and the World Economy* 16: 35–54.

Marjit, S. 2006. 'Protection, skill formation and income distribution.' *Asia-Pacific Journal of Accounting and Economics* 13(2): 135–39.

Marjit, S. and S. Kar. 2011. 'International Capital Flow, Finite Change and Two-sided Wage Inequality.' Working Paper 2, Centre for Studies in Social Sciences, Kolkata.

Meschi, E. and M. Vivarelli. 2009. 'Trade and income inequality in Developing Countries.' *World Development* 37(2): 287–302.

Pan, L. and Y. Zhou. 2013. 'International factor mobility, environmental pollution and skilled–unskilled wage inequality in developing countries.' *Economic Modelling* 33: 82–831.

Tsai, P. 1995. 'Foreign Direct Investment and income inequality: Further evidence.' *World Development* 23(3): 469–83.

Yabuuchi, S. and S. Chaudhuri. 2009. 'Skill formation, capital adjustment and wage inequality.' *Review of Urban and Regional Development Studies* 21(1): 2–13.

Yabuuchi, S., H. Beladi, and G. Wei. 2005. 'Foreign Investment, Urban Unemployment, and Informal Sector.' *Journal of Economic Integration* 20(1): 123–38.

6

Skilled Migration and Foreign Aid in a General Equilibrium Model of Monopolistic Competition

Dambar Uprety and Sajal Lahiri

Introduction

Many aspects of foreign aid has been studied in the theory of international trade. The effect of foreign aid on welfare has been examined for more than 80 years, ever since the debate between Keynes (1929) and Ohlin (1929).[1,2] One of the most discussed results is the so-called transfer paradox; that is, the donor benefiting and the recipient losing because of foreign aid.[3,4] The main reason behind the paradox is aid-induced changes in the international terms of trade. Later on, there have been contributions that focused on the welfare effect of tied aid.[5,6]

However, the welfare effect of foreign aid is not the only issue that economists have been concerned with. Allocation of aid has also been studied extensively. Alesina and Dollar (2000) examine the motives of giving aid. Lahiri and Raimondos

---

[1] For surveys of the literature, see, for example, Kemp (1992) or Brakman and van Marrewijk (1998).

[2] Some believe that foreign aid should be replaced by better access to trade for the aid-recipient countries. For a discussion of the relevant issues see, for example, Johnson (1967) and Kemp and Shimomura (1991).

[3] Professor Ron Jones has made extensive and important contributions to this literature. See, for example, Jones, (1970, 1975, 1976, 1984, 1985, and 1987).

[4] The first formal analysis of the problem was undertaken by Samuelson (1954). The possibility of the paradox in distorted economies was also demonstrated by, for example, Ohyama (1974), Brecher and Bhagwati (1982), Bhagwati, Brecher and Hatta (1985), Dixit (1983), Jones (1985), and Turunen-Red and Woodland (1988).

[5] See, for example, Kemp and Kojima (1985), Schweinberger (1990), Lahiri and Raimondos (1995, 1997b), and Lahiri *et al.* (2002).

[6] There is also a growing empirical literature that examines the effectiveness of aid. See, for example, Burnside and Dollar (2000) and Easterly (2003).

(1997a) have examined how trade policies in the recipient countries affect allocation. Lahiri and Raimondos-Møller (2000) have focused on how the allocation of aid is determined by lobbying of the various ethnic groups. Another strand of the literature analyzes how aid can be provided to compensate losers in the process of trade liberalization.[7] Gayton-Fregoso and Lahiri (2000) are concerned with the effect of aid on illegal immigration. Hatzipanayotou *et al.* (2002) have examined the relationship between foreign aid and pollution in the presence of cross-border pollution. Becsi and Lahiri (2007) have examined how aid can be used to reduce intercountry conflicts.

In this chapter, we shall concentrate on the effect of foreign aid on skilled immigration.

In the case of Transfer Paradox literature, the effect will be via aid-induced changes in incomes in the aid-recipient and aid-giving countries; however, unlike in the Transfer Paradox literature, here, there will be no terms-of-trade effect. In fact, to avoid unrewarding complications, we shall rule out goods trade. We shall build upon a model of international migration by Iranzo and Peri (2009), who consider a two-sector model with one of the sectors being a monopolistically competitive one, similar to love-of-the-variety type of Dixit and Stiglitz (1977). The key feature of the model is the heterogeneity of skills among the workers. In addition, the productivity of workers is monotonic with skills.

The literature of skilled migration is concerned mainly with its welfare effects. The exodus of highly-skilled people, commonly known as brain drain, could influence the economies of both source and destination countries. The effects on the source countries have received a lot of attention in the literature, which examines both the detrimental and the beneficial effects of brain drain. The early literature focused on the negative effects. Bhagwati (1976) proposed a brain drain tax to mitigate the adverse effects of brain drain on the source countries. The negative effects of brain drain arise mainly from four sources, according to Brock and Blake (2014). First, a country that is the source of highly-skilled migrants loses its human capital. Second, skilled people tend to contribute more in tax revenue than they receive through government expenditures. The emigration of skilled people reduces net government revenue. Third, skilled workers have spillover effects on others in the economy. When they leave the country, these positive externalities disappear. Fourth, skilled people are indispensable for building institutions, which are crucial for development. Thus, their departure is detrimental for development.

Brain drain, however, has some positive effects on the source country. For example, a highly-skilled diaspora can be a potential force for developing the home

---

[7] See, for example, Sachs and Warner (1995), Lahiri and Raimondos (1997b), Nanivazo and Lahiri (2015), and Fischer (2003).

country through reducing trade barriers, enhancing foreign direct investment (FDI), and facilitating information sharing and transferring of knowledge. There may be a possibility of spurring net human capital in the home country with migration of skilled people. Stark and Bloom (1985) argued that the possibility of migration can induce people to acquire human capital. Migrants' remittances could be the prominent one. As Bollard *et al.* (2011) point out, a skilled migrant could remit a large amount back[2] to their country of origin, increasing savings and investments in the source country. However, Faini (2007) pointed out that skilled migrants may have a lower propensity to remit from a given flow of earnings. This is because skilled migrants are likely to spend more time abroad and to reunite with their close family in the host country.

We shall not consider remittances, but foreign aid would affect demand and supply of the differentiated product via income effects. These, in turn, would affect the wage rates of skilled labor in the two countries, inducing further migrations. The model and the equilibrium are spelt out in the next section. This is followed by Section 3, which analyzes the effect of foreign aid on the level of skilled migration.

The Theoretical Framework

We start by considering two economies that have no international trade in goods and services; however, migration is free between them. One of the countries is more developed than the other and is the recipient of skilled migration, as well as the source of foreign aid. This country is labeled as Country 1. The other country— labeled as Country 2—is the source of skilled migration and the recipient of foreign aid. Each country produces two goods: a traditional homogeneous good (Y) and a modern differentiated good (X). The homogeneous sector has constant return to scale technology of production while differentiated goods are produced by using increasing returns to scale for more skilled workers than in the traditional sector. A developed country has higher total factor productivity (TFP)[8] than a developing country.

All consumers in both countries have identical preferences. They consume both goods. The preferences of a representative consumer in each country are described by a Constant Elasticity of Substitution (CES) utility function over X and Y as follows:

$$u_j = \left[(1 - \beta) Y_j^{\frac{\theta-1}{\theta}} + \beta X_j^{\frac{\theta-1}{\theta}} \right]^{\frac{\theta}{\theta-1}} \tag{1}$$

---

[8] The portion of output is not explained by the amount of inputs used in production. It is larger in the economy that uses inputs more efficiently and intensely.

where $j = 1; 2$; the parameter θ (> 1) represents the elasticity of substitution between Goods X and Y, and β is the consumption share of Good X.

The aforementioned variable X_j represents the consumption of the composite good, obtained by aggregating over the varieties as follows:

$$X_j = \left[\int_0^{N_j} x_j(i)^{\frac{\sigma-1}{\sigma}} di \right]^{\frac{\sigma}{\sigma-1}} \tag{2}$$

where σ stands for the elasticity of substitution across the varieties of the differentiated good. The consumption of Variety i in Country j is $x_j(i)$. The varieties of X are closer substitutes of each other than the substitution between X and Y. Thus, $\sigma > \theta > 1$. N_j is the number of varieties of Good X is Country j.

Each representative consumer in Country j maximizes u_j given in equation (1), subject to the budget constraint and subject to foreign aid included income of Country j as follows:

$$Y_j + P_{Xj}X_j = Ej, j = 1, 2 \tag{3}$$

E_j represents income in Country j, and this includes aid inflows, if it is a migrant-sending country, and aid outflows, if it is a migrant-receiving country. The price of the composite Good X_j is P_{Xj}, and the homogeneous good is taken to be the numeraire good so that its price is unity in both countries.

A consumer finds the optimal level of each variety of Good X by maximizing as follows:

$$\underset{x_j(i)}{Max} \left[\int_0^{N_j} x(i)^{\frac{\sigma-1}{\sigma}} di \right]^{\frac{\sigma}{\sigma-1}} \tag{4}$$

Subject to the sub-budget constraint

$$\int_0^{N_j} p_j(i)x_j(i)dj = S\left(P_{X_j}\right)E_j \tag{5}$$

where $S\left(P_{X_j}\right)$ is the share of expenditure on good X, and is given by

$$S\left(P_{X_j}\right) = \frac{\beta^{\theta} P_{X_j}^{1-\theta}}{\beta^{\theta} P_{X_j}^{1-\theta} + (1-\beta)^{\theta}},$$

where the price index of good X over its varieties is

$$P_{X_j} = \left[\int_0^{N_j} P_j(i)^{1-\sigma} di \right]^{\frac{1}{1-\sigma}} \tag{6}$$

and the overall price index, P is equal to

$$P = \left[\beta^{\theta} P_{X_j}^{1-\theta} + (1-\beta)^{\theta} \right]^{\frac{1}{1-\theta}} \tag{7}$$

From the optimization problem of the consumers, the demand for goods Y and X are obtained as:

$$Y_j^D = (1 - \beta)^\theta \frac{E_j}{P_j} \left(\frac{1}{P_j}\right)^{-\theta} \tag{8}$$

$$X_j^D = \frac{\beta^\theta E_j}{P_j} \left(\frac{P_{X_j}}{P_j}\right)^{-\theta} \tag{9}$$

$$X_j^D(i) = \frac{s\left(P_{X_j}\right) E_j}{P_{X_j}} \left(\frac{P_j(i)}{P_{X_j}}\right)^{-\sigma} \tag{10}$$

Turning to the production side, there is a continuum of worker of size M_j in country ($j = 1, 2$), and they are differentiated by their skill level, which we index by z. The larger the value of z, more skilled the worker is. Skill index z is normalized, and the highest level of this index is 1. The index z can be interpreted as having observable characteristics in workers such as education attainment or unobservable characteristics such as ability and quality in the workers. The skill distribution of workers in each country is exogenously given. The probability density function (pdf) of workers' skill in Country j is $g_j(z)$. Thus, the probability of that a worker in Country j has a skill level of at least Z is given by $\int_0^z g_j(z)dz$, and expected wage income of each worker in that range is $\int_0^Z W_j(z)g_j(z)dz = \int_0^Z W_j(z)dG_j(z)$, where $G_j(z)$ is the cumulative distribution function (cdf). The total wage income of country j is $M_j \int_0^Z W_j(z)dG_j(z)$, where M_j represents the size of workers in each country ($j = 1, 2$).

The skill threshold point of worker in the developing country (country 2) is $\overline{Z}_{2H}$: workers with level above this threshold migrate out to the developed country (country 1). Therefore, the size of migrant workers is $M_2 \int_{\overline{Z}_{2H}}^1 dG_2(z)$. The threshold pint $\overline{Z}_{2H}$ will be endogenously determined.

There is a single factor of production, which is labor. Constant return-to-scale technology is used for the production of the traditional homogeneous Good Y. Variety i of Good X incurs fixed costs F_i and there is free entry and exit of firms. Each firm produces only one variety of X. Each worker with skill z produces $A_x(z)$ and $A_y(z)$ amounts of Goods X and Y, respectively. Production technology is skill-biased, and the differentiated goods sector has a more skill-biased technology than the homogeneous sector, that is, $\left(\partial A_x(Z)/\partial Z\right) > \left(\partial A_y(Z)/\partial Z\right) > 0$. However, the least-skilled workers ($z = 0$) produce the same amount in both sectors, which is $A_x(0) = A_y(0)$.

The production function in each sector is guided by the Mincerian assumption that labor productivity depends exponentially on the years of schooling (Mincer, 1974), and thus we assume labor productivities to take the form as follows:

$$A_x(z) = \Lambda_j e^{g_{yj}z} \text{ and } A_y(z) = \Lambda_j e^{g_{yj}z},$$

where L_j is the total factor productivity (TFP) in Country j (j = 1; 2), and g_{yj} and g_{xj} are the technological parameters with $g_{xj} > g_{yj}$. These parameters g_{yj} and g_{xj} are marginal returns to skill for workers in the two sectors. This reflects the imperfect substitutability between workers of different skills, that is, skill price varies with the level of skill. The national income of migrant-sending and migrant-receiving countries are respectively given by

$$I_2 = M_2 \left(1 - \int_{Z_{2H}}^1 dG_2(z)\right)\left[\Lambda_2 \int_0^{Z_2} \exp(g_{y2}z) dG_2(z) + C_{x_2}\Lambda_2 \int_{Z_2}^{Z_{2H}} \exp(g_{x_2}z) dG_2(z)\right],$$

$$\tag{11}$$

$$I_2 = \Lambda_1 M_2 \int_0^{Z_1} \exp(g_{y_1}z) dG_1(z) + \left(M_1 + M_2 \int_{Z_1}^1 dG_2(z)\right)\Lambda_1 C_{x1}\int_{Z_1}^1 \exp(g_{x_1}z) dG_1(z),$$

$$\tag{12}$$

where the threshold skill $\overline{Z}_j$ separates workers in the traditional sector and the differentiated goods sector in Country j (j = 1; 2). We now turn to the determination of these threshold values.

Labor markets are assumed to be perfectly competitive, and labor is the only factor of production. Therefore, the wage rates of a worker with skill level z in the two sectors are given by the following equation:

$$W_{y_j}(z) = \Lambda_j e^{g_{y_j}z} \text{ and } W_{x_j}(z) = C_{x_j}\Lambda_j e^{g_{x_j}z} \tag{13}$$

Because workers can move freely between the two sectors, the threshold value of skill is $\overline{Z}_j$. This is the threshold at which workers are indifferent between working in Sector Y or Sector X (Yeaple, 2005). Using equation (13), the threshold values must satisfy

$$C_{x_j} = \frac{e^{g_y Z_j}}{e^{g_x \overline{Z}_j}}, \quad j = 1, 2 \tag{14}$$

Substituting (14) in (13), we find

$$W_{x_j}(z) = \frac{e^{g_{y_j}Z_j}}{e^{g_{x_j}\overline{Z}_j}}\Lambda_j e^{g_{x_j}z}\Lambda_j e^{(g_{y_j}-g_{x_j})\overline{Z}_j}e^{g_{x_j}z} \tag{15}$$

There is another threshold point of skill level in a developing country at which workers are indifferent between working in the country or migrate-out of the country and work in Country 1.

We denote such a point by $\overline{Z}_{2H}$. Workers with skill $Z_2 < \overline{Z}_{2H}$ work in home country while with skill $Z_2 > \overline{Z}_{2H}$ emigrate. Therefore the complete wage schedule of developing country, $W_2(z)$ is as follow:

$$
W_2(z) = \begin{cases} \Lambda_2 e^{g_{y_2} z} & \text{if } 0 < z \le \overline{Z}_2, \\[2mm] \Lambda_2 e^{(g_{y_2} - g_{x_2})\overline{Z}_{2} e^{g_{x_2} z}} & \text{if } \overline{Z}_2 < z \le \overline{Z}_{2H} \quad (16) \\[2mm] \Lambda_1 C_{x_1} e^{g_{x_1} z} & \text{if } \overline{Z}_{2H} < z \le 1 \end{cases}
$$

These threshold points $\overline{Z}_2$ and $\overline{Z}_{2H}$ are endogenous and will be determined later.

There are three skill threshold points as follows: one is interindustry skill threshold point in each of the two countries, and the other is the migration threshold point in the migrant-sending country. Therefore, we need three independent equations to solve for these three threshold points. At skill level $\overline{Z}_{2H}$ workers in developing countries are indifferent between working home country industry X or emigrate to developed foreign country and work in industry X there. From wage schedule (16), cross-country wage equalization yields $C_{x_2} \Lambda_2 e^{g_{x_2} \overline{Z}_{2H}} = C_{x_1} \Lambda_1 e^{g_{x_1} Z_1}$, which be manipulated to obtain

$$
\overline{Z}_{2H} = \frac{1}{g_{x_2}} \left[ln\left(\frac{\Lambda_1 C_{x_1}}{\Lambda_2 C_{x_2}} \right) + g_{x_1} \overline{Z}_1 \right] \tag{17}
$$

We now provide a diagrammatic representation of wage schedules. Figure 6.1 depicts the three different cases of wage schedules as follows: wages in homogeneous sector (blue line), in composite differentiated sector in home country (red line), and in differentiated sector in foreign country (black line). Logarithm of wage is piecewise linear function with kinks at $\overline{Z}_2$ and $\overline{Z}_{2H}$.

The first kink represents the interindustry threshold point of skills while the latter represents the migration threshold point.

The slope of wage schedule, g_{x_2}, in the differentiated sector, is larger than that in the homogeneous sector in both countries, because $g_{x_2} > g_{y_2}$ as shown by the red and the blue lines, respectively. Thus, wage rate in the differentiated sector is greater than in the homogeneous sector as indicated by the greater slope. Once again, $g_{x1} > g_{x2}$, because a developed country has more advanced technology than that of a developing one. Therefore, returns to skills are greater in a developed country than in developing countries. Skill threshold points, Z_2 and Z_{2H} are endogenous in the model. At skill level Z_2, we can find the unit cost C_{x_2} and the wage rate in each industry. Workers with skill level less than Z_2 higher wage in Y sector than working in sector X, as depicted by solid-blue and left extended dashed-red line respectively. Workers with skills between Z_2 and Z_{2H} have comparitve advantage working in X sector than in sector Y, as shown by solid-red and left elongated-black lines. Workers whose skill level is higher than $\overline{Z}_{2H}$ choose to migrate out to developed country since wage rate is higher there as represented by the black line. Logarithm of total factor productivity (TFP) determines the intercept of wage schedule in sector Y. Logarithm of unit cost in sector X determine the intercept of wage schedule of skilled workers in sector X. Similarly, the sum of both of these logarithms constitutes the intercept of wage schedule for migrant workers aboard.

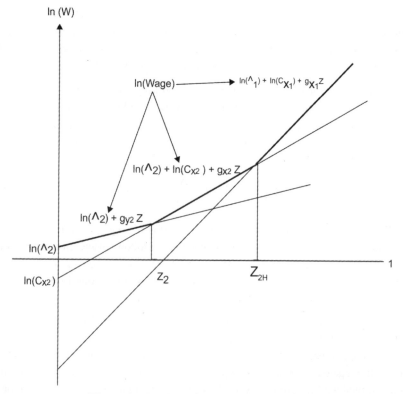

Figure 6.1 Workers skills and wage schedule

We now turn to the determination of price and output of each variety. Profit of an individual firm in the monopolistic competitive industry is given by

$$\Pi_j(i) = p_j(i)x_j(i) - C_{x_j}x_j(i) - F_j \quad (18)$$

where $p_j(i)$ is the price, $x_j(i)$ the output, and F_j is the fixed cost of production for the ith variety, and C_{x_j} is the marginal cost of production. Individual firm chooses price $p_j(i)$ to maximize profit given the industry price. So, profit maximization of a firm implies

$$\frac{\partial \Pi_j(i)}{\partial p_j(i)} = p_j(i)\frac{\partial x_j(i)}{\partial p_j(i)} + x_j(i) - \frac{\partial x_j(i)}{\partial p_j(i)}C_{x_j} = 0 \quad (19)$$

One of the features of monopolistic competition with CES preference is that the price elasticity of demand is constant. We can easily see from (1) that elasticity of demand, $\left(\partial x_j / \partial p_j\right)\left(x_j / p_j\right) = -\sigma$. Using this, from (19) we find

$$p_j(i) = \frac{\sigma - 1}{\sigma}C_{x_j} \quad (20)$$

From free entry and exit of firms in the differentiated goods sector, gives $\Pi_j(i) = 0$, and this gives

$$x_j(i) = \frac{F_j}{p_j(i) - C_{x_j}} \quad (21)$$

From equations (20) and (21), it follows that the prices and the output of a variety are the same across the varieties, that is, $p_j(i) = p_j$ and $x_j(i) = x_j$ for all i. Therefore, it can be shown that the industry price index P_{X_j} (given in equation (6)) simplifies to

$$P_{X_j} = p_j\left(N_j\right)^{\frac{1}{1-\sigma}} \quad (22)$$

Using equations (10), (21), and (22), we solve for the number of varieties in the two countries as

$$N_j = \frac{S\left(P_{X_j}\right)E_j}{\sigma F_j}$$

which gives

$$N_1 = \frac{M_1\Lambda_1\int_Z^1 e^{g_{X1}z}dG_1(z)}{\sigma F_1} \quad (23)$$

$$N_2 = \frac{\Lambda_2}{\sigma F_2}\left(M_2 - M_2\int_{Z2H}^1 dG_2(z)\right)\int_{Z2}^{\overline{Z}2H} e^{g_{X2}z}dG_2(z)$$

Now, only the intersectoral threshold points in skills in the two countries, that is, $\bar{Z}_1$ and $\bar{Z}_2$, remain to be determined. Note that the other threshold point, the immigration threshold point, is determined from equation (17) once $\bar{Z}_1$ is determined. It was also noted that there is a positive relationship between the two. The two equations that would determine $\bar{Z}_1$ and $\bar{Z}_2$ are the market-clearing conditions for the numeraire good in the two countries.[9]

The disposable income levels, E_1 and E_2 (defined in equation (3)), are respectively $I_1 - A$ and $I_2 + A$, where A is the level of foreign aid given by Country 1 to Country 2, and I_i ($i = 1, 2$) are defined in equations (11) and (12). With these, excess demand of the numeraire good in the two countries are set to zero, that is

$$H\left(\bar{Z}_1, \bar{Z}_2, A\right) = \left[1 - S\left(P_{x_2}\right)\right] E_2 - M_2 \left(1 - \int_{Z_{2H}}^1 dG_2\left(z\right)\right) \Lambda_2 \int_0^{Z_2} e^{g_{y2} z} dG_2\left(z\right) = 0,$$

$$\widetilde{H}\left(\bar{Z}_1, \bar{Z}_2, A\right) = \left[1 - S\left(P_{x_1}\right)\right] E_1 - M_1 \Lambda_1 \int_0^{Z_1} e^{g_{y1} z} dG_1\left(z\right) = 0,$$

which with suitable substitutions reduce to

$$H\left(\bar{Z}_1, \bar{Z}_2, A\right) = \int_0^{Z_2} e^{g_{y2} z} dG_2\left(z\right) - \left(\frac{1-\beta}{\beta}\right)^\theta \left(\frac{\sigma F_2}{M_2 \Lambda_2}\right)^{\frac{1-\theta}{\sigma-1}} \left(\frac{\sigma}{\sigma-1}\right)^{\theta-1}$$

$$\left(1 - \int_{Z_{2H}}^1 dG_2\left(z\right)\right)^{\frac{\theta-1}{1-\sigma}}$$

$$e^{\left(g_{y2} - g_{x2}\right)\theta Z_{2H}} \left(\int_2^{Z_{2H}} e^{g_{x2} z} dG_2\left(z\right)\right)^{\frac{\sigma-\theta}{\sigma-1}} - A\Lambda_2^{\frac{\sigma+\theta-2}{1-\sigma}} \left(\frac{1-\beta}{\beta}\right)^\theta \left(\frac{\sigma F_2}{M_2}\right)^{\frac{\theta-1}{\sigma-1}} \left(\frac{\sigma}{\sigma-1}\right)^{\theta-1} \quad (25)$$

$$e^{\left(g_{y2} - g_{x2}\right)(\theta-1)Z_{2H}} \left(1 - \int_{Z_{2H}}^1 dG_2\left(z\right)\right)^{\frac{\sigma+\theta-2}{1-\sigma}} \left(\int_{Z_2}^{Z_{2H}} e^{g_{x2} z} dG_2\left(z\right)\right)^{\frac{\sigma-\theta}{\sigma-1}} = 0$$

$$\widetilde{H}\left(\bar{Z}_1, \bar{Z}_2, A\right) = \int_0^{Z_1} e^{g_{y1} z} dG_1\left(z\right) - \left(\frac{1-\beta}{\beta}\right)^\theta \left(\frac{\sigma}{\sigma-1}\right)^{\theta-1} \left(\frac{\sigma F_1}{M_1 \Lambda_1}\right)^{\frac{\theta-1}{\sigma-1}} e^{\left(g_{y1} - g_{x1}\right)\theta Z_1}$$

$$\left[1 + \frac{M_2}{M_1} \int_{Z_{2H}}^1 dG_2\left(z\right) - \frac{e^{\left(g_{x1} - g_{y1}\right)Z_1}}{M_1} A\right] \left(\int_{Z_1}^1 e^{g_{x1} z} dG_1\left(z\right)\right)^{\frac{\sigma-\theta}{\sigma-1}} = 0 \quad (26)$$

This completes the description of the theoretical framework. In the next section, we shall examine the effect of increasing the amount of foreign aid A on the skilled migration.

---

[9] The market-clearing conditions for the differentiated good will be satisfied due to the Walras's Law.

Foreign Aid and Skilled Migration

To examine the effect of foreign aid on immigration, we totally differentiate equations (25) and (26) to obtain the following:

$$H_1 d\overline{Z}_1 + H_2 d\overline{Z}_2 = -H_3 dA$$

$$\overline{H}_1 d\overline{Z}_1 + \overline{H}_2 d\overline{Z}_2 = -\widetilde{H}_3 dA,$$

where

$$H_1 = a\frac{\theta-1}{\sigma-1}\left(1 - \int_{Z_{2H}}^{1} dG_2(z)\right)^{\frac{\theta+\sigma-2}{1-\sigma}} e^{(g_{y2}-g_{x2})\theta Z_{2H}}\left(\int_{Z_2}^{Z_{2H}} e^{(g_{x2}z)} dG_2(z)\right)^{\frac{\sigma-\theta}{1-\sigma}}$$

$$+a\left(1 - \int_{Z_{2H}}^{1} dG_2(z)\right)^{\frac{\theta-1}{\sigma-1}} \left(g_{x2} - g_{y2}\right)(\theta-1) e^{(g_{y2}-g_{x2})(\theta-1)Z_{2H}}\left(\int_{Z_2}^{Z_{2H}} e^{(g_{y2}z)} dG_2(z)\right)^{\frac{\sigma-\theta}{1-\sigma}}$$

$$+a\frac{\sigma-\theta}{\sigma-1}\left(1 - \int_{Z_{2H}}^{1} dG_2(z)\right)^{\frac{\theta-1}{\sigma-1}} e^{(g_{y2}-g_{x2})\theta Z_{2H}}\left(\int_{Z_2}^{Z_{2H}} e^{(g_{x2}z)} dG_2(z)\right)^{\frac{2\sigma-\theta-1}{1-\sigma}} e^{g_{x2}Z_{2H}} g_{x2}$$

$$+bA\frac{\sigma+\theta-2}{1-\sigma} e^{(g_{y2}-g_{x2})(\theta-1)Z_{2h}} \left(1 - \int_{Z_{2H}}^{1} dG_2(z)\right)^{\frac{2\sigma+\theta-3}{1-\sigma}}\left(\int_{Z_2}^{Z_{2H}} e^{(g_{x2}z)} dG_2(z)\right)^{\frac{\theta-1}{1-\sigma}}$$

$$+bA\frac{\sigma+\theta-2}{1-\sigma} e^{(g_{y2}-g_{x2})(\theta-1)Z_{2H}} \left(1 - \int_{Z_{2H}}^{1} dG_2(z)\right)^{\frac{2\sigma+\theta-3}{1-\sigma}}\left(\int_{Z_2}^{Z_{2H}} e^{(g_{x2}z)} dG_2(z)\right)^{\frac{\theta-1}{1-\sigma}}$$

$$+bA\frac{\theta-1}{\sigma-1} e^{(g_{y2}-g_{x2})(\theta-1)Z_{2H}} \left(1 - \int_{Z_{2h}}^{1} dG_2(z)\right)^{\frac{\sigma+\theta-2}{1-\sigma}} e^{g_{x2}Z_{2H}} g_{x2} > 0$$

$$H_2 = e^{g_{y2}Z_2} g_{y2} + a\frac{\sigma-\theta}{\sigma-1} e^{(g_{y2}-g_{x2})(\theta-1)Z_{2H}} \left(\int_{Z_2}^{Z_{2H}} e^{(g_{x2}z)} dG_2(z)\right)^{\frac{2\sigma-\theta-1}{1-\sigma}} e^{g_{x2}Z_2} g_{x2}$$

$$-bA\frac{\theta-1}{\sigma-1} e^{(g_{y2}-g_{x2})(\theta-1)Z_{2H}} \left(1 - \int_{Z_{2H}}^{1} dG_2(z)\right)^{\frac{\sigma+\theta-2}{1-\sigma}}\left(\int_{Z_2}^{Z_{2H}} e^{(g_{x2}z)} dG_2(z)\right)^{\frac{\sigma+\theta-2}{1-\sigma}} e^{g_{x2}Z_2} g_{x2},$$

$$H_3 = -e^{(g_{x2}-g_{x2})(\theta-1)Z_{2H}} b\left(1 - \int_{Z_{2H}}^{1} dG_2(z)\right)^{\frac{\sigma+\theta-2}{1-\sigma}}\left(\int_{Z_2}^{Z_{2H}} e^{(g_{x2}z)} dG_2(z)\right)^{\frac{\theta-1}{1-\sigma}} < 0$$

$$\widetilde{H}_1 =$$

$$b\frac{\sigma-\theta}{\sigma-1} e^{(g_{y1}-g_{x1})\theta Z_1}\left[1 + \frac{AM_2}{M_1}\int_{\theta Z_1}^{1} dG_2(z) - \frac{e^{(g_{x1}-g_{y1})Z_1}}{M_1}\right]\left(\int_{Z_1}^{1} e^{(g_{x1}z)} dG_2(z)\right)^{\frac{1-\theta}{\sigma-1}} e^{(g_{x1}z)} g_{x1}$$

$$+b\frac{AM_2}{M_1}e^{\left(g_{y_1}-g_{x_1}\right)\theta Z_1}\left(\int_{Z_1}^{1}e^{\left(g_{x_1}z\right)}dG_1\left(z\right)\right)^{\frac{\sigma-\theta}{\sigma-1}}\left(1+e^{\left(g_{x_1}-g_{y_1}\right)\theta Z_1}\right)\left(g_{x_1}-g_{y_1}\right)\theta+e^{g_{y_2}z}g_{y_1}$$

$$+\left(\int_{Z_1}^{1}e^{\left(g_{x_1}z\right)}dG_1\left(z\right)\right)^{\frac{\sigma-\theta}{\sigma-1}}\left[1+\frac{AM_2}{M_1}\int_{\theta Z_1}^{1}dG_2\left(z\right)-\frac{e^{\left(g_{x_1}-g_{y_1}\right)Z_1}}{M_1}\right]e^{\left(g_{y_1}-g_{x_1}\right)\theta Z_1}\left(g_{y_1}-g_{x_1}\right)\theta>0$$

$$\widetilde{H}_2=0,$$

$$\widetilde{H}_3=be^{(1+\theta)Z_1}\left(\int_{Z_1}^{1}e^{\left(g_{x_1}z\right)}dG_1\left(z\right)\right)^{\frac{\sigma-\theta}{\sigma-1}}>0,$$

where

$$a=\left(\frac{1-\beta}{\beta}\right)^{\theta}\left(\frac{\sigma F_2}{M_2\Lambda_2}\right)^{\frac{1-\theta}{\sigma-1}}\left(\frac{\sigma}{\sigma-1}\right)^{\theta-1}>0$$

$$b=\left(\frac{1-\beta}{\beta}\right)^{\theta}\left(\frac{\sigma}{\sigma-1}\right)^{\theta-1}\left(\frac{\sigma F_1}{M_1\Lambda_1}\right)^{\frac{\theta-1}{\sigma-1}}>0.$$

Solving the above two equations we obtain

$$\frac{d\overline{Z}_1}{dA}=\frac{H_2\widetilde{H}_3-H_3\widetilde{H}_2}{H_1\widetilde{H}_2-H_2\widetilde{H}_1}=\frac{-\widetilde{H}_3}{\widetilde{H}_1},\tag{27}$$

$$\frac{d\overline{Z}_2}{dA}=\frac{H_3\widetilde{H}_1-H_1\widetilde{H}_3}{H_1\widetilde{H}_2-H_2\widetilde{H}_1}=\frac{H_3\widetilde{H}_1-H_1\widetilde{H}_3}{-H_2\widetilde{H}_1},\tag{28}$$

The denominator in (27) and (28), $H_1\widetilde{H}_2-H_2\widetilde{H}_1=-H_2\widetilde{H}_1$, must be positive for the stability of the equilibrium. Since $\widetilde{H}_1>0$, this condition implies that $H_2<0$. To summarize then, we have $H_1>0,H_2<0,H_3<0,\widetilde{H}_1>0,\widetilde{H}_2=0,$ and $\widetilde{H}_3>0$. It then follows from (27) and (28) that $\frac{d\overline{Z}_1}{dA}<0$, and $\frac{d\overline{Z}_2}{dA}<0$.

Finally from (17) it then follows that $\frac{d\overline{Z}_{2H}}{dA}<0$

That is, an increase in foreign aid unambiguously raises the level of skilled migration. Formally,

Proposition 1 *An increase in foreign aid unambiguously raises the level of skilled migration from the aid-recipient country to the aid-giving country.*

We shall now explain the aforementioned result intuitively. Income in Country 2 rises with an increase in foreign aid, and this, in turn, increases the relative demand for the differentiated goods. This results in an expansion of Sector X, as a larger market allows for more varieties. This has the effect of reducing the price of the composite Good X, as P_{Xj}, because of more competition. In addition, consumers shift their expenditure more toward Good X than that for the homogeneous goods. Therefore, the share of expenditure spent on Good X, which is $S(P_{Xj})$, increases. The expansion in output of X raises the demand for labor and, therefore, wages. This increases the unit cost as C_{Xj}. The wage schedule in Sector X shifts up, whereas the wage schedule for Sector Y remains unchanged. Some workers shift from Sector Y to Sector X. This causes the interindustry skill threshold point of an aid-recipient country to move to the left.

Foreign aid reduces income in the donor country. The loss of income in the developed country lowers the demand for the traditional good less than that for the modern good, thereby causing a relative increase in the production of the traditional good. Because the production of the traditional good now requires more labor, the marginal worker in the skill distribution moves rightward along the skill distribution in the developed country. Therefore, the wage for the marginal worker in the modern sector increases. The opposite happens in the migrant-sending country, where the wage for the marginal worker in the modern sector decreases. The wage gap for the marginal workers in the two countries increases, inducing more migration from the developing to the developed country.

Conclusion

This study examines the effect of foreign aid on skilled migration from a source country to a destination country. The source country is a developing one and the destination country is developed. In both countries, the population/workers are distributed according to their skill levels. This distribution is distributed in three ranges in the source country as follows: (i) people in the first range produce a traditional homogeneous good, (ii) those in the middle range work in a differentiated goods sector, and (iii) the people in the third range—the most-skilled group—migrate to the developed country. The people in the developed country are divided in two ranges according to their place in the skill distribution. The lower-skilled group work in the homogeneous good sector, and the higher-skilled ones in the differentiated goods sector. We develop a general equilibrium model in which the differences between the groups of workers in the two countries are endogenously determined.

Having characterized the equilibrium, we examine the effect of foreign aid (from the destination country to the source country) on the level of migration of skilled workers. We find that the effect is unambiguously positive. This happens because the increase in income in the developing country and a reduction of income in the developed country expands the traditional sector in the developed country and the composite good sector in the developing country. This increases the wage between the marginal workers in the two countries, inducing more migration.

This study has a number of limitations. Future research by the authors will try to overcome these limitations. First, we assume the skill distribution of workers to be exogenous. This can potentially be extended to incorporate skill formation. Second, we do not allow for any international trade in goods. Third, we do not allow for any remittances by the migrants. Finally, we assume that migrants can move freely between countries. All these shortcomings of this analysis can be dealt with in an extended framework, albeit at the cost of significant complications in the analysis.

References

Alesina, A. and D. Dollar. 2000. 'Who gives aid to whom and why?' *Journal of Economic Growth* 5: 33–63.

Becsi, Z. and S. Lahiri. 2007. 'Bilateral war in a multilateral world: carrots and sticks for conflict resolution.' *Canadian Journal of Economics* 40(4): 1168–87.

Bhagwati, J. N. 1976. 'Taxing the Brain Drain.' *Challenge* 19(3): 34–38.

Bhagwati, J. N., R. Brecher, and T. Hatta. 1985. 'The generalized theory of transfers and welfare: exogenous (policy-imposed) and endogenous (transfer-induced) distortions.' *Quarterly Journal of Economics* 160(3): 697–714.

Bollard, A., D. McKenzie, M. Morten, and H. Rapoport. 2011. 'Remittances and the brain drain revisited: The microdata show that more educated migrants remit more.' *The World Bank Economic Review.*

Brock, G. and M. Blake. 2014. *Debating Brain Drain: May Governments Restrict Emigration?* Oxford University Press.

Brakman, S. and C. van Marrewijk. 1998. *The Economics of International Transfers.* New York: Cambridge University Press.

Brecher, R. and J. N. Bhagwati. 1982. 'Immiserizing transfers from abroad.' *Journal of International Economics* 13: 353–64.

Burnside, C. and D. Dollar. 2000. 'Aid, policies and growth.' *American Economic Review* 90: 847–68.

Dixit, A. 1983. 'The multi-country transfer problem.' *Economics Letters* 13: 49–53.

Dixit, A. K. and J. E. Stiglitz. 1977. 'Monopolistic Competition and Optimum Product Diversity.' *American Economic Review* 67(3): 297–308.

Easterly, W. 2003. 'Can foreign aid buy growth?' *Journal of Economic Perspectives* 17: 23–48.

Faini, R. 2007. 'Remittances and the Brain Drain: Do more skilled migrants remit more?' *The World Bank Economic Review* 21(2): 177–91.

Fischer, S. 2003. 'Globalization and its challenges.' Richard T. Ely Lecture. *American Economic Review* 93(2): 1–30. DOI: 10.1257/000282803321946750.

Gaytan-Fregoso, H. and S. Lahiri. 2000. 'Foreign Aid and Illegal Immigration.' *Journal of Development Economics* 63(2): 515–27.

Hatzipanayotou, P., S. Lahiri, and M. S. Michael. 2002. 'Can Cross-Border Pollution Reduce Pollution?' *The Canadian Journal of Economics* 35(4): 805–18.

Iranzo, S. and G. Peri. 2009. 'Migration and trade: Theory with an application to the Eastern–Western European integration.' *Journal of International Economics* 79(1): 1–19.

Johnson, H. G. 1967. *Economic policies toward less developed countries.* Washington, DC: The Brookings Institute.

Jones, R. W. 1970. 'The Transfer Problem Revisited.' *Economica.*

—————. 1975. 'Presumption and the Transfer Problem.' *Journal of International Economics.*

—————. 1976. 'Terms of Trade and Transfers: The Relevance of the Literature.' In *The International Monetary System and the Developing Nations,* edited by D. Leipziger. Washington, DC: AID.

—————. 1984. 'The Transfer Problem in a Three-Agent Setting.' *Canadian Journal of Economics* 17: 1–14.

—————. 1985. 'Income effects and paradoxes in the theory of international trade.' *The Economic Journal* 95: 330–44.

—————. 1987. 'The Population Monotonicity Property and the Transfer Paradox.' *Journal of Public Economics* 32: 125–32.

Kemp, M. C. 1992. 'The static welfare economics of foreign aid: A consolidation.' In *Equity and Efficiency in Economic Development: Essays in Honor of Benjamin Higgins,* edited by D. Savoie and I. Brecher. Montreal: McGill-Queens University Press.

Kemp, M. C. and S. Kojima. 1985. 'Tied aid and the paradoxes of donor-enrichment and recipient-impoverishment.' *International Economic Review* 26(3): 721–29.

Kemp, M. C. and K. Shimomura. 1991. "Trade" or "Aid"?' In *Trade Policy and International Adjustments,* edited by A. Takayama, M. Ohyama, and H. Ohta. San Diego: Academic Press.

Keynes, J. M. 1929. 'Mr. Keynes' Views on the Transfer Problem. III. A Reply.' *The Economic Journal* 39(155): 404–09.

Lahiri, S. and P. Raimondos. 1995. 'The welfare effect of aid under quantitative trade restrictions.' *Journal of International Economics* 39: 297–315.

—————. 1997a. 'Competition for aid and trade policy.' *Journal of International Economics* 43(3): 369–85.

—————. 1997b. 'On the tying of aid to tariff reform.' *Journal of Development Economics* 54: 479–91.

—————. 2000. 'Lobbying by Ethnic Groups and Aid Allocation.' *The Economic Journal* 110(462): 62–79.

Lahiri, S., P. Raimondos, K. Y. Wong, and A. Woodland. 2002. 'Optimal Foreign Aid and Tariffs.' *Journal of Development Economics* 67: 79–99.

Mincer, J. 1974. 'Schooling, Experience, and Earnings.' *Human Behavior and Social Institutions* 2.

Nanivazo, M. and S. Lahiri. 2015. 'Promoting Trade Liberalization: Theoretical Analysis of Foreign Aid as Prize.' *Review of Development Economics* 19(3): 748–57.

Ohlin, B. 1929. 'Mr. Keynes' Views on the Transfer Problem. II. A Rejoinder.' *The Economic Journal* 39(155): 400–04.

Ohyama, M. 1974. 'Tariffs and the transfer problem.' *Keio Economic Studies* 11: 29–45.

Sachs, J. and A. Warner. 1995. 'Economic Reform and the Process of Global Integration.' *Brooking Papers on Economic Activity* 26(1): 1–118.

Samuelson, P. A. 1954. 'The transfer problem and transport costs II: analysis of effects of trade impediments.' *Economic Journal* 64: 264–89.

Schweinberger, A. G. 1990. 'On the welfare effects of tied aid.' *International Economic Review* 31(2): 457–62.

Stark, O. and D. E. Bloom. 1985. 'The New Economics of Labor Migration.' *The American Economic Review* 75(2): 173–78.

Turunen-Red, A. H. and A. D. Woodland. 1988. 'On the multilateral transfer problem: existence of Pareto improving international transfers.' *Journal of International Economics* 22: 57–64.

Yeaple, S. R. 2005. 'A simple model of firm heterogeneity, international trade, and wages.' *Journal of international Economics* 65(1): 1–20.

7

Trade, Factor Flows, and Product Variety in a Small Open Economy

Anwesha Aditya[1]

Introduction

This chapter provides an explanation of asymmetry in policy changes regarding commodity trade, capital inflow, and immigration of labor in terms of their asymmetric impacts on product variety and diversification of export basket.

Recent years have witnessed a remarkable push toward globalization. The global economy is more open than before. Yet, noticeable differences in the magnitude of changes in volumes of trade, international capital flows, and immigration can be observed (Findlay and O'Rourke, 2002; Obstfeld and Taylor, 2002). The extraordinary increase in trade volumes in the post-World War II era has not been matched by a parallel rise in labor movement (Mayda, 2004).

This is primarily because of asymmetric policies, preferences, and perceptions of countries toward commodity trade liberalization, and immigration of labor or capital inflow. Historically, domestic policies of nations regarding goods trade and labor flows have moved in opposite directions. In the post-World War I era, immigration policies have experienced tightening relative to the previous century, whereas trade policies have increasingly been liberalized especially after World War II (Faini, 2002).

Empirical evidence suggests that the economic forces driving the supply side of international immigration—cross-country wage and income differentials, reduced transport, communication and information costs, and opportunities for risk

[1] An earlier draft of the chapter was presented at the Conference entitled '50 years of Simple General Equilibrium Models and Policy Implications for Open Developing Economies – Historical and Emerging Issues', held during November 17–18, 2015 at the Centre for Studies in Social Sciences, Calcutta. I thank Eric Bond, Ronald Jones, Saibal Kar, Ngo Van Long, Sugata Marjit, and other participants for their comments. The usual disclaimer applies, however.

diversification—have become stronger in the last two decades. Hence, as pointed out by Faini (2002), restrictive policies play a key role in explaining the relatively small scale of international immigration.

The reasons for such a preference of asymmetric policy may be more than one. Trade and migration patterns are driven largely by the differences in the relative endowments of skilled and unskilled labor in different countries as suggested by the Heckscher–Ohlin–Samuelson (denoted as HOS hereafter) theory. This theory predicts that the migration of skilled labor is less anti-trade and anti-immigration in more skill-abundant countries (which are the richer countries) than in more unskilled labor-abundant countries (poorer countries). This theoretical prediction is also empirically verified and confirmed by some recent studies of O'Rourke (2003) and Mayda (2004) rejecting the earlier view that only noneconomic considerations shape attitudes toward foreigners. Mayda (2004), in particular, brings out the importance of the economic factors, which play key and robust role in preference formation on immigration policy, thereby controlling for the impacts of noneconomic factors.

The importance of economic factors is explicitly taken into account by Bilal *et al.* (2003) who developed a three-factor (capital, as well as low- and high-skilled labor), two-household (low- and high-skilled individuals), and a two-sector trade model, in which preferences toward immigration are determined by the natives' perception of the impact of immigration on wages. This study highlights the importance of factor intensities in shaping attitudes toward immigration by incorporating explicitly the role of capital ownership and the skill level of potential immigrants in the United States.

Asymmetric welfare implications of commodity trade and factor flows may also govern policy differences concerning the two. However, gains from commodity trade and the underlying conditions are well established in trade theory, which dates back to the writings of Ricardo (1867) and in modern times to the writings of Markusen and Melvin (1989), as well as Melitz (2003), in which welfare implications of factor flows is less clear. Nevertheless, welfare changes are nonmonotonic with respect to the amount of factor flows even for a small open economy (Bhagwati, 1997). Even the type of factor flows may matter. For example, in a standard HOS model, international labor migration should have similar effects as the capital flow on the composition of aggregate output without leading to any change in factor prices. However, in contrast to that in the specific factors model developed by Jones (1971) with three factors and two commodities, it was noted that at given commodity prices, changes in factor endowments have direct effect on factor returns; in addition, labor immigration may have depressing effect on domestic wage rates. Even in the standard HOS model, welfare implications may be asymmetric depending on whether the benefits of the migrants accrue to the home country or host country. Host countries gain from immigration, but also must bear the negative consequences such as population surge, pressure on employment, and threats on national identity and national security. Similar to capital inflow, labor immigration augments the value of aggregate output of the host country. However, the home country gains when the emigrants' incomes are considered as part of its national income, which is the case for *temporary emigrants*. Conversely, the incomes earned by *permanent emigrants* should be a part of the national income of the host country. The issue, however, becomes complicated when permanent immigrants to a host country retain their ties with their country of origin, which has been the case, for example, with a large number of highly educated and skilled Indian immigrants in the United States.

This might be one reason why, in contrast to policies regulating trade and capital flows, immigration policies of destination countries continue to be highly protectionist, and migration flows has so far been not very significant, especially when compared with the second half of the nineteenth century. Immigrant countries attempt to attract specific types of talent from certain countries in terms of visa requirements. This is important even for the host countries, which are structurally dependent on immigrant labor, such as the Gulf oil-producing states in the Middle East or Malaysia. The H1-B visa system in the United States for highly skilled workers is enthusiastically supported by the corporate sector. This is despite the fact that the Mode 4 trade involving movement of people is enthusiastic about enhancing merchandise trade flows (Jansen and Piermartini, 2005). [2]

Although all these dimensions of impacts of commodity trade and factor flows are relevant for understanding trade and migration policies, an important dimension that has so far been not taken into account is their impacts on product diversification or varieties of differentiated goods produced domestically and traded with the rest of the world. This dimension has two broader implications that make it worthwhile to consider as an explanation for policy preferences that result in international factor movements being far less than commodity movements. The first one is in the context of asymmetric welfare implications as an explanation for asymmetric policies toward commodity trade and factor flows, on the one hand, and toward capital inflow and immigration of skilled or unskilled labor, on the other hand.

---

[2] Mode 4 can increase goods trade via the following four channels: the *preference effect* (changed preference pattern toward the foreign countries' product when they move back home), the *information effect* (reduce informal barriers to trade, as well as network search costs, using their connections with the local business network), the *contract enforcement effect* (with better knowledge of local business law and practices, foreign workers can facilitate stronger enforcement of international contracts eliminating partly the uncertainties connected with international transactions), and by improving the quality and reducing the cost of services (such as transport services or telecommunication services).

The comparable set of welfare results is mostly confined to gains or losses at the *intensive margin* from commodity trade and factor flows. A comparison of variety gains or gains at *extensive margin* from trade and factor flows is rather scarce. There have been studies that analyzed variety gains from commodity trade (such as Krugman (1979), Helpman (1981), Feenstra (1992), Feenstra and Kee (2005), Feenstra and Ma (2014), Romer (1994), Klenow and Rodriguez-Clare (1997), Broda and Weinstein (2004), and Aditya and Acharyya (2015)). Both Krugman (1979) and Helpman (1981), for example, established that opening up of trade between two countries increases the domestically produced number of varieties of a differentiated good in both the countries. Feenstra (1992) and Romer (1994) suggested that a fall in the number of goods available could add substantially to the costs of protection. Empirically Broda and Weinstein (2004) found unmeasured growth in product variety from US imports to be an important source of gains from trade during 1972–2001. Hence, the gains from trade, as suggested by Krugman, are important. Romer (1994) showed that the welfare losses operating through reduced variety in response to higher tariffs may be greater in magnitude than those associated with the standard trade analysis. Consistent with Romer's hypothesis, Klenow and Rodriguez-Clare (1997) found that trade liberalization in Costa Rica during 1986 to 1992 led to an increase in import variety, that is, the estimated welfare gains from trade are 50 percent more when the impact of trade liberalization on variety is considered. Feenstra and Ma (2014), on the other hand, examined the link between trade facilitation (using port efficiency) and export variety at a cross-country level during 1991–2000 and found that the bilateral import tariff appeared to discourage expansion in export variety; however, it only has insignificant impact on the intensive margin. With heterogeneous firms, Melitz and Ottaviano (2008) also found increased varieties being exported by countries after trade opened up.

In a recent study, Aditya and Acharyya (2015) demonstrated that for a country producing a continuum of homogeneous goods and different varieties of a differentiated good, a reduction of tariff on imports of the subset of the continuum of homogeneous goods may lead to variety gains or gains at the extensive margin. However, there is almost no theoretical analysis or empirical study to analyze variety gains from factor flows.

The second relevance of analyzing the impacts of commodity trade and factor flows on product variety and export diversity is to have an understanding on the prospects of growth. New Growth Theories (Grossman and Helpman, 1991; Young, 1991), as well as recent cross-country studies (Agosin, 2007; Hesse, 2008; Lederman and Maloney, 2007; and Aditya and Acharyya, 2013), bring out the role of product variety and export diversity in augmenting growth rates of open economies. For example, Hesse (2008) and Aditya and Acharyya (2013) found evidences of a non-linear relationship between export diversification and output growth at cross-country level. This means that diversification is more important for the developing countries, whereas the advanced countries gain by specializing. Caselli *et al.* (2011), on the other hand, argue that diversification through trade causes less macroeconomic volatility due to trade openness. The larger the number of goods exported by a country, movements in the world prices of individual goods offset each other, and the country's export price level tends to be relatively stable. In contrast, the terms of trade of a country is expected to fluctuate more when the extent of commodity concentration is greater (Michaely, 1962; Hesse, 2008). These results suggest that asymmetric impacts of commodity trade and factor flows on product diversity, if at all present, essentially mean different growth prospects that the two could bring about.

Given these perspectives, this chapter examines whether commodity trade and factor flows indeed have asymmetric impacts on the number of varieties of a horizontally differentiated export good produced and exported by a small country. Hence, the chapter can provide a different explanation for asymmetric policy toward the two in terms of gains at the extensive margin in the short run and growth prospects in the long run. By highlighting on these two dimensions of observed asymmetric policies toward the movement of goods, capital inflow, and immigration of labor, this chapter differentiates it with the existing analysis in the aforementioned two relevant strands of literature.

For the purpose, we consider a small open economy producing three traded goods with the following three factors of production—skilled labor, unskilled labor, and capital. Two of the three goods are homogeneous goods—one is an import-competing good and the other is an export good—which are produced under constant returns-to-scale technology and perfectly competitive conditions. The third good is a horizontally differentiated good with distinct set of varieties, which is produced under increasing returns to technology and monopolistically competitive conditions. Different varieties of this good are exported and imported; therefore, inter- and intra-industry trade coexists in this analysis. The subsystem comprising the two traded homogeneous goods has a specific factor production structure, a la Jones (1971), with unskilled and skilled labor as the two specific factors. In addition, physical capital is used in the production of both. The different varieties of the horizontally differentiated good, on the other hand, are developed and produced by capital and skilled labor. The number of such varieties produced and exported by our small economy is endogenously determined, and preference for those displays love-of-variety, as suggested by Dixit and Stiglitz (1977) and Krugman (1979). The unskilled money wage is assumed to be fixed whereas the rate of return to capital and skilled wage are market determined. In a later part, we consider real wage rigidity in place of fixed money wage, which produces no *qualitative* change in our result.

In such a setup, two sets of thought experiments are considered—commodity trade liberalization through a reduction of tariff on import of the homogeneous good, and *small* factor flows through partial relaxation of restrictions on capital inflow and immigration of skilled and unskilled workers. With production of all goods and varieties competing for capital and a subset of goods competing for skilled labor, effects of such policy changes on the number of varieties of the differentiated export good work through reallocation of these scarce resources across different sectors.

However, the resource allocation effect of trade liberalization policies on the number of varieties and gains at the extensive margin that we emphasize in this chapter has not been explicitly explored in the existing theories. The only notable exception is that of Feenstra *et al.* (2005), who argue that tariff reduction may boost export variety by moving resources into the exporting sectors. However, Krugman (1979) talked about the resource constraint in the sense that the number of variety is proportional to country size, though there was no scope for allocation of resources. Aditya and Acharyya (2015), on the other hand, examined whether in a resource-constrained economy that produces many goods and product varieties, trade liberalization in terms of tariff reduction by releasing resources from the import-competing sectors can make its export basket more diversified. However, there is no as such study on the impact of factor flow through its resource reallocation effect on product variety. Given this context, we establish the following results.

First, we show that the impact of tariff reduction and factor flows on changes in export variety depends on the factor intensity assumption. We establish that tariff reduction and capital inflow will lead to increased variety of the differentiated export good when the import-competing homogeneous good is relatively *skilled labor* intensive.

It is further shown that immigration of labor (both skilled and unskilled) lowers the number of differentiated varieties under the particular factor intensity assumption making the export basket less diversified. Thus, capital inflow and labor *immigration* (both skilled and unskilled) can be shown to have just the opposite effect because in either case the net capital to skilled labor endowment ratio rises for the small open economy.

The chapter is organized as follows: The second section describes the assumptions and analytical structure of the model of a small open economy. The third examines the implications of tariff reductions and factor flows on product variety. We begin with analyzing the impact of tariff reduction on product variety and then examines the impact of factor flow. The impacts of capital, as well as skilled and unskilled labor movements, are also analyzed in the third section. In the fourth section, we propose real wage rigidity instead of money wage rigidity, which provides a robustness check of the results derived in the third section. The fifth section discusses how the main results derived in the third and the fourth sections explain asymmetry in policy toward commodity trade and factor flows. Finally, concluding remarks are provided along with discussion of possible extensions in the sixth section.

The Analytical Framework

Consider a small open economy producing two homogeneous goods Y and Z and a differentiated good X. The homogeneous good Z is produced using skilled labor (S) and capital per unit of output, whereas the production of good Y requires unskilled labor (L) and capital per unit of output. For example, good Y can be considered as an unskilled labor-intensive manufacture (say, textiles), whereas good Z as skill-based manufacture (say, machinery). Both these goods are produced with constant returns-to-scale (CRS) technology under perfectly competitive conditions. The country imports the homogeneous good Z, subject to an ad-valorem tariff, $t \in (0,1)$, and exports good Y. The third one, that is, the horizontally differentiated good X, is produced under increasing returns-to-scale (IRS) technology and monopolistically competitive conditions, with skilled labor used in fixed proportion per unit of output of each variety, and capital in fixed amount per variety of the good being produced. The number of endogenously determined varieties of good X produced is denoted by n and are distinctly different from each other due to IRS.[3] Preference for the differentiated good displays love-of-variety. By the IRS production technology, it is easy to check that under free trade in good X, varieties domestically produced will be distinctly different from those produced in the rest of the world. This coupled with love-of-variety preference means that there will be intraindustry trade in different varieties of good X.

More precisely, let per unit production of the homogeneous good Z require a_{KZ} units of capital and a_{SZ} units of skilled labor and that of good Y require a_{KY} units of capital and a_{LY} units of unskilled labor.

On the other hand, as specified in Aditya and Acharyya (2015), let a fixed amount of capital (ρ) be required to develop a new design or specification or to make a variation in the design of an existing variety to create a newer variety.[4] After developing the new design, or making a variation on the existing one, production of that new variety requires only β units of skilled labor per unit of output. This production technology resembles that of Krugman (1979), apart from the fact that instead of labor being used as both the fixed and variable factors of production there, in this case capital is considered as the fixed factor.

---

[3] It is this IRS property that implies there would be n number of domestic firms each producing distinct varieties of Good X.

[4] Following Krugman (1979), newer varieties are developed inhouse without any learning-by-doing effect.

Endowment of (skilled and unskilled) labor and capital is exogenously given. The return to capital (r) and skilled wage are fully flexible. However, the unskilled wage is assumed to be fixed institutionally ($\overline{w}$). As we will see later, this assumption is needed to close the model, because along with outputs of goods Y and Z, the number of varieties of good X (or the number of firms in X sector) is also endogenously determined. The rigid unskilled wage assumption is, however, not at odds with prevalence of official minimum wage rates for unskilled and semi-skilled workers in many countries across the globe, including the OECD countries. [5]

The economy under consideration is small, in the sense that it is a price taker in the world market for the homogeneous goods. Thus, world prices of the two homogeneous goods are exogenously given. However, because of the IRS, the i-th variety will be produced by only one firm in the small open economy under consideration, as well as in the world. Therefore, if that particular variety is produced domestically and exported, the firm concerned will be a price-setter in the world market.

Given the aforementioned set of assumptions, the following conditions specify the domestic market equilibrium conditions in this small country. First, perfect competition in the homogeneous good sectors implies that producers earn zero profit at the long-run equilibrium:

$$(1 + t)P_Z^W = a_{SZ}w_S + a_{KZ}r \tag{1}$$

$$p_Y^W = a_{LY}\overline{w} + a_{KY}r \tag{2}$$

where $0 < t < 1$ is the ad-valorem tariff rate, P_Z^W and P_Y^W are respectively the world prices of good Z and good Y, w_S is the skilled wage, and r is the rate of return to capital.

Second, we have the least-cost input choices with flexible coefficient production technology as follows:

$$a_{LY} = a_{LY}\left(\overline{w}/r\right) \tag{3}$$

$$a_{Kj} = a_{Kj}\left(w/r\right), j = Y, Z \tag{4}$$

$$a_{SZ} = a_{SZ}\left(w_S/r\right) \tag{5}$$

Third, free entry and monopolistic competition erode any profit opportunity in the X sector as well. However, because of IRS, the price of each variety (P_{Xi}) equals its average cost as follows:

$$p_x = \beta w_S + \frac{\rho r}{x_i} \tag{6}$$

[5] Note that, the ILO encourages its member States to adopt minimum wage to reduce poverty and provide social protection for vulnerable employees.

The other equilibrium condition in the market for good X is the equality between marginal revenue (MR) and marginal cost (MC), which reflects the monopoly power that each firm has over the variety that it produces as

$$p_x = \left(\frac{\varepsilon_i}{\varepsilon_i - 1}\right)\beta w_S \tag{7}$$

where ε_i is the price elasticity of demand for the i-th variety faced by the individual firm.

Finally, the following full-employment conditions for capital and skilled and unskilled labor determine together the output of the homogeneous import-competing good and the number of varieties of the export good as follows:

$$K = a_{KZ}Z + a_{KY}Y + n\rho \tag{8}$$

$$L = a_{LY}Y \tag{9}$$

$$S = a_{SZ} + n\beta x \tag{10}$$

Using the symmetric equilibrium condition for the number of varieties of good x, $\sum_i x_i = nx$.

Given P_Z^W, P_Y^W, and $\overline{w}$, the aforementioned set of ten equations (actually there are eleven equations as equation (4) holds for both goods Y and Z) determine the following eleven variables: r, w_s, x, P_x, Y, Z, n, and the four *aijs*. It is now clear that we need to fix the money wage to close the model. As evident from equations (1)–(7), given the unskilled wage, the prices and outputs of different varieties, the input requirements, skilled wage, and the rate of return to capital are determined solely and uniquely by the world prices of goods Y and Z, independent of the factor market equilibrium conditions. The zero-profit conditions for goods Y and Z determine the rate of return to capital, as well as skilled wage, given the institutionally fixed unskilled wage and the ad-valorem tariff rate, t. The two equilibrium conditions for good X then determine the price and output of each variety.

Three comments are warranted at this point. First, for any given number of domestically produced varieties (and firms, n), the subsystem comprising the two homogeneous traded goods displays production structure of a specific factor model, a la Jones (1971). Despite an embedded specific factor production structure, due to the fixed unskilled wage, the skilled wage and the rate of return to capital are solely determined by commodity prices and the tariff rate, independent of factor endowment conditions. Thus, the endowment of factor of production does not have any direct impact on factor prices, as in a standard HOS model. Second, as evident from equation (7), the price of each variety of good X is a markup over the (constant) skilled wage cost. To keep things simple, we assume constant price elasticity of demand, so that the price of each variety will be a *constant* markup over the wage cost and, therefore, will be invariant with respect to changes in the tariff rate. Third, because all firms in sector X share the same technology and face the same factor prices, therefore, $x_i = x_j$, and consequently, $P_{xi} = P_{xj} \; \forall \; i \neq j$. Thus, we have a symmetric equilibrium as suggested in Krugman (1979).

Once the output of each variety of good X is determined in the independent subsystem comprising conditions, as in equations (1)–(7), the full-employment conditions, as in equations (8)–(10), determine the output levels of goods Y and Z and the number of varieties of good X (and the number of firms producing good X). Note that, despite wage rigidity, unskilled labor is fully employed, because any excess supply of unskilled labor can be absorbed through adjustment of the number of varieties and hence the number of firms. Of course, during the adjustment toward full employment, whether n rises and Z falls or the reverse happens depends on the factor intensity assumption.[6]

Figure 7.1 illustrates the determination of the equilibrium number of variety and the output of the homogeneous good Z. From equation (8), substituting the expression for good Y in the full-employment condition of capital, we can rewrite the condition, noted in equation (11), as $\tilde{K} = a_{KZ}Z + n\rho$, where $\tilde{K} = K - \dfrac{a_{KY}}{a_{LY}} L$

is the net capital available for good Z and n is the number of varieties of good X. This is the net capital availability constraint. Note that, unskilled labor being specific to the production of good Y, the output of good Y is determined by the availability of unskilled labor and the choice of technique, as reflected in a_{LY}.

In Figure 7.1a, the two constraints are drawn under the assumption that the production of good Z is skilled labor intensive relative to differentiated varieties, in the sense that the ratio of labor requirement per unit of output of good Z to labor requirement per variety is larger than the ratio of the capital requirement per unit of output of good Z to capital requirement per variety as follows: $\dfrac{a_{SZ}}{\beta x} > \dfrac{a_{KZ}}{\rho}$.

Figure 7.1b, alternatively, represents the situation when good Z is relatively capital intensive compared to good X. The equilibrium in both the cases is at E_0, where n_0 number of differentiated varieties and Z_0 level of output of the import-competing homogeneous good Z are produced. What emerges from Figure 7.1a (or 7.1b) is that the number of varieties and the extent to which export basket is diversified are constrained by the availability of skilled labor, net capital stock $\tilde{K}$, and the choice of techniques (which, in turn, depends on world commodity prices).

---

[6] The model displays the HOS properties so that the nature of adjustments in case of excess supply of labor (or capital) are analogous to output magnification effect of an increase in the endowment of labor (or capital) in a standard HOS model.

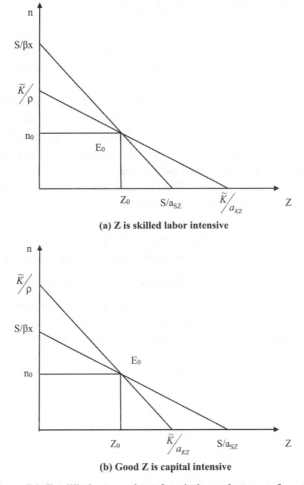

(a) Z is skilled labor intensive

(b) Good Z is capital intensive

Figure 7.1 Equilibrium number of varieties and output of good Z

Given the aforementioned specifications, in the next section we examine the impact of commodity trade liberalization and factor flows on the equilibrium number of domestically produced and exported varieties of good X.

Impact of Tariff and Factor Flows on Varieties

In the aforementioned setup, we consider two broad policy changes. One is commodity trade liberalization through a reduction of tariff on imports of good Z, and the other is allowing capital inflow and immigration of skilled and unskilled labor. We begin with implications of tariff reduction on export diversification.

Diversification Effect of Tariff Reduction

A reduction of tariff on import of good Z affects the number of varieties produced and exported through the resource reallocation effect that it triggers across the sectors. The resource reallocation effect of tariff reduction can be traced out as follows.

At the initial world price of good Y, with the unskilled wage being fixed, the rate of return to capital remains unchanged. This is evident from the zero-profit condition (2). Now given the world price of good Z, a tariff reduction causes the domestic tariff-inclusive price to fall below the average (and marginal) cost. With return to capital being tied to the given world price of good Y, the skilled wage falls through competitive forces. This, in turn, lowers skilled wage cost in the differentiated manufacturing sector X, inducing a scale expansion there. Note that at the initial equilibrium, given the output level of each variety, the fall in skilled wage lowers the average cost of producing each variety by *less than* proportionately, $\theta_{SX}\hat{W}_S$, whereas given the constant markup, it lowers the price of each variety proportionately, $\hat{P}_x = \hat{W}_S$. This induces each incumbent firm to increase its output to the extent necessary to reduce the average cost through economies of scale and to break even. As shown in the Appendix, the required output (or scale) expansion is exactly proportional to the fall in skilled wage as follows:

$$\hat{x}_i = -\hat{W}_S = -\frac{1}{\theta_{SZ}}\hat{T} \tag{11}$$

where $\theta_{SZ} = \dfrac{a_{SZ}W_s}{P_Z^W}$ is the cost share of skilled labor in the unit production of Z

sector, and $\hat{T} = \dfrac{d(1+t)}{1+t}$ denotes the proportional change in ad-valorem tariff rate.

However, scale expansion of the existing varieties require additional skilled labor, which can be obtained either through scale contraction in the import-competing sector Z or through a fall in the number of domestically produced varieties of good X. On the other hand, lower skilled wage and unchanged return to capital induce producers to use more skilled labor and less capital in per unit production of good Z. Therefore, Z sector will release some capital, which may be used for either scale expansion for Z or production of newer varieties of X. If all existing varieties together require less skilled labor per unit of (industry) output than the Z sector, then output of Z must contract so that the skilled labor released on that account, along with capital released due to the technique effect, can sustain development and production of newer varieties. Otherwise, if Z good is relatively capital intensive, then the amount of skilled labor released by it through scale contraction will not be sufficient to sustain production of newer varieties of good X. In such a case, Z sector expands and the number of varieties of good X fall at the new equilibrium. This sounds like an output magnification effect with the direction of changes in good Z and n depending on the factor-intensity ranking of goods.

Given this chain of adjustments and reallocation of skilled labor and capital across sectors, the final changes in the output of the import-competing good and the number of varieties of the differentiated export good X are illustrated in Figure 7.2. These are illustrated under the assumption that the import-competing good is relatively skilled labor intensive. By the technique effect in Z sector (reflected in lower a_{KZ} and higher a_{SZ}) and scale expansion in X sector (higher output per variety) induced by lower skilled wage, the skilled labor constraint shifts to the left, whereas the net capital availability constraint rotates outward. At the new full-employment equilibrium E_1, the country produces and exports a larger set of varieties. That is, tariff reduction makes export basket more diversified.

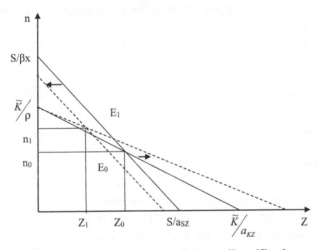

Figure 7.2 Tariff reduction and export diversification

Algebraically (as shown in the Appendix), the expressions for the *equilibrium* changes in the output of import-competing good Z, and the number of varieties produced and exported by the small open economy is given as follows:

$$\hat{Z} = \frac{\alpha}{|\lambda|}\hat{T} \tag{12}$$

$$\hat{n} = -\frac{\lambda_{KZ}(\lambda_{SX} + \sigma_Z\lambda_{SZ})}{\theta_{SZ}|\lambda|}\hat{T} \tag{13}$$

$$\text{where } \alpha = \frac{\lambda_{KX}\left[\lambda_{SX} + \sigma_Z\left\{\lambda_{SZ}\theta_{KZ} + \dfrac{\lambda_{SX}\lambda_{KZ}}{\lambda_{KX}}\theta_{SZ}\right\}\right]}{\theta_{SZ}}, \; |\lambda| = \lambda_{SZ}\lambda_{KX} - \lambda_{SX}\lambda_{KZ},$$

$\lambda_{Sj} = \dfrac{a_{Sj}X_J}{S}$, $j = X$ and Z, which is the share of sector j in total skilled labor

employment, $\lambda_{Kj} = \dfrac{a_{Kj}X_J}{K}$, wherein $j = X$ and Z, which is the share of sector j in

total capital employment. σ_Z is the elasticity of substitution between skilled labor and capital in the production of good Z.

Because a tariff reduction means $\hat{T} < 0$; therefore, $\hat{n} > 0$ and $\hat{Z} < 0$ if $|\lambda| > 0$, that is, if Z is skilled labor intensive. Otherwise, $|\lambda| < 0$, in which case the number of variety will fall, and the Z sector will expand.

The seemingly paradoxical result that the output of good Z increases despite the fall in its tariff-inclusive price deserves some explanations. Note that given the fixed unskilled money wage, the rate of return to capital is tied down to the given world price of the homogeneous export good Y. Thus, reduction in tariff rate lowers the skilled wage regardless of the factor-intensity ranking of the import-competing good Z. In addition, from the zero-profit condition of the homogeneous import-competing sector and the marginal condition in the differentiated good sector, it follows that tariff reduction unambiguously lowers the price of each variety proportionately with the fall in skilled wage (because price is a constant markup over wage cost), simultaneously raising the output of each variety. The fall in price of each variety necessitates an increase in output level, because scale expansion would achieve economies of scale and lower average cost commensurate to the price fall. The fall in skilled wage induces the producers of good Z to use relatively more skilled labor-intensive techniques of production, thereby raising the demand for skilled labor and lowering the demand for capital per unit of output. On the other hand, scale expansion in the X sector also raises the demand for skilled labor, but it does not require any additional capital. Thus, overall, at the initial output of good Z, there arises an excess supply of capital (and an excess demand for skilled labor). Because the output of good Y is fixed by the number of unskilled workers specific to this sector (and there would be no change in technique of production there as well), this excess supply of capital can be absorbed either through a scale expansion in Z sector or through an increase in the number of varieties produced. If good Z is relatively capital intensive, in the sense that capital required per unit of output is larger than the capital required to develop a variety of good X, then increase in the number varieties cannot absorb capital released from Z sector due to adoption of more skilled labor-intensive production techniques there. Moreover, the development of additional varieties require skilled labor to produce such varieties, which, given that both the scale expansion in X sector and change in technique in Z sector require additional skilled labor, would be available only if output of good Z falls. But again, good Z being capital intensive, it would release less skilled labor per unit of output than would be required for per unit output of each newer variety. All these mean that to maintain full employment, the output of good Z must rise, and the number of varieties of good X must fall after tariff reduction.[7]

This perverse response of output of good Z to the fall in its tariff-inclusive price is due to the distortion that fixed unskilled money wage causes. If it had not been fixed so that the rate of return to capital could also vary, we would expect that a fall in tariff-inclusive price of good Z would lower the rate of return to capital relative to the skilled wage, if good Z is capital intensive.[8] Therefore, a reduction in tariff would induce the adoption of relatively capital-intensive techniques of production instead. In such a case, there would have arisen an excess supply of skilled labor at initial output of good Z, which in turn would have lowered the output of good Z for reasons similar to those aforementioned. In addition, there would have been a usual supply response to a fall in price, that is, the fixed unskilled money wage distorts the choice of production technique in Z sector leading to a perverse supply response to a fall in tariff-inclusive price of good Z when it is relatively capital intensive. However, when it is relatively skilled labor intensive, the choice of production technique is not distorted (at least directionally, if not in magnitude). This is because a fall in tariff-inclusive price lowers the skilled wage relative to the rate of return to capital just as it would have caused had the unskilled money wage been flexible and correspondingly the rate of return to capital could change. Accordingly, we have the usual supply response in case of good Z being relatively skilled labor intensive.

Therefore, from the results derived in equations (12) and (13), we can state Proposition 1 as follows:

Proposition 1. *In this setup with fixed unskilled wage, a reduction of tariff on import of the homogeneous good unambiguously increases output per variety of*

---

[7] This is similar to the output magnification effect in a standard 2x2 HOS model: an excess supply of capital raises the output of Good Z and lowers the number of varieties of good X if good Z is relatively capital intensive.

[8] Note that given the endowment of unskilled workers, and correspondingly the output of good Y and the capital requirement there, the Z–X subsystem displays HOS production structure. And in a 2x2 HOS model, by price magnification effect, a fall in tariff would lower the rate of return to capital and raise the skilled wage if the import-competing good is relatively capital intensive.

the horizontally differentiated export good, but increases the number of varieties only if the import-competing good is relatively skilled labor intensive.

This result suggests that for countries that import relatively skilled intensive goods and export relatively capital intensive varieties of a differentiated good, trade liberalization through tariff reductions can lead to gains at the extensive margin. On the other hand, the consequent diversification of the country's export basket improves its long-run growth prospects.

Factor Movement and Diversification

When the country allows international factor movement or factor trade, the direction and type of factor flows will depend, among others, on domestic factor prices vis-à-vis those prevailing in the rest of the world. Note that, even in the present framework, factor prices are solely determined by commodity prices, and tariffs prohibit commodity prices to equalize across nations. Consequently, cross-country differences in factor prices persist creating scope for factor flows. However, without presuming anything about whether rate of return to capital and wages are higher or lower in the small country under consideration vis-à-vis the rest of the world, we consider in turn impacts of capital inflow and immigration of skilled and unskilled labor given our purpose discussed earlier. Impacts of reverse factor flows would just be mirror images of the results that we derive below.

However, we consider that our host country allows only limited or small amount of capital inflow or immigration so that changes in composition of output that such flows bring about are not large enough to cause complete specialization in either of the two homogeneous traded goods (Y and Z). This means that the skilled wage and the rate of return to capital are still determined solely by the world prices of these two traded goods. Because our host country is assumed to be small in the world market for the homogeneous goods, changes in its trade volumes consequent upon factor-flow-induced changes in the composition of output will have no impact on world commodity prices, and hence on domestic factor prices. Therefore, small factor flows—capital inflow or immigration (or reverse flows)—will leave factor prices unchanged.[9]

This factor price invariance (or no-impact) aspect of small factor flows, along with the assumption of constant price elasticity of demand for each variety of the export good X, also means that the output levels of each variety will not change either. With unchanged factor prices, the cost of production of good X does not

---

[9] This is similar to the no-impact result in a 2x2 HOS model: as long as capital inflow is small to change the commodity composition within the cone of diversification for the host country, factor prices there do not change (Bhagwati, 1997).

change making price and output per variety constant. The logic is simple. With constant price elasticity of demand for each variety of the export good X, the price of each variety of the export good is cost-determined or a (constant) markup over the constant wage cost. With prices thus tied to the constant wage cost, the output of each variety is inversely proportional to the rate of return to capital. Consequently, a small factor flow that leaves the rate of return to capital unchanged does not affect the output of each variety.

What all these mean is that by assuming small factor flows, we need to examine only the pattern of reallocation of resources through *scale expansion or contraction* without being concerned regarding the factor substitution or technique effects. However, as we see in the forthcoming paragraphs, the pattern of reallocation of resources differs with the type of factor flow that takes place. In the next subsection, we begin with a discussion on capital inflow.

Capital Inflow

A ceteris paribus capital inflow changes only the output of the import-competing good and the number of varieties of the export good. The direction of such changes, however, depends on the factor-intensity ranking of the import-competing good and the export good. With the increased availability of capital, the number of variety will increase if production of good Z is relatively skilled labor intensive in the sense as defined earlier. However, for increased number of variety, more skilled labor is required, which is released from the Z sector. Consequently the Z sector contracts, which will further release some capital. Hence, the net availability of capital for a number of variety is greater than the amount of capital inflow into this small host country, resulting in a more than proportionate increase in the variety of good X than the rate of capital inflow. Figure 7.3 graphically depicts the shift in the capital constraint and changes in output of good Z and number of variety. Algebraically this can be verified from the following expressions (see Appendix):

$$\hat{Z} = -\frac{\lambda_{SX}}{|\lambda|}\hat{K} \tag{14}$$

$$\hat{n} = \frac{\lambda_{SZ}}{|\lambda|}\hat{K} \tag{15}$$

where $|\lambda| = \lambda_{SZ}\lambda_{KX} - \lambda_{SX}\lambda_{KZ}$ is the employment share matrix between homogeneous good Z and differentiated good X.

Proposition 2. *In the present setup, a capital inflow will increase the number of variety of the differentiated export good if good Z is relatively skilled labor intensive, that is, $|\lambda| > 0$.*

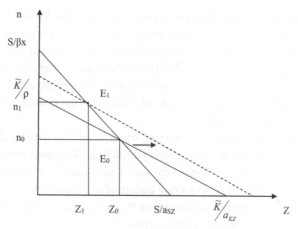

Figure 7.3 Impact of capital inflow

Immigration of Skilled Labor

Consider now the immigration of skilled labor, ceteris paribus, which means an increase in size of the skilled workforce: $\hat{S} > 0$. In the subsystem comprising the import-competing sector Z and the differentiated export sector X, for any given output of each variety, the output of good Z and the number of varieties of good X are determined by the net availability of capital and size of the skilled workforce, as shown earlier. More precisely, similar to standard HOS model, the size of skilled workforce relative to net capital availability is what that matters for the level of output of good Z and the number of varieties of good X. Given the number of unskilled workers in our host country, and choice of technique remaining the same in other parts of the world due to unchanged factor prices for reasons spelled out earlier, the output of the homogeneous export good Y and its capital requirement remain the same. On the other hand, output of each variety remaining invariant as well, and skilled labor requirement for production of the existing varieties of good X does not change either. All these mean that immigration of skilled labor raises the endowment ratio $\frac{S}{K}$ in contrast to a capital inflow lowering the endowment ratio $\frac{S}{K}$. Thus, we can expect that immigration of skilled labor will have exactly the opposite effects on the number of varieties of good X produced and exported by the host country compared to a capital inflow. Therefore, if the import-competing good is relatively skilled labor intensive, then immigration of skilled labor should lower the number of varieties of the differentiated export good X and consequently make the export basket less diversified. This can be verified from the following equilibrium changes worked out in the Appendix:

$$\hat{Z} = \frac{\lambda_{KX}}{|\lambda|} \hat{S} \qquad (16)$$

$$\hat{n} = -\frac{\lambda_{KZ}}{|\lambda|} \hat{S} \qquad (17)$$

Thus, $\hat{n} < 0$ if $|\lambda| > 0$, unlike in case of a capital inflow. However, even though the direction of changes are reversed as expected, magnification effects still hold, that is, the rise in the output of good Z is more than proportional to the number of skilled immigrants.[10]

Intuitively, if the production of good Z is relatively skilled labor intensive, the immigration of skilled labor and a consequent increase in the size of skilled workforce should raise the output of good Z. If on the contrary, had the output of good Z contracted, it would have released some skilled labor workforce in the process, which together with the immigrants could not have been absorbed in X sector through expansion of the number of varieties. Thus, by the factor intensity assumption, at the new equilibrium, the output of good Z must increase to employ the new migrants. However, such expansion requires capital as well, which in turn necessitates a fall in the number of varieties of good X being produced (and exported). The consequent laying off of skilled workers from X sector then makes it possible for a further increase in the output of good Z. At the final equilibrium, therefore, the rise in output of good Z is more than proportionate to the number of skilled immigrants. This is illustrated in Figure 7.4.

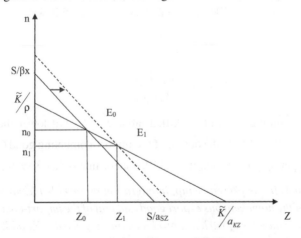

Figure 7.4 Immigration of skilled labor

---

[10] In case of *emigration* of skilled labor under $|\lambda| > 0$ or immigration of skilled labor under $|\lambda| < 0$, the number of varieties would have increased more than proportionately.

Therefore, we propose the following.

Proposition 3: *Small immigration of skilled labor ($\hat{S} > 0$) will lower the number of varieties ($\hat{n} < 0$) and raise the output of the import-competing good ($\hat{Z} > 0$) more than proportionately if the import-competing good Z is relatively skilled labor intensive ($|\lambda| > 0$).*

Immigration of Unskilled Labor

Unlike in cases of capital inflow and immigration of skilled labor, ceteris paribus immigration of unskilled labor increases the output of the homogeneous export good. As long as immigration of unskilled labor is small in the sense defined earlier so that factor prices do not change, the increase in the output of good Y will be proportional to the immigration of unskilled labor: $\hat{Y} = \hat{L} > 0$. Because such production expansion requires capital as well, the net capital availability for the Z and X sectors thus falls. Therefore, the endowment ratio $\frac{S}{K}$ rises similar to immigration of skilled labor. Accordingly, the impact of immigration of unskilled labor on the number of varieties of good X produced and exported by our host country would be the similar to that of immigration of skilled labor. If good Z is relatively skilled labor intensive, then with immigration, the number of varieties of good X will fall.

Algebraically, the equilibrium changes in output of good Z and number of variety due to movement of unskilled labor can be obtained as follows:

$$\hat{Z} = \frac{\lambda_{KY}\lambda_{SX}}{\lambda_{LY}|\lambda|}\hat{L} \tag{18}$$

$$\hat{n} = -\frac{\lambda_{KY}\lambda_{SZ}}{\lambda_{LY}|\lambda|}\hat{L} \tag{19}$$

Therefore, immigration of unskilled labor ($\hat{L} < 0$) will lower the number of varieties ($\hat{n} < 0$) and raise the output of the import-competing good ($\hat{Z} > 0$) if the import-competing good is relatively skilled labor intensive ($|\lambda| > 0$).[11]

Proposition 4. *In the present setup, immigration of unskilled labor will increase the output of the homogeneous export good and that of the import-competing good, but lowers the number of varieties produced and exported, if good Z is relatively skilled labor intensive.*

---

[11] Conversely, emigration of unskilled labor $\hat{n} > 0$ will increase the number of varieties ($\hat{n} > 0$).

Case of Fixed Real Wage

Instead of fixed money wage, suppose the real wage is fixed in terms of the basic (or homogeneous) goods:

$$\frac{W}{P} = \varpi \qquad (20a)$$

where $P = \left(P_Z^w\right)^\delta \left(P_Y^w\right)^{1-\delta}$ $\qquad$ (20b)

Thus, using equation (20a), we can rewrite the zero-profit condition in Y sector as,

$$p_Y^w = a_{LY}\left(\varpi P\right) + a_{KY}r \qquad (2a)$$

By the assumption of fixed real wage, with any change in the tariff rate, *the money wage, as well as the rate of return to capital, changes unlike the previous case of fixed money wage.* However, because the money wage varies proportionately with the price index (but less than proportionately with the domestic price of the import good for any given world price of the basic or homogeneous export good),

$$\hat{W} = \hat{P} = \delta\hat{T} + (1 - \delta)\hat{P}_Y^w = \delta\hat{T} \qquad (20c)$$

so again, the one-to-one correspondence between commodity price changes and factor price changes holds. Accordingly, factor flows, ceteris paribus, have no bearing on the factor prices in this small host or native country (as the case may be), and impacts of such flows on the number of varieties and output levels remain the same.

However, the effect of a reduction in tariff will produce additional effects, as it will now change the money wage (as indicated above) and with it the rate of return to capital for a given world price of the basic/homogeneous export good Y. Substantial part of such additional effects of a tariff reduction will be arising in this sector itself in terms of a factor-price substitution effect induced by the change in wage–rental ratio. In addition, there will arise a corresponding scale effect because this sector uses unskilled labor as a specific factor. These effects had not arisen in the previous case because fixed money wage also tied down the rate of return to capital, and accordingly there had been no changes whatsoever in the Y sector. But now, with the money wage falling with the tariff reduction, the rate of return to capital rises,

$$\hat{r} = -\delta\frac{\theta_{LY}}{\theta_{KY}}\hat{T} > 0 \qquad (21)$$

so that producers now use relatively more (unskilled) labor-intensive techniques to produce good Y. With unskilled labor being specific in use, the output of good Y must fall due to more intensive use of unskilled labor per unit of output. Therefore, on account of these factor substitution and scale contraction effects induced by tariff in the Y sector, some capital will be released to be used in the rest of the economy. In the import-competing sector, on the other hand, the rise in capital cost now leads to a larger decline in the skilled wage (given the fall in the tariff-inclusive price) than in the case of fixed money wage:

$$\hat{W}_S = \frac{\theta_{KY} + \delta\theta_{KZ}\theta_{LY}}{\theta_{KY}\theta_{SZ}}\hat{T} < 0 \qquad (22)$$

The tariff reduction induced factor substitution effect, whereby capital will be released (at initial level of output of good Z), will now be larger than before.

However, because the output of each variety increases as well (similar to the fixed money wage case)

$$\hat{x}_i = -\left[\frac{A}{\theta_{SZ}\theta_{KY}} + \frac{\delta\theta_{LY}\theta_{KX}}{\theta_{KY}}\right]\hat{T} > 0 \qquad (23)$$

where $A \equiv \theta_{KY} + \delta\theta_{KZ}\theta_{LY}$. Therefore, a larger factor substitution effect in the import-competing sector also means that a larger demand for skilled labor, which can be made available by either of the following similar to the fixed money wage case: a fall in the output of good Z or a fall in the number of varieties of good X. Again, the factor-intensity ranking of good Z and good X determines which one of these alternatives will be consistent with full-employment equilibrium (see Appendix). Thus, the real wage rigidity does not alter our results *qualitatively* compared to the rigid money wage case, and thus the results derived under such an assumption are robust in this respect.

Asymmetric Diversification Impacts of Commodity Trade and Factor Flows

From the aforementioned results derived, it is evident that commodity trade has similar diversification effect as capital inflow but contrasting effects compared to immigration of skilled and unskilled workers. In particular, although tariff reduction and capital inflow both raise the number of varieties of good X produced and exported if the import-competing good is skilled labor intensive relative to good X, immigration of skilled and unskilled labor lowers the number of varieties. This means gains at the *extensive* margin in the short run, and potential augmentation of growth rate in the long run can be obtained through commodity trade liberalization and allowing capital inflow under such factor-intensity ranking, but not through immigration of labor, both skilled or unskilled. Emigration of labor would then be a more preferred policy for a country importing relatively skilled intensive goods.

These contrasting results may provide an alternative theoretical explanation for observed policy asymmetry toward commodity trade and factor flows on the one hand, and between capital inflow and immigration of labor, on the other hand. At the same time, at least for most of the developing countries that typically import high skill-intensive goods, these results reveal the potential gains that these countries may have through commodity trade liberalization and allowing foreign capital inflow. These countries are also the potential exporters of labor, both skilled and unskilled. The growth objective that can be realized through export diversification can then form the basis of why the developing countries may be keen on exporting labor through mode IV of GATS. On the other hand, the same logic should explain why the developed and rich nations are averse to immigration of unskilled labor from the developing and poor countries.

Conclusion

This chapter examines the implications of trade liberalization policies such as tariff reduction and factor flows on export diversification in terms of increased product variety. By doing so, it offers an altogether different explanation of the observed asymmetry in policy changes regarding commodity trade, capital inflow, and immigration of labor. Though there are studies such as Mayda (2004), Bilal *et al.* (2003), and Faini (2002), who bring out the importance of economic factors along with noneconomic factors in explaining the asymmetric attitude, the channel of export diversification in explaining the asymmetric attitude toward migration has not been explored in the existing literature. We find out the asymmetric impacts of not only commodity trade and factor flows but also between capital and labor flow on the number of varieties of a horizontally differentiated export good produced and exported by a small country. The result thus provides a different explanation for asymmetric policy toward the two in terms of gains at the extensive margin in the short run and growth prospects in the long run.

In particular, it is seen that the impact of trade liberalization, through its resource reallocation effect, depends on the factor-intensity condition. Tariff reduction and capital inflow will lead to diversified export basket by increasing the number of variety if the import-competing homogeneous good is relatively skilled labor intensive, whereas immigration of labor (skilled as well as unskilled) lowers the number of variety. The results remain unchanged qualitatively when unskilled money wage rigidity is replaced with rigid money wage. Therefore, for many developing countries that are usually an importer of high skill-intensive goods and potential exporters of labor, the growth objective that can be realized through export diversification can then explain why such countries are interested in commodity trade liberalization and allowing foreign capital inflow while exporting labor through mode IV of GATS.

Some enriching extension of the chapter would be to consider variable elasticity of demand instead of constant demand elasticity and two-country world economy in place of a small open economy to take into account the impact of terms of trade.

Appendix

A.1. Diversification Effect of Tariff Reduction

Totally differentiating and taking logarithm, that is, hat operation of the zero-profit condition of good Z in equation (1), yields the following:

$$\hat{T} = \theta_{SZ}\hat{W}_S + \theta_{KZ}\hat{r} \tag{A.1}$$

For a small open economy, $\hat{P}_Y = 0$, which makes

$$\hat{r} = 0 \tag{A.2}$$

as evident from the condition in equation (2).

Therefore, (A.1) gives the change in skilled wage in terms of tariff reduction as follows:

$$\hat{W}_S = \frac{\hat{T}}{\theta_{SZ}} \tag{A.3}$$

Hat operation of the two equilibrium conditions in equations (3) and (4) yields the following:

$$\hat{P} = \theta_{SX}\hat{W}_S - \theta_{KX}\hat{x}_i = \frac{\theta_{SX}}{\theta_{SZ}}\hat{T} - \theta_{KX}\hat{x}_i \tag{A.4}$$

and

$$\hat{P} = \hat{W}_S = \frac{\hat{T}}{\theta_{SZ}} \tag{A.5}$$

Using (A.4) and (A.5) we can write

$$\frac{\hat{T}}{\theta_{SZ}} - \frac{\theta_{SX}}{\theta_{SZ}}\hat{T} = -\theta_{KX}\hat{x}_i,$$

or

$$-\theta_{KX}\hat{x}_i = \frac{(1 - \theta_{SX})\hat{T}}{\theta_{SZ}} = \frac{\theta_{KX}}{\theta_{SZ}}\hat{T},$$

or

$$\hat{x}_i = -\frac{1}{\theta_{SZ}}\hat{T} \tag{11}$$

Thus, output per variety rises due to reduction of tariff on the import-competing good Z irrespective of factor-intensity ranking.

With exogenously given endowment of unskilled labor, the change in the output of good Y can be obtained from the full-employment condition of unskilled labor in equation (9) as follows:

$$\hat{Y} = -\hat{a}_{LY} \tag{A.6}$$

Similarly, from the full-employment condition of capital in equation (8) we have the following:

$$0 = \lambda_{KZ}(\hat{a}_{KZ} + \hat{Z}) + \lambda_{KX}\hat{n} \tag{A.7}$$

Thus,

$$\hat{n} = -\frac{\lambda_{KZ}}{\lambda_{KX}}(\hat{a}_{KZ} + \hat{Z}) \tag{A.8}$$

Proceeding similarly with the full-employment condition of skilled labor in equation (10), we obtain the following:

$$0 = \lambda_{SZ}(\hat{a}_{SZ} + \hat{Z}) + \lambda_{SX}(\hat{n} + \hat{x}) = \lambda_{SZ}(\hat{a}_{SZ} + \hat{Z}) + \lambda_{SX}\hat{n} - \frac{\lambda_{SX}}{\theta_{SZ}}\hat{T} \tag{A.9}$$

Putting the expression for $\hat{n}$ from (A.8) into (A.9), we can write as follows:

$$\lambda_{SZ}\hat{Z} = -\lambda_{SZ}\hat{a}_{SZ} + \frac{\lambda_{SX}}{\theta_{SZ}}\hat{T} + \frac{\lambda_{SX}\lambda_{KZ}}{\lambda_{KX}}(\hat{a}_{KZ} + \hat{Z})$$

$$\frac{\lambda_{SZ}\lambda_{KX} - \lambda_{SX}\lambda_{KZ}}{\lambda_{KX}}\hat{Z} = \frac{\lambda_{SX}}{\theta_{SZ}}\hat{T} - \lambda_{SZ}\hat{a}_{SZ} + \frac{\lambda_{SX}\lambda_{KZ}}{\lambda_{KX}}\hat{a}_{KZ} \tag{A.10}$$

To solve for the change in the number of varieties produced and exported, we proceed as follows.

First note that by cost-minimization rule in the Z sector, $(\theta_{KZ}\hat{a}_{KZ} + \theta_{SZ}\hat{a}_{SZ})$

$= 0$, where $\theta_{SZ} = \dfrac{a_{SZ}W_S}{P_Z}$ and $\theta_{KZ} = \dfrac{a_{KZ}r}{P_Z}$ are the respective shares of skilled

labor and capital in unit cost such that $\theta_{SZ} + \theta_{KZ} = 1$. Therefore, we can write

changes in skill-labor and capital intensities there as,

$$\hat{a}_{KZ} = \hat{a}_{KZ} - (\theta_{KZ}\hat{a}_{KZ} + \theta_{SZ}\hat{a}_{SZ})$$

$$= \theta_{SZ}(\hat{a}_{KZ} - \hat{a}_{SZ})$$

$$= \theta_{SZ}\sigma_Z(\hat{W}_S - \hat{r}) = \theta_{SZ}\sigma_Z\hat{W}_S \tag{A.11}$$

$$\hat{a}_{SZ} = \hat{a}_{SZ} - (\theta_{KZ}\hat{a}_{KZ} + \theta_{SZ}\hat{a}_{SZ})$$

$$= \theta_{KZ}(\hat{a}_{SZ} - \hat{a}_{KZ})$$

$$= \theta_{KZ}\sigma_Z(\hat{r} - \hat{W}_S) = -\theta_{KZ}\sigma_Z\hat{W}_S \tag{A.12}$$

where $\sigma_Z \equiv \dfrac{\hat{a}_{KZ} - \hat{a}_{SZ}}{\hat{W}_S - \hat{r}} > 0$ is the elasticity of factor substitution in the production

of good Z.

Substituting these two in equation (A.10):

$$\frac{|\lambda|}{\lambda_{KX}}\hat{Z} = \frac{\lambda_{SX}}{\theta_{SZ}}\hat{T} + \lambda_{SZ}\theta_{KZ}\sigma_Z\hat{W}_S + \frac{\lambda_{SX}\lambda_{KZ}}{\lambda_{KX}}\theta_{SZ}\sigma_Z\hat{W}_S \qquad (A.13)$$

where $|\lambda| = \lambda_{SZ}\lambda_{KX} - \lambda_{SX}\lambda_{KZ}$ is the employment share matrix between import-competing homogeneous good Z and differentiated export good X.

$$\psi\hat{Z} = \frac{\lambda_{SX}}{\theta_{SZ}}\hat{T} + \sigma_Z\frac{\hat{T}}{\theta_{SZ}}\left[\lambda_{SZ}\theta_{KZ} + \frac{\lambda_{SX}\lambda_{KZ}}{\lambda_{KX}}\theta_{SZ}\right]$$

$$= \frac{\hat{T}}{\theta_{SZ}}\left[\lambda_{SX} + \sigma_Z\left\{\lambda_{SZ}\theta_{KZ} + \frac{\lambda_{SX}\lambda_{KZ}}{\lambda_{KX}}\theta_{SZ}\right\}\right]$$

Thus, $\displaystyle\hat{Z} = \frac{\left[\lambda_{SX} + \sigma_Z\left\{\lambda_{SZ}\theta_{KZ} + \frac{\lambda_{SX}\lambda_{KZ}}{\lambda_{KX}}\theta_{SZ}\right\}\right]}{\psi\theta_{SZ}}\hat{T} = \frac{\alpha}{|\lambda|}\hat{T} \qquad (12)$

Using the expressions of $\hat{Z}$ from equation (A.13) and $\hat{W}_S$ from equation (A.3), we can write equation (A.8) in the following way:

$$\hat{n} = -\frac{\lambda_{KZ}\theta_{SZ}\sigma_Z}{\lambda_{KX}\theta_{SZ}}\hat{T} - \frac{\lambda_{KZ}\lambda_{SX}}{|\lambda|\theta_{SZ}}\hat{T} - \frac{\lambda_{KZ}\lambda_{SZ}\theta_{KZ}\sigma_Z}{|\lambda|\theta_{SZ}}\hat{T} - \frac{\lambda_{SX}\lambda_{KZ}^2\theta_{SZ}\sigma_Z}{|\lambda|\lambda_{KX}\theta_{SZ}}\hat{T}$$

$$= -\frac{\lambda_{KZ}}{|\lambda|\theta_{SZ}}\left(\lambda_{SX} + \lambda_{SZ}\theta_{KZ}\sigma_Z\right)\hat{T} - \frac{\lambda_{KZ}\sigma_Z}{\lambda_{KX}}\left(1 + \frac{\lambda_{SX}\lambda_{KZ}}{|\lambda|}\right)\hat{T}$$

$$= -\frac{\lambda_{KZ}}{|\lambda|\theta_{SZ}}\left(\lambda_{SX} + \lambda_{SZ}\theta_{KZ}\sigma_Z\right)\hat{T} - \frac{\lambda_{KZ}\lambda_{SZ}\sigma_Z}{|\lambda|}\hat{T} \text{ as } |\lambda| = \lambda_{SZ}\lambda_{KX} - \lambda_{SX}\lambda_{KZ}$$

$$= -\frac{\lambda_{KZ}\left(\lambda_{SX} + \sigma_Z\lambda_{SZ}\right)}{\theta_{SZ}|\lambda|}\hat{T} \text{ because } \theta_{KZ} + \theta_{SZ} = 1 \qquad (13)$$

A.2. Diversification Effect of Capital inflow

For a price-taking country with rigid unskilled wage, the zero-profit condition for good Y in equation (2) shows that the rate of return to capital remains unchanged due to capital inflow as follows:

$$\hat{r} = 0 \qquad (A.14)$$

With unchanged return to capital, in a small open economy:

$$\hat{W}_S = 0 \qquad (A.15)$$

Given r and w_s, output per variety remains unchanged as follows from the condition in equation (6):

$$\hat{x}_i = 0 \qquad (A.16)$$

With constant price elasticity of demand, price per variety also does not change as is evident from the condition in equation (7) as follows:

$$\hat{P} = 0 \qquad (A.17)$$

From the full-employment condition of capital in equation (8):

$$\hat{K} = \lambda_{KZ}\hat{Z} + \lambda_{KX}\hat{n}$$

$$\text{(because } \hat{W}_S = \hat{r} = 0, \hat{a}_{KZ} = 0 \text{)} \quad (A.18)$$

Again the full-employment condition of skilled labor in equation (10) becomes:

$$0 = \lambda_{SZ}(\hat{a}_{SZ} + \hat{Z}) + \lambda_{SX}\hat{n}$$

Thus,
$$\hat{n} = -\frac{\lambda_{SZ}}{\lambda_{SX}}\hat{Z} \quad \text{(because } \hat{W}_S = \hat{r} = 0, \hat{a}_{SZ} = 0 \text{)} (A.19)$$

Substituting the value of $\hat{n}$ in equation (A.18), we get

$$\hat{K} = \lambda_{KZ}\hat{Z} - \frac{\lambda_{KX}\lambda_{SZ}}{\lambda_{SX}}\hat{Z}$$

$$\Rightarrow \quad \frac{\lambda_{SX}\lambda_{KZ} - \lambda_{SZ}\lambda_{KX}}{\lambda_{SX}}\hat{Z} = \hat{K}$$

Thus, equilibrium changes in output of good Z due to capital inflow is given by the following:

$$\hat{Z} = -\frac{\lambda_{SX}}{|\lambda|}\hat{K} \qquad (14)$$

From equations (A.18) and (14), the equilibrium changes in the number of variety can be obtained as follows:

$$\hat{n} = \frac{\lambda_{SZ}}{|\lambda|}\hat{K} \qquad (15)$$

A.3. Immigration of Skilled Labor

From the full-employment condition of capital in equation (8):

$$0 = \lambda_{KZ}\hat{Z} + \lambda_{KX}\hat{n} \qquad \text{(because } \hat{a}_{KZ} = 0 \text{)}$$

Thus,
$$\hat{n} = -\frac{\lambda_{KZ}}{\lambda_{KX}}\hat{Z} \qquad (A.20)$$

The full-employment condition of skilled labor in equation (10) gives us:

$$\hat{S} = \lambda_{SZ}\hat{Z} + \lambda_{SX}\hat{n}$$

$$= \lambda_{SZ}\hat{Z} - \frac{\lambda_{SX}\lambda_{KZ}}{\lambda_{KX}}\hat{Z}$$

$$= \frac{\lambda_{SZ}\lambda_{KX} - \lambda_{SX}\lambda_{KZ}}{\lambda_{KX}}\hat{Z}$$

$$\therefore \qquad \hat{Z} = \frac{\lambda_{KX}}{|\lambda|}\hat{S} \qquad (16)$$

From equations (A.20) and (16), the equilibrium changes in the number of variety due to skilled labor are given by:

$$\hat{n} = -\frac{\lambda_{KZ}}{|\lambda|}\hat{S} \qquad (17)$$

A.4. Immigration of Unskilled Labor

From full-employment condition of unskilled labor in equation (9), the change in output of good Y is given by:

$$\hat{Y} = \frac{\hat{L}}{\lambda_{LY}} - \hat{a}_{LY} \qquad (A.21)$$

Now from the full-employment condition of capital in equation (8), we have:

$$\hat{K} = \lambda_{KZ}\hat{Z} + \lambda_{KY}\left(\hat{Y} + \hat{a}_{KY}\right) + \lambda_{KX}\hat{n}$$

$$= \lambda_{KZ}\hat{Z} + \lambda_{KY}\frac{\hat{L}}{\lambda_{LY}} + \lambda_{KY}\left(\hat{a}_{KY} - \hat{a}_{LY}\right) + \lambda_{KX}\hat{n}$$

$$\Rightarrow \qquad 0 = \lambda_{KZ}\hat{Z} + \lambda_{KY}\frac{\hat{L}}{\lambda_{LY}} + \lambda_{KX}\hat{n} \qquad (A.22)$$

$$(\text{because } \hat{a}_{KY} = 0 \text{ and } \hat{a}_{LY} = 0)$$

Now from equation (10)

$$0 = \lambda_{SZ}\hat{Z} + \lambda_{SX}\hat{n}$$

Thus, $\hat{n} = -\dfrac{\lambda_{SZ}}{\lambda_{SX}}\hat{Z}$ (A.23)

Substituting the value of $\hat{n}$ from equation (A.23) into (A.22) yields the equilibrium change in the output of good Z as follows:

$$\hat{Z} = \frac{\lambda_{KY}\lambda_{SX}}{\lambda_{LY}|\lambda|}\hat{L} \qquad (18)$$

Again substituting the expression of $\hat{Z}$ back into equation (A.23) gives the equilibrium change in the number of horizontally differentiated variety as follows:

$$\hat{n} = -\frac{\lambda_{KY}\lambda_{SZ}}{\lambda_{LY}|\lambda|}\hat{L} \qquad (19)$$

A.5. Fixed Real Wage

Using equations (2a) and (20b) given $\hat{P}_Y = 0$, we can write

$$0 = \delta\theta_{LY}\hat{T} + \theta_{KY}\hat{r}$$

$$\Rightarrow \qquad \hat{r} = -\delta\frac{\theta_{LY}}{\theta_{KY}}\hat{T} > 0 \qquad\qquad (A.24)$$

Substitution in equation (A.1) yields the change in skilled wage as specified in the text. On the other hand, rewriting equation (A.4) with $\hat{r} \neq 0$ using changes in skilled age and rate of return, we obtain the change in the level of output of each variety as,

$$\hat{P} = \theta_{SX}\hat{W}_S + \theta_{KX}(\hat{r} - \hat{x}_i)$$

$$\Rightarrow \qquad (1 - \theta_{SX})\hat{W}_S = \theta_{KX}(\hat{r} - \hat{x}_i)$$

$$\Rightarrow \qquad \frac{\theta_{KX}A}{\theta_{KY}\theta_{SZ}}\hat{T} = -\frac{\delta\theta_{LY}\theta_{KX}}{\theta_{KY}}\hat{T} - \theta_{KX}\hat{x}_i,$$

where $A = \theta_{KY} + \delta\theta_{LY}\theta_{KZ}$

$$\Rightarrow \qquad \hat{x}_i = -\left[\frac{A}{\theta_{SZ}\theta_{KY}} + \frac{\delta\theta_{LY}\theta_{KX}}{\theta_{KY}}\right]\hat{T} = -D\hat{T} > 0,$$

where $D = \dfrac{A}{\theta_{SZ}\theta_{KY}} + \dfrac{\delta\theta_{LY}\theta_{KX}}{\theta_{KY}}$

Now, using equation (A.6), we can rewrite equation (A.7) as follows:

$$0 = \lambda_{KZ}(\hat{a}_{KZ} + \hat{Z}) + \lambda_{KY}(\hat{Y} + \hat{a}_{KY}) + \lambda_{KX}\hat{n}$$

$$= \lambda_{KZ}(\hat{a}_{KZ} + \hat{Z}) + \lambda_{KY}(\hat{a}_{KY} - \hat{a}_{LY}) + \lambda_{KX}\hat{n} \qquad (A.7a)$$

Thus,

$$\hat{n} = -\frac{\lambda_{KZ}}{\lambda_{KX}}(\hat{a}_{KZ} + \hat{Z}) - \frac{\lambda_{KY}}{\lambda_{KX}}\sigma_Y(\hat{W} - \hat{r}) = -\frac{\lambda_{KZ}}{\lambda_{KX}}(\hat{a}_{KZ} + \hat{Z}) - \sigma_Y\frac{\lambda_{KY}}{\lambda_{KX}}\frac{\delta\theta_{LY}}{\theta_{KY}}\hat{T}$$

$$(A.8a)$$

Similarly, using equation (A.8a), (A.9) can be rewritten as follows:

$$0 = \lambda_{SZ}(\hat{a}_{SZ} + \hat{Z}) + \lambda_{SX}(\hat{n} + \hat{x})$$

$$= \lambda_{SZ}(\hat{a}_{SZ} + \hat{Z}) - \lambda_{SX}D\hat{T} - \frac{\lambda_{SX}\lambda_{KZ}}{\lambda_{KX}}(\hat{a}_{KZ} + \hat{Z}) - \sigma_Y\frac{\lambda_{SX}\lambda_{KY}}{\lambda_{KX}}\frac{\delta\theta_{LY}}{\theta_{KY}}\hat{T}$$

$$(A.9a)$$

Putting equation (A.8a) in (A.9a), we can write:

$$\frac{\lambda_{SZ}\lambda_{KX} - \lambda_{SX}\lambda_{KZ}}{\lambda_{KX}} \hat{Z} = \tilde{D}\hat{T} - \lambda_{SZ}\hat{a}_{SZ} + \frac{\lambda_{SX}\lambda_{KZ}}{\lambda_{KX}}\hat{a}_{KZ} \qquad (A.10a)$$

where $\tilde{D} = \lambda_{SX}D + \sigma_Y \dfrac{\delta}{\theta_{KY}} \dfrac{\lambda_{SX}\lambda_{KY}}{\lambda_{KX}}$

Substitution of values from equations (A.11) and (A.12) and using expressions for changes in skilled and unskilled wages and in rate of return, this boils down to the following:

$$\psi\hat{Z} = \left[\sigma_Z\left\{ \lambda_{SZ}\theta_{KZ} + \frac{\lambda_{SX}\lambda_{KZ}}{\lambda_{KX}}\theta_{SZ} \right\}\left\{ \frac{\delta\theta_{LY}}{\theta_{KY}} \right\} + \tilde{D} \right]\hat{T}$$

From equation (A.8a) then we obtain,

$$\hat{n} = -\frac{\lambda_{KZ}}{\lambda_{KX}}\left[\frac{\sigma_Z\left\{ \lambda_{SZ}\theta_{KZ} + \frac{\lambda_{SX}\lambda_{KZ}}{\lambda_{KX}}\theta_{SZ} \right\}\left\{ \frac{\delta\theta_{LY}}{\theta_{KY}} \right\} + \tilde{D}}{\psi} \right]\hat{T} -$$

$$- \frac{\lambda_{KZ}}{\lambda_{KX}}\sigma_Z\theta_{SZ}\left\{ \frac{\delta\theta_{LY}}{\theta_{KY}} + A \right\}\hat{T} - \sigma_Y\frac{\delta}{\theta_{KY}}\frac{\lambda_{KY}}{\lambda_{KX}}\hat{T}$$

$$= -\frac{\lambda_{KZ}\theta_{KY}\left[\lambda_{SZ}\sigma_Z\left\{ \frac{\delta\theta_{LY}}{\theta_{KY}} + A \right\} + \lambda_{SX}D \right] + \delta\sigma_Y\lambda_{SZ}\lambda_{KY}}{\theta_{KY}\lambda_{KX}\psi}\hat{T}$$

Thus, as in case of fixed money wage, $\hat{n} > 0$ if $|\lambda|$.

References

Aditya, A. and R. Acharyya. 2013. 'Export Diversification, Composition and Economic Growth: Evidence from Cross-Country Analysis.' *The Journal of International Trade and Economic Development* 27(2): 959–92.

_____. 2015. 'Trade Liberalization and Export Diversification.' *International Review of Economics and Finance* 39: 390–410.

Agosin, M. R. 2007. 'Export Diversification and Growth in Emerging Economies.' Working Paper 233, Departamento de Economía, Universidad de Chile.

Bhagwati, J. N. 1997. 'Writings on International Economics.' In *International Factor Movements and National Advantage*, edited by V.N. Balasubramanyam. New Delhi: Oxford University Press.

Bilal, S., J. M. Grether, and J. D. Melo. 2003. 'Determinants of Attitudes towards Immigration: A Trade-Theoretic Approach.' *Review of International Economics* 11(2): 253–67.

Broda, C. and D. A. Weinstein. 2004. 'Globalization and the Gains from Variety.' NBER Working Paper 10314.

Faini, R. 2002. Discussion of 'International migration and the integration of labor markets.' In *Globalization in Historical Perspective*, edited by B. Chiswick and T. Hatton. Chicago: University of Chicago Press.

Feenstra, R. C. 1994. 'New Product Varieties and the Measurement of International Prices.' *The American Economic Review* 84(1): 157–77.

Feenstra, R. and H. L. Kee. 2005. *Trade Liberalization and Export Variety: A Comparison of China and Mexico*. Washington, DC: World Bank.

Feenstra, R. C. and H. Ma. 2014. 'Trade Facilitation and the Extensive Margin of Exports.' *Japanese Economic Review* 65(2): 158–77.

Findlay, R. and K. H. O'Rourke. 2002. 'Commodity Market Integration 1500–2000.' In *Globalization in Historical Perspectives*, edited by A. Taylor and J. Williamson. Chicago, IL: University of Chicago Press.

Grossman, G. and E. Helpman. 1991. *Innovation and Growth in the Global Economy*. Cambridge: MIT Press.

Helpman, E. 1981. 'International Trade in the Presence of Product Differentiation, Economies of Scale, and Monopolistic Competition: A Chamberlin-Heckscher-Ohlin Approach.' *Journal of International Economics* 11: 305–40.

Hesse, H. 2008. 'Export Diversification and Economic Growth.' Working Paper 21, Commission on Growth and Development, World Bank.

Hummels, D. and P. J. Klenow. 2005. 'The Variety and Quality of a Nation's Exports.' *The American Economic Review* 95(3): 704–23.

Jansen, M. and R. Piermartini. 2005. 'The Impact of Mode 4 Liberalization on Bilateral Trade Flows.' Staff Working Paper ERSD-2005–06, World Trade Organization Economic Research and Statistics Division.

Jones, R. W. 1971. 'A Three-Factor Model in Trade, Theory, and History.' In *Trade, Balance of Payments and Growth: Essays in Honour of C. P. Kindleberger,* edited by J. N. Bhagwati, R. W. Jones, R. A. Mundell and J. Vanek. Amsterdam: North-Holland Publishing.

Klenow, P. and A. Rodriguez-Clare. 1997. 'Quantifying Variety Gains from Trade Liberalization.' University of Chicago, Graduate School of Business Working Paper.

Krugman, P. R. 1979. 'Increasing Returns, Monopolistic Competition and International Trade.' *The Journal of International Economics* 9: 469–79.

Lederman, D. and W. F. Maloney. 2007. 'Trade Structure and Growth.' In *Natural Resources: Neither Curse Nor Destiny,* edited by D. Lederman and W. F. Maloney. Palo Alto, CA: Stanford University Press.

Markusen, J. R. and J. R. Melvin. 1989. 'The Gains-from-Trade Theorem with Increasing Returns to Scale.' In *Monopolistc Competition and International Trade,* edited by H. Kierzkowski. Oxford: Clarendon Press.

Melitz, M. J. 2003. 'The Impact of Trade on Intra-Industry Reallocations and Aggregate Industry Productivity.' *Econometrica* 71(6): 1695–725.

Melitz, M. J. and G. I. P. Ottaviano. 2008. 'Market Size, Trade and Productivity.' *Review of Economic Studies* 75: 295–316.

Mayda, A. M. 2004. 'Who is Against Immigration? A Cross-Country Investigation of Individual Attitudes toward Immigrants.' IZA Discussion Paper No. 1115.

Michaely, M. 1962. *Concentration in International Trade*. Amsterdam: North Holland Publishing Company.

Obstfeld, M. and A. M. Taylor. 2002. 'Globalization and Capital Markets.' In *Globalization in Historical Perspective,* edited by A. M. Taylor and J. G. Williamson. Chicago, IL: University of Chicago Press.

O'Rourke, K. H. 2003. 'Heckscher-Ohlin Theory and Individual Attitudes towards Globalization.' IIIS Discussion Paper No. 07.

Romer, P. M. 1994. 'New Goods, Old Theory, and the Welfare Costs of Trade Restrictions.' *The Journal of Development Economics* 43(1): 5–38.

8

Product Differentiation, Quality of Innovation, and Capital Mobility

A General Equilibrium Analysis[1]

Sudeshna Mitra, Tonmoy Chatterjee, and Kausik Gupta

Introduction

Most of the theories of international trade show that a larger economy exports more in absolute terms than a smaller economy. However, trade theories differ in analyzing the fact as to how larger economies export more. Models that assume Armington's (1969) kind of national differentiation emphasize on the concept of intensive margin. It implies that an economy, when twice the size of another economy, exports twice that of the other economy, it does not export a wider variety of goods. Models based on monopolistic competition similar to the work of Krugman (1981) stress on the *extensive* margin, that is, economies twice the size of another country produce and export twice the range of goods of the other economy. Vertical differentiation models, such as those proposed by Flam and Helpman (1987) and Grossman and Helpman (1991), feature a quality margin, namely that richer countries produce and export higher-quality goods. The large extensive margins are inconsistent with Armington's (1969) type of models, which have no extensive margin and imply that larger economies face lower export prices. In contrast, Krugman's (1981) style of models with firm-level product differentiation predict that larger economies will produce and export more varieties, consistent with the observed large extensive margins (assuming a strictly increasing relationship

[1] An earlier version of the chapter has been presented as a paper in an International Conference on '*50 Years of Simple General Equilibrium Models and Policy Implications for Open Developing Economies – Historical and Emerging Issues,*' organized by the Centre for Studies in Social Sciences, Calcutta during 17–18 November 2015. The authors are extremely indebted to all the participants of that Conference, especially to Professor Eric Bond and Professor Noritsugu Nakanishi for their valuable comments. However, the authors are solely responsible for any remaining error in the chapter.

between varieties produced and varieties exported). However, these models predict that variety will expand in proportion to an exporter's size, which overstates the size of the observable extensive margin in the data.

It is a very commonly held view among trade theoretician that the gains from trade are larger than what quantitative general equilibrium models of trade can explain. A recurring goal in the trade literature has been to find new channels through which trade models can generate larger gains. A prominent example is suggested by Romer (1994), who stated that trade allows for the consumption of a large variety of goods, and this generates additional benefits not included in standard general equilibrium trade models. Furthermore, Romer (1994) has also performed a numerical exercise to show in terms of Harberger Triangles, in response to higher tariffs, that welfare losses operating through reduced variety may be larger than losses in standard trade analysis. Arkolakis, Demidova, Klenow, and Rodriguez-Clare (2008) have showed that very small gains from trade may occur due to strong heterogeneity across the imported goods. As a result of trade liberalization, they find that the new varieties are imported in small quantities, which would, hence, lead to improvement in welfare. The aforementioned works mentioned do not take into account the effect of trade liberalization on domestic variety. However, it seems reasonable to think that an increase in import competition would cause a decline in domestic variety as domestic firms exit. In fact, Tybout (2003) has shown some evidences that trade liberalization leads to the exit of domestic firms. Studies by economists such as Melitz (2003), Chaney (2007), Eaton, Kortum, and Kramarz (2007), and Arkolakis (2008) explain that domestic variety is endogenous and falls with a decline in trade costs. However, studies related to firm-level increasing returns, differentiated products, monopolistic competition, endogenous variety, and free entry show that, as in the study by Baldwin and Forslid (2004), total variety (including both domestic and imported) can either increase, decrease, or remain constant with trade liberalization. More importantly, the gains from trade do not depend on what happens to total variety.

Our study is motivated by the missing link noted in the analysis of the impact of capital market liberalization on domestic variety. Moreover, the issue of quality in the era of liberalization has also not been linked with variety, produced within the domestic economy, in the existing theoretical literature in this field. In this chapter, we focus on these issues related to the choice of variety as well as product quality as a result of liberalization. For this purpose, we model a three-sector small open economy with one Research and Development sector producing innovations of different quality for the modern manufacturing import-competing sector, which produces products of different variety. It is assumed here that each variety requires innovation with certain level of quality as input. The other sector of the economy is assumed to be the composite exportable good-producing sector. The capital endowment of the economy is assumed to be classified in two categories—traditional capital, used by the export sector, and modern or advanced capital, used by the import-competing and Research and Development sectors. Labor is assumed to be homogeneous for the entire economy, and it is mobile across the three sectors.

The present chapter has been developed on the basis of the idea presented in the works of Sen, Ghosh, and Barman (1997) and Acharyya and Jones (2001). Imperfect competition and differentiated product, in an otherwise general equilibrium model, has been depicted on the basis of the work of Sen, Ghosh, and Barman (1997). However, our model is widely different from the works of the aforementioned authors. The difference lies in the fact that these authors have not captured quality differentiation, which is dealt with in our model. The issue of quality of innovation in our model has been developed on the basis of the idea of export quality in a general equilibrium framework, similar to what we find in the works of Acharyya and Jones (2001). In this chapter, unlike the one by Acharyya and Jones (2001), we have considered quality of innovation in the Research and Development (R&D) sector along with product variety. Both these issues are very much relevant in the context of trade liberalization in developing economies. Apart from this, the idea of analyzing quality of innovation, quality differentiation, and product differentiation in a general equilibrium setup is something new in the literature. The issue becomes more important when we examine such a structure under the regimes of both international capital immobility and international capital mobility. The striking result that this study has observed is that trade liberalization in the form of international capital mobility enhances the quality of the product/service of the R&D sector and also increases the number of varieties produced by the advanced import-competing (manufacturing) sector, though the output of each firm in the import-competing sector falls. Our model thus takes into account of various avenues of new trade theory in a general equilibrium framework on one hand and on the other hand provides valuable insights regarding the importance of trade liberalization in developing economies. Combination of these two issues shows the significance of this chapter in the context of the literature on trade theory.

The chapter is organized as follows: The basic model is described in the second section. The case of international immobility of advanced capital is explained in the third section. The fourth section analyzes the implications of liberalization in terms of perfect international advanced capital mobility. Finally, the concluding remarks are contained in the fifth section.

The Model

To illustrate the issues related to product differentiation and quality of innovation, we consider a small open economy in which there exists an advanced manufacturing sector and an intermediate quality-attached Research and Development (R&D) sector. To be more specific, we assume a small open economy that consists of three sectors in a Heckscher–Ohlin–Samuelson (HOS) type general equilibrium framework. We also consider that the goods produced in two of the three sectors of our small open economy are traded goods whereas the product/service of the third sector, the R&D sector, is a non-traded intermediate product/service. The two sectors that produce traded goods are the exportable composite good (X_A) (other than R&D services) producing competitive Sector A and the other is the differentiated goods producing import-competing Sector M. Sector A uses labor (L) and traditional capital (K) as its inputs, and Sector M, for producing modern import competing good (X_M), uses labor (L) and modern or advanced capital (N) along with innovation as the third factor of production (it is the product/service of the R&D sector). Innovation is considered here as a non-traded intermediate input used by Sector M. There are different firms producing different varieties of the product of Sector M, and each variety-producing firm of Sector M follows a markup pricing rule. Innovation (X_Z) with certain level of quality (Q) is produced by the third sector (Sector Z) of our representative economy, using labor (L) and advanced capital (N). We refer to Sector Z as the Research and Development sector (R&D sector hereafter) of the aforementioned hypothetical small open economy. It is to be noted that the R&D sector is a producer of innovation of different quality, and hence quality differentiation is considered for this sector.[2] The quality (Q) of innovation can be indexed in a closed interval ranging from zero to one. There is no open unemployment, because workers cannot survive without jobs, and hence the labor market always appears to be clear without unemployed laborers.

Product markets of Sectors A and Z (for given quality) are competitive, whereas for Sector M, we assume increasing returns to scale and imperfect competition (as in Krugman (1979) and Helpman and Krugman (1985)) characterized by the type of preferences and product differentiation as suggested by Dixit–Stiglitz (1977). In Sector M, we have, thus, a monopolistic competition type of market structure, in which the producers are guided by profit motive, and profit maximization for each variety implies markup pricing rule. Hence, for this sector, we have some modification of the competitive equilibrium condition. For Sector A, we have considered variable coefficient technology. However, for Sectors M and Z, we have considered fixed coefficient technology.[3] For given factor prices, we can thus say

---

[2] Note that product differentiation is considered in Sector M, whereas quality differentiation is considered in Sector Z of our representative small open economy. For any given level of Q, the competitive equilibrium condition holds well in the product market of Sector Z.

[3] This is just a simplifying assumption.

that average variable cost is fixed, and it is equal to marginal cost. We set the profit maximization condition as the equality between marginal revenue and marginal cost. Free entry into the differentiated goods sector causes the supernormal profits to fall to zero (the Chamberlin large group case); therefore, the condition assuming that price equals to average cost has also been considered. For Sector Z, we have assumed that unit capital requirement for Sector Z is sensitive to change in the level of quality.[4] The fact that Sector Z behaves similar to a competitive sector only when the quality is given, when we have quality differentiation, the buyers are willing to pay a higher price for any given quantity that they buy, if the quality of the product is higher than what they would be willing to pay if the quality is lower. This provides incentives to the firms to raise the quality of the product. Thus, there is some element of imperfectly competitive market structure when we have quality differentiation. Here, we find that marginal willingness-to-pay by the buyers and the cost of quality are the two basic forces underlying the choice of product quality. From the point of view of the producers, the firms will vary product quality in a manner such that the optimum quality is obtained from the profit maximizing condition (with respect to quality), which is given by marginal revenue from quality equal to the marginal cost of quality.

Before introducing the model, we would prefer a glance at the microfoundation from the point of view of consumers, as shown in the paper by Sen, Ghosh, and Barman (1997).[5] They have considered a Cobb–Douglas utility function of the consumers with usual budget constraint for a homogeneous good and an aggregate differentiated good. They have also considered the subutility function of the aggregate differentiated good of the Dixit–Stiglitz (1977) type. On the basis of these assumptions, they have shown that elasticity of substitution between varieties (σ) is greater than unity, and it is also the elasticity of demand facing each firm. For our purpose, we have used this idea and shall consider σ as the elasticity of demand facing each firm (apart from its usual interpretation of elasticity of substitution between varieties) at the time of considering markup pricing by the differentiated good import-competing sector.

We use following notations to describe the set of equations of our model:

P^*_i = world price of commodity i

P_i = domestic price of commodity i

L = labor endowment

---

[4] It is reasonable to assume that high-quality innovation requires more of capital per unit of output.

[5] It is not explicitly shown in this chapter. Interested readers can go through the work of Sen, Ghosh, and Barman (1997).

N_d = domestic modern or advanced capital stock of the economy

N_f = foreign modern or advanced capital stock of the economy

K_f = foreign traditional capital stock

K_d = domestic traditional capital stock

W = competitive wage rate

r = rate of return to traditional capital

R = rate of return to modern or advanced capital

σ = elasticity of demand facing each variety firm. Also interpreted as elasticity of substitution between varieties

n = number of varieties produced by Sector M at home

a_{ji} = quantity of the *j*th factor for producing one unit of output in the ith sector; $j = L, K, N$ and

$i = A, M, Z$

F_N = amount of (advanced) capital required as fixed input (for each variety) of variety producing modern import-competing sector

θ_{ji} = distributive share of the jth input in the ith sector; $j = L, K, N$ and $i = A, M, Z$

λ_{ji} = proportion of the jth factor used in the production of the ith sector; $j = L, K, N$ and $i = A, M, Z$

Q = level of quality of the product of Sector Z

We assume the price of the product of Sector A as numeraire; therefore, $P_A = P^*_A = 1$. It is also assumed that $P^*_M = P_M$, as the import-competing sector is not protected by tariff.

The competitive equilibrium condition for Sector A is given by:

$$a_{LA}W + a_{KA}r = 1 \tag{1}$$

For Sector M, profit maximization for each variety implies markup pricing rule, and it is given by:

$$a_{LM} W + a_{NM} R + a_{ZM}P_Z(Q) = P_M(1 - 1/\sigma) \tag{2}$$

σ1 implies elasticity of substitution between different varieties of the product of Sector M. It is also the elasticity of demand facing each variety firm.[6] Here, it is assumed that all the input–output coefficients are fixed, and advanced capital is the only component of fixed cost. Equation (2) represents the equality between marginal cost and marginal revenue under markup pricing. The LHS of equation

---

[6] The idea behind equation (2) follows from the work of Sen, Ghosh, and Barman (1997). Readers should not confuse σ with elasticity of substitution between factors, rather it is the elasticity of substitution between different varieties of the product of Sector M.

(2) implies the marginal cost as well as the average variable cost, which is given[7] for w and R. Equation (2) thus represents the unit cost equation for each variety with markup pricing rule, which implies the presence of fixed cost with increasing returns to scale. Chamberlin's group equilibrium implies that average cost equals to price (apart from equality of marginal revenue and marginal cost), and it is considered in this model later in terms of equation (8).

For given quality, the competitive equilibrium condition for Sector Z is given by the following equation:[8]

$$a_{LZ} W + a_{NZ}(Q)R = P_Z(Q) \tag{3}$$

Here, a_{LZ} is assumed to be fixed for different qualities, but the production technology in Sector Z is such that innovations of high quality are more advanced capital intensive than low-quality augmented innovations. Hence, $a_{NZ} = a_{NZ}(Q)$ where $a_{NZ}{}' > 0$ and $a_{NZ}{}'' > 0$. Again this R&D sector will not compromise with quality, as its innovation will be demanded by the advanced import-competing Sector M. Therefore, Sector Z should experience an increasing P_Z with respect to Q and, hence, $P_Z{}' > 0$. It implies that higher is the quality, for a given level of the product of Sector Z, the buyers of the product (here Sector M) are willing to pay a higher price. It is to be noted that as Sector Z is assumed to be a non-traded intermediate goods sector, its price P_Z is endogenously determined.[9]

Full-employment conditions are as follows:

$$a_{LA}X_A + a_{LM}X_M n + a_{LZ}X_Z = L \tag{4}$$

$$a_{KA}X_A = K \tag{5}$$

$$a_{NM}X_M n + a_{NZ}(Q) X_Z = N_d + N_f = N \tag{6}$$

$$a_{ZM}X_M n = X_Z \tag{7}$$

---

[7] Total variable cost (TVC) is homogeneous of degree one in output. As the input–output coefficients are fixed, for given w and R, average variable cost (AVC) is same as that of marginal cost (MC). The idea here is similar to that of usual cost function that we find in text books of industrial organization. For example if total cost function (C) is given as C = F + cq_i (symbols having usual significance) for $q_i > 0$, where F is total fixed cost (TFC) and cq_i is TVC, we find that AVC = c = MC, and average total cost (ATC) is given by ATC(q_i) = (F/q_i) + c such that we find that when Chamberlin's group equilibrium takes place at the falling part of ATC, the demand curve is tangent to the ATC curve. The assumption of fixed coefficient technology helps us to equate AVC with MC, so that the LHS of equation (2) can easily be achieved. Fixed coefficient technology is thus also no impediment to achieve group equilibrium.

[8] The idea behind equation (3) follows the work of Acharyya and Jones (2001).

[9] This is true as Q is endogenous in the system.

It is assumed that a_{NM} represents the requirement of both fixed and variable advanced capital stocks to produce one unit of each variety[10] by Sector M. Free entry into Sector M drives down the supernormal profit to zero in the Chamberlin group equilibrium case. Hence, for each variety, excess of revenue over total variable cost exactly offsets the fixed cost incurred. Assuming advanced capital is the only component of fixed cost, we get equation (8).[11]

$$F_N R = (P_M X_M / \sigma) \qquad (8)$$

In this setup, we have eight equations with eight unknowns: W, r, R, Q, X_A, X_M, X_Z, and n. Hence, the system can be solved.

International Advanced Capital Immobility

In our hypothetical small open economy, initially we have assumed that international advanced capital is immobile.[12]

Equation (8) implies that fall in R leads to a fall in X_M. Again, using equation (7) in equation (4) we get[13]

$$[\{a_{LM} / a_{ZM}\} + a_{LZ}] X_Z = L - a_{LA}(R) X_A(R) = L' \qquad (4.1)$$

From equation (4.1), we find that a fall in R leads to an increase in X_Z to maintain the equality condition[14], as $a_{LA}' > 0$ and $X_A' > 0$. When R falls, $a_{LA} X_A$

---

[10] Presence of fixed advanced capital for each variety of Sector M can be incorporated in the advanced capital allocation condition (as shown by equation (6)) and can be written as $n F_N + a_{NM} X_M n + a_{NZ}(Q) X_Z = N_d + N_f = N$. However, it can easily be checked that such modification of equation (6) will not make any difference in the present analysis. Hence, we have not considered explicitly the fixed cost component in equation (6) and have not modified equation (6) of the text.

[11] Equation (8) actually follows from equation (2). From equation (8), we find that average fixed cost $= (F_N R)/X_M = (P_M / \sigma)$. As average cost consists of average fixed cost and average variable cost and as Chamberlin group equilibrium implies price = average cost, we find from equation (2) $a_{LM} W + a_{NM} R + a_{ZM} P_Z(Q) + (P_M / \sigma) = P_M$

[12] International advanced capital immobility is a situation in which domestic rate of return on foreign advanced capital (R) is greater than the rate of return on foreign advanced capital in the international market (R*), and there is restriction on the entry of foreign advanced capital to the domestic economy.

[13] We derive this result for given quality.

[14] For given Q, from equation (2), we find that when R falls, W increases. From equation (1), we find that W and r are inversely related, so that $r = r(W)$ where $r' < 0$. Again from equation (2), we find that, for given Q, $W = W(R)$ where $W' < 0$. Thus $a_{LA} = a_{LA}(W, r(W)) = a_{LA}(W) = a_{LA}(W(R)) = a_{LA}(R)$. As a_{LA} and W are inversely related and as W and R also inversely related, we find that when $a_{LA} = a_{LA}(R)$, we have $a_{LA}' > 0$. Similarly, it can be shown that $a_{KA} = a_{KA}(R)$ and $a_{KA}' < 0$. From equation (5), we thus find that a fall in R implies an increase in a_{KA} and hence reduces X_A. Thus $X_A' > 0$.

falls, and thus increases $L^{/}$. To maintain equality, we find that X_Z must increase. In other words, from equation (4.1), we find that $X_Z = X_Z(R)$ where $X_Z^{/} < 0$. As from equation (8), we find that a fall in R leads to a fall in X_M, and as a fall in R raises X_Z, from equation (7), we find that a fall in R causes n to increase in order to maintain the equality condition of equation (7). Therefore, from here, we can establish the following lemma:

Lemma: There exists an inverse relationship between R and n.

We now consider change in quality in the form of quality differentiation in the R& D sector. In case of quality differentiation, the profit maximizing behavior of the producers of quality differentiated sector, that is, Sector Z (R&D), gives us

$$a_{NZ}^{/}(Q) R = P_Z^{/}(Q) \tag{9}$$

Equation (9) implies that marginal cost of quality is equal to the marginal revenue from quality. Here, we assume $a_{NZ}^{//}(Q)R > P_Z^{//}(Q)$, which implies that quality enhancement raises the costs further and faster than the price of the product[15]. From equation (9), we find that an increase in Q leads to an increase in both $a_{NZ}^{/}(Q) R$ and $P_Z^{/}(Q)$, but an increase in $a_{NZ}^{/}(Q)$ will be higher compared to increase in $P_Z^{/}(Q)$ because we assume $a_{NZ}^{//}(Q) R > P_Z^{//}(Q)$. Therefore, R declines to maintain the equality condition of equation (9). Hence, we can derive a negative locus of R and Q for which profit maximizing condition with respect to quality of Sector Z is satisfied. This locus may be named as R-$Q_{(1)}$ schedule, which is shown in Figure 8.1.

Again, using equation (7) in equation (6), one can obtain

$$[(a_{NM}/a_{ZM}) + a_{NZ}(Q)] X_Z(R) = N \tag{6.1}$$

From equation (6.1), we find that a reduction in R leads to an increase in X_Z (as derived from the labor market full-employment condition). As a consequence, the value of the LHS of equation (6.1) will go up. Therefore, a_{NZ} has to decrease for maintaining the equality condition of equation (6.1), and it is possible if Q goes down. Thus, we get a positive relation between Q and R for which advanced

---

[15] This assumption has been borrowed from the work by Acharyya and Jones (2001). See Acharyya and Jones (2001) for interpretation in detail of equation (9).We remind the readers once more that though we have considered competitive equilibrium conditions for Sector Z for a given quality (as shown by equation (3)), for quality differentiation we find some elements of imperfect competition, and we consider the profit-maximizing condition, that is, the equality between marginal cost of quality and marginal revenue from quality. The choice of product qualities by a single firm and a perfectly competitive industry was first analyzed independently by Mussa and Rosen (1978) and Gabszweicz and Thisse (1979). The subsequent literature grew out of these two seminal works. Our assumption regarding the R&D sector is close to that of the works of Mussa and Rosen (1978) and Gabszweicz and Thisse (1979).

capital market will be in equilibrium. This can be represented in terms of a locus, which may be named as $R\text{-}Q_{(2)}$ schedule, and it is positively sloped, as shown in Figure 8.1.

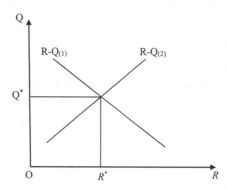

Figure 8.1 Determination of quality and return to capital

The intersection point between $R\text{-}Q_{(1)}$ and $R\text{-}Q_{(2)}$ locus in Figure 8.1 gives us the equilibrium values of R and Q. Next, the system can be solved as follows:

When Q is known, P_Z is also known, as it is an increasing function of Q. Then, W and r can be determined from equations (2) and (1), respectively. When factor prices are determined, input–output coefficients of Sector A can also be determined. Next, from equations (5) and (8), X_A and X_M can be solved, respectively. Using equation (7), we can substitute for X_M n as (X_Z/a_{ZM}) and, hence, X_Z can be determined from equation (4). Next, we can solve for n from equation (6).

International Advanced Capital Mobility

In this section, we shall analyze the impact of liberalization in terms of allowing perfect international advanced capital mobility within the assumed small open economy.

The presence of international advanced capital immobility implies a situation in which domestic rate of return on advanced capital is set at a level higher than the rate of return of the same at international market, that is, $R > R^*$, where R^* is the given return on international advanced capital in the international market. In such a situation, we have no foreign advanced capital inflow. If R falls to, where $R \gg R^*$, we find that there is some amount of inflow of advanced capital (N) from foreign part, and at last we will reach at the equilibrium level[16] of N, where

---

[16] At $R = R^*$, we have the equilibrium level of international advanced capital inflow due to equilibrium in the international advanced capital market.

$R = R^*$. From the aforementioned arguments, we can conclude that when there is international advanced capital mobility, N is treated as an endogenous variable, because R is fixed at R^*. Thus, the total number of independent equations and unknowns remains the same, and the system can also be solved in the regime of international advanced capital mobility.

Movement from regime of international advanced capital immobility to a regime of international advanced capital mobility leads to a continuous reduction in R, until R reaches at R^*. Therefore, we can use reduction in R as an instrument through which impact of international advanced capital mobility can be captured. As we have stated in the lemma that R and n are inversely related with each other, hence for given Q, a reduction in R due to an increase in N leads to an increase in the number of variety, n, produced by the advanced manufacturing import-competing Sector M.

From equation (6.1), it is observed that a fall in R leads to increase in X_Z, thereby leading to an increase in the value of LHS of the same equation. Again, in the present regime, a fall in R implies an increase in N. Hence, the equality of equation (6.1) can be manageable even if Q remains fixed. Thus, for given Q, a reduction in R implies a leftward shift of the $R\text{-}Q_{(2)}$ schedule, which is shown in Figure 8.2. However, there will be no movement of the $R\text{-}Q_{(1)}$ locus for an increase in N. It is to be noted that a fall in R lowers the marginal cost of production in Sector Z, for any given quality. Because quality enhancement raises costs further and faster than the price of the product as we have assumed $a_{NZ}{}''(Q) R > P_Z{}''(Q)$, profit will be maximized now at a higher quality.[17] Hence, there will be a movement along the $R\text{-}Q_{(1)}$ schedule for an increase in N.

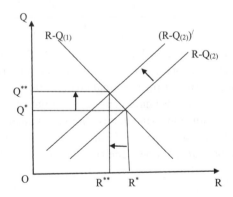

Figure 8.2 Change in Q* and R* when capital is mobile

[17] See Acharyya and Jones (2001) for more details.

From Figure 2, we see that a movement from a regime of advanced capital immobility to a regime of advanced capital mobility leads to an increase in the quality level, Q, of the product produced by Sector Z. In other words, with perfect mobility of international advanced capital, more quality-enhanced product/service is innovated in Sector Z, which is used as input in Sector M. The fall in R raises the value of X_Z and reduces the value of X_M. Hence, from equation (7), it implies that there will be an increase in the number of domestic variety produced by the differentiated good import-competing sector[18] given by 'n.' This leads us to the following proposition.

Proposition: *Trade liberalization in the form of perfect international mobility of advanced capital leads to an increase in the quality of innovation of the R &D sector and also an increase in the number of variety produced by the differentiated good import-competing sector. It also promotes expansion of the R&D sector. However, the output of the differentiated good import-competing sector falls.*

Concluding Remarks

In this chapter we have analyzed the effects of liberalization, in terms of perfect international capital (advanced or modern capital) mobility, on the number of domestic variety and the level of quality of the innovation of the R&D sector of a representative small open economy. For this purpose, we have considered a general equilibrium framework, in which we have introduced elements of imperfect competition in the form of product differentiation and quality differentiation. Various attempts have been done earlier to incorporate elements of imperfect competition in an otherwise general equilibrium framework. The significance of the present exercise is that it includes both product differentiation and quality differentiation in a general equilibrium framework, and these are studied in the context of trade liberalization. Such an attempt is something new in the context of the literature on trade theory. Moreover, in our framework instead of capturing trade liberalization in terms of infinitesimal changes (in the form of traditional comparative static exercises), we have considered 'finite changes' by comparing the regimes of 'no liberalization' (in the form of international capital immobility) with that of 'full liberalization' (in the form of perfect mobility of international capital). This is not only an additional contribution in the context of the literature

---

[18] Using equations (2), (3), and (9), under some reasonable assumptions as we have assumed here, we find that when Q increases, R falls. From equation (8), we find that fall in R implies a fall in X_M and, from equation (4.1), using equation (1), we find that a fall in R implies an increase in X_Z. Hence, at the new equilibrium, we find that X_M falls and X_Z increases. Thus from equation (7), we find that the value of 'n' must rise at the new equilibrium level.

on trade theory, it also provides some new insights to the researchers who are interested to study the impact of trade liberalization on domestic product variety and quality of innovation in the economy's R&D sector. Our model shows that in the era of liberalization, greater number of variety is produced by the advanced manufacturing import-competing sector, and more quality enhanced product/ service is innovated by the R&D sector. It also shows that the product/service of the R&D sector expands as a result of trade liberalization. However, the output of each firm in the advanced manufacturing import-competing sector falls due to liberalization. These results are not only interesting and new contributions from the point of view of research in trade theory, but also these results are very much important for the policymakers who are interested in analyzing the impact of trade liberalization in developing economies. Finally, our model shows that general equilibrium structure is capable to capture issues such as product differentiation and quality differentiation, which are usually analyzed by researchers in terms of partial equilibrium framework. General equilibrium structures not only help us to analyze the aforementioned issues but also provide valuable insights on intersectoral linkages, which are very much relevant so far as research on trade theory for developing economies is concerned.

References

Acharyya, R. 2005. *Product Standards, Employment and Exports: An Analytical Study.* Heidelberg: Physica/Springer Verlag.

Acharyya, R. and R. W. Jones. 2001. 'Export Quality and Income Distribution in a Small Dependent Economy.' *Internatinal Review of Economics and Finance* 10: 337–51.

Arkolakis, C. 2008. 'Market Penetration Costs and the New Consumers Margin in International Trade.' http://www.econ.yale.edu/~ka265/research/Arkolakis03Feb08.pdf

Arkolakis, C., S. Demidova, P. J. Klenow, and A. Rodriguez-Clare. 2008. 'Endogenous Variety and the Gains from Trade.' *American Economic Review* 98(4): 444–50.

Armington, P. S. 1969. 'A Theory of Demand for Products Distinguished by Place of Production.' *International Monetary Fund Staff Papers* 16(1): 159–78.

Baldwin, R. E. and R. Forslid. 2004. 'Trade Liberalization with Heterogeneous Firms.' Center for Economic Policy Research Discussion Paper 4635.

Broda, C. and D. E. Weinstein. 2006. 'Globalization and the Gains from Variety.' *Quarterly Journal of Economics* 121(2): 541–85.

Chaney, T. 2007. 'Distorted Gravity: The Intensive and Extensive Margins of International Trade.' http://home.uchicago.edu/~tchaney/research/DistortedGravity.pdf.

Demidova, S. and A. Rodríguez-Clare. 2007. 'Trade Policy under Firm-Level Heterogeneity in a Small Economy.' NBER Working Paper 13688.

Dixit, A. and J. E. Stiglitz. 1977. 'Monopolistic Competition and Optimum Product Diversity.' *American Economic Review* 67: 297–305.

Eaton, J. and S. Kortum. 2002. 'Technology, Geography, and Trade.' *Econometrica* 70(5): 1741–79.

Eaton, J., S. Kortum, and F. Kramarz. 2007. 'An Anatomy of International Trade: Evidence from French Firms.' http:// www.econ.umn.edu/~kortum/papers/ekk1005.pdf.

Flam, H. and E. Helpman. 1987. 'Vertical Product Differentiation and North–South Trade.' *American Economic Review* 77(5): 810–22.

Funke, M. and R. Ralf. 2001. 'Product Variety and Economic Growth: Empirical Evidence for the OECD Countries.' *IMF Staff Papers*, 48(2): 225–42.

Gabszweicz, J. J. and J. F. Thisse. 1979. 'Price Competition, Quality and Income Disparities.' *Journal of Economic Theory* 20: 340–59.

Grossman, G. M. and E. Helpman. 1991. *Innovation and Growth in the Global Economy.* Cambridge, MA: MIT Press.

Feenstra, R. C. 1994. 'New Product Varieties and the Measurement of International Prices.' *American Economic Review* 84(1): 157–77.

Helpman, E. and P. Krugman. 1985. *Market Structure and International Trade.* Cambridge, MA: MIT Press.

Hummels, D. and P. J. Klenow. 2002. 'The Variety and Quality of a Nation's Trade.' NBER Working Paper 8712.

Kehoe, T. J. and K. J. Ruhl. 2003. 'How Important Is the New Goods Margin in International Trade.' Federal Reserve Bank of Minneapolis Staff Report 324.

Klenow, P. J. and A. Rodríguez-Clare. 1997. 'Quantifying Variety Gains from Trade Liberalization.' http://klenow.com/QuantifyingVariety.pdf.

Krugman, P. 1979. 'Increasing Returns, Monopolistic Competition and International Trade.' *Journal of International Economics* 9: 469–79.

––––––––. 1980. 'Scale Economies, Product Differentiation, and the Pattern of Trade.' *American Economic Review* 70(5): 950–59.

Melitz, M. J. 2003. 'The Impact of Trade on Intra-Industry Reallocations and Aggregate Industry Productivity.' *Econometrica* 71(6): 1695–725.

Mussa, M. and S. Rosen. 1978. 'Monopoly and Product Quality.' *Journal of Economic Theory* 18: 301–17.

Romer, P. 1994. 'New Goods, Old Theory, and the Welfare Costs of Trade Restrictions.' *Journal of Development Economics* 43(1): 5–38.

Tybout, J. 2003. 'Plant- and Firm-level Evidence on the "New" Trade Theories.' In *Handbook of International Trade*, edited by E. K. Choi and J. Harrigan. Oxford: Basil- Blackwell.

Schott, P. K. 2004. 'Across-Product versus Within-Product Specialization in International Trade.' *Quarterly Journal of Economics* 119(2): 647–78.

Sen, P., A. Ghosh, and A. Barman. 1997. 'The Possibility of Welfare Gains with Capital Inflows in a Small Tariff-Ridden Economy.' *Economica* 64: 345–52.

9

Cross-Border Mergers and International Trade

A Vertical GOLE Model

Hamid Beladi, Avik Chakrabarti, and Sugata Marjit[1]

Introduction

How does the vertical structure of an industry affect the links between cross-border mergers and international trade? To answer this question, we construct a tractable vertical general equilibrium (VGOLE) model of an oligopolistic industry. In a vertically related industry, firms are located at different stages of production or distribution, with some firms supplying inputs used by others. Mergers in vertically related industries have been drawing increasing attention of regulators, anti-trust authorities, as well as those in the media and academics. This is so because cross-border mergers between firms in such industries add more complexities for competition within and across open economies.[2]

Although the theoretical literature on cross-border mergers[3] is still at its infancy, to the best of our knowledge, our VGOLE construct is the first *general equilibrium* model to explore the implications of vertical structures for the links between cross-border mergers and international trade in oligopolistic industries. The vertical structure of an industry injects a distinction between the foreign and domestic firms, even in the absence of transport costs, because mergers can affect competition in input markets creating, in addition to the usual *market power*

---

[1] The usual disclaimer applies. Sugata Marjit is indebted to the Reserve Bank of India (RBI) endowment at the CSSSC for financial support, but the chapter does not implicate the RBI in any way.

[2] The most prominent recent example was the attempted $42 billion merger between General Electric (GE) and Honeywell that was approved by the US authorities but not by the European Commission. See Beladi *et al.* (2010, 2013).

[3] Some notable contributions include the works of Long and Vousden (1995), Head and Ries (1997), Falvey (1998), Marin and Verdier (2002), Jovanovic and Rousseau (2003), Reuer *et al.* (2004), Neary (2003, 2007), and Qiu (2010).

motive, an *input-market concentration* effect. Our key results, stemming from a direct comparison of the pattern of specialization and the incentives for cross-border mergers with and without the possibility of vertically integration, are that a) the extensive margin of trade shrinks in the face of vertical integration; and b) cross-border mergers mitigate the effect of vertical integration on the extensive margins of trade by facilitating specialization toward the direction of comparative advantage. Intuitively, as the disintegrated home firms become less competitive, it allows foreign firms to compete in a larger subset of sectors, wherein, without vertical integration, home would have a comparative advantage. The impact of a merger, on the extensive margins of trade, is magnified when the merger takes place between two disintegrated firms across borders compared to a merger between a disintegrated firm in one country and a vertically integrated firm in another.

The rest of the chapter is organized as follows. In the next section, we present our VGOLE model and results. In the third section, we discuss the welfare implications of our construct and cover some caveats. In the final section, we draw key conclusions.

Model and Propositions

In the forthcoming paragraphs, we present our VGOLE model that keeps the general equilibrium analysis tractable and allows us to study specialization according to comparative advantage in the tradition of the neoclassical models of international trade. Our construct preserves the key characteristic of a typical general equilibrium model of an oligopolistic industry (GOLE) to the extent that we are looking at a continuum of atomistic industries, within each of which firms have market power and interact strategically. In doing so, we recognize that a partial equilibrium approach provides an incomplete basis for an understanding of cross-border mergers in the face of any economy-wide shock, because the intensification of cross-border mergers continues to be facilitated by extensive financial liberalization policies and regional agreements. As such, from an analytical standpoint, our VGOLE construct is a natural follow-up of the partial equilibrium analyses presented in Beladi *et al.* (2013).

Consider a stylized world containing two countries, each with a continuum of atomistic industries indexed by $z \in [0.1]$ each producing a homogeneous final good. Following the Dornbusch–Fischer–Samuelson (DFS) exposition of the Ricardian theory, let countries differ in their access to technology reflected in unit labor requirements denoted by $\beta(z)$ and $\beta^*(z)$, with wages w and w^* at home and abroad, respectively. For expositional convenience, we assume that $\beta(z)$ is increasing and $\beta^*(z)$ is decreasing in z, which can then be interpreted as an index of foreign comparative advantage with home's relative productivity $\left(\dfrac{\beta^*(z)}{\beta(z)} \right)$ decreasing as z

increases. Each industry is vertically related with 2 upstream firms ($M_i : i = 1, 2$) competing (`a la Bertrand) to supply a homogeneous intermediate input to n downstream firms ($R_j : j = 1, 2, ..., n$) located at home, and 2 upstream firms (M_i^*: $i = 1, 2$) supplying the same intermediate input to n^* downstream firms ($R_i^*: i = 1, 2, ..., n^*$) located in a foreign country.[4] Fixed costs are set to zero which, otherwise, would provide a trivial rationale for mergers. The intermediate input is not traded internationally, and its marginal cost (uniform across borders) of production is set to zero, without loss of generality. All downstream firms (competing `a la Cournot), in a given location, have identical marginal costs of transforming the intermediate input into the final good: $c(z) = w\beta(z)$ for home firms and $c^*(z) = w^*\beta^*(z)$ for foreign firms. Let $\bar{y}(z)$ and $\bar{y}^*(z)$ be the industry outputs of the final good at home and abroad, respectively.

Let the demand side be characterized by an additive utility function of the form

(1) $\quad U\left[\{x(z)\}\right] = \int_0^1 \left[\rho_1 x(z) - \frac{1}{2}\rho_2 x(z)^2\right] dz$

Let there be a single representative consumer, in each country, who maximizes (1) subject to the budget constraint

(2) $\quad \int_0^1 p(z)x(z)dz \leq I$

where I is aggregate income. This yields, for each country, an inverse demand ($\bar{x}$) function for each good, which is linear in its own price conditional on the marginal utility of income (λ).

(3) $\quad p(z) = \frac{1}{\lambda}\left[\rho_1 - \rho_2\bar{x}(z)\right]$

where $\lambda = \dfrac{a\mu_1^p - bI}{\mu_2^p}$.

The effects of prices on λ are summarized by the first and second moments of the distribution of prices as follows:

(4) $\quad \mu_1^P \equiv \int_0^1 p(z)dz$

(5) $\quad \mu_2^P \equiv \int_0^1 p(z)^2 dz$

It follows that the world inverse demand curve for each good is

---

[4] Restricting upstream competition to two firms, within the borders of each country, is intended to highlight the importance of the vertical structure.

(6) $p(z) = a - b\bar{x}(z)$

where $a = \dfrac{\rho_1 + \rho_1^*}{\lambda + \lambda^*}$, $b \equiv \dfrac{\rho_2}{\bar{\lambda}}$, and $\bar{x} = \left(x + x^*\right)$ with ρ_1 and ρ_1^* being the

intercepts and ρ_2 the common slope for home demand $(x(z))$ and foreign demand $\left(x^*(z)\right)$, respectively. $\bar{\lambda}$ is the world marginal utility of income, which we choose as the *numeraire*. We will, hereinafter, normalize the wages to $W = \bar{\lambda}w$ and $W^* = \bar{\lambda}w^*$.

Wages are determined by the full employment conditions as follows:

(7) $L = \int\limits_0^{z^*} \beta(z)n\,\tilde{y}(W,z,n)\Big|_C \, dz + \int\limits_z^{z^*} \beta(z)n\,\tilde{y}(W,W^*,z,n,n^*)\Big|_C \, dz$

(8) $L^* = \int\limits_z^1 \beta^*(z)n^*\,\tilde{y}^*(W^*,z,n^*)\Big|_C \, dz + \int\limits_z^{z^*} \beta(z)n^*\,\tilde{y}^*(W,W^*,z,n,n^*)\Big|_C \, dz$

where L and L^* measure the supply of labor at home and in the foreign country, respectively.

In the absence of any possibility of vertical integration, the Nash equilibrium price charged by each upstream firm will be equal to its (zero) marginal cost. Each domestic downstream firm will

> *Maximize:* $\Pi_i = \left(a - b\left(\tilde{y}(z) + \tilde{y}^*(z)\right) - c(z)\right)y_i(z)$
> $\{y_i\}$

Each foreign downstream firm will

> *Maximize:* $\Pi_i^* = \left(a - b\left(\tilde{y}(z) + \tilde{y}^*(z)\right) - c^*(z)\right)y_i^*(z)$
> $\{y_i^*\}$

A domestic firm finds it profitable to produce *iff* its unit cost does not exceed a weighted average of the demand intercept and the unit cost of foreign firms, where the weight attached to the former is decreasing in the number of foreign firms:

(9) $c \le \xi_0 a + \left(1 - \xi_0\right)c^*$

where $\xi_0 = \left(\dfrac{1}{n^* + 1}\right) \in (0,1)$.

Analogously, a foreign firm finds it profitable to produce *iff* its unit cost does not exceed to a weighted average of the demand intercept and the unit cost of domestic firms, where the weight attached to the former is decreasing in the number of foreign firms:

(10) $c^* \le \xi_0^* a + \left(1 - \xi_0^*\right)c$

where $\xi_0^* = \left(\dfrac{1}{n+1}\right) \in (0,1)$.

Let us now consider the possibility, at home, of one of the upstream firms (say, M_1) becoming integrated with one of the downstream firms (say, R_1). The joint profit of the vertically integrated M_1-R_1 will be maximized *iff* M_1 supplies the intermediate input internally at (zero) marginal cost to its downstream segment (R_1) and withdraws[5] from competing in the input market in order to increase its profit by raising the cost of its downstream rivals at home, as M_2 will then charge a price $\left(\dfrac{a - (n^* + 1)c + n^* c^*}{2(n^* + 2)}\right)$ for supplying the intermediate input to any disintegrated downstream firm at home.

A domestic firm finds it profitable, notwithstanding its vertical structure, to produce *iff*

(11) $\quad c \leq \xi_0 a + \left(1 - \xi_0\right)c^*$

A foreign firm finds it profitable to produce *iff*

(12) $\quad c^* \leq \xi_0^{*\,\prime} a + \left(1 - \xi_0^{*\,\prime}\right)c$

where $\xi_0^{*\,\prime} = \left(\dfrac{3 + 2n^* + n}{4n + 4 + nn^* + 3n^*}\right) \in (\xi_0^*, 1)$.

Foreign downstream firms become more competitive and the disintegrated domestic downstream firms less competitive in the international market. This is mainly because of vertical integration at home, because the *relative* cost differential between foreign and domestic firms shrinks. As the new vertically integrated domestic firm withdraws from upstream competition, raising the cost of its downstream rivals, the output of each disintegrated domestic firm shrinks. The output of the new vertically integrated domestic firm as well as that of the foreign firm rises as the relative cost of their disintegrated rivals rises.

Let us now turn to the possibility of mergers.[6] It may be noted, at the outset, that notwithstanding the vertical structure of an industry,

---

[5] See Ordover *et al.* (1990) for the original exposition of the integrated firm's foreclosure strategy to raise rivals' costs. An analogous argument could be developed, based on exclusivity contracts between downstream and upstream firms, if a multinational firm offers exclusivity contracts to its suppliers with the objective of raising domestic firms' costs.

[6] Lemmas 1 through 4, presented in Appendix B, help simplify the derivation of the results to follow. The appendices draw on our companion paper (Beladi *et al.* (2013)), in which we presented a *partial equilibrium* model of the incentives for and implications of cross-border horizontal mergers in a vertically related oligopolistic industry.

$$\left(n + n^*\right) > 2$$

imposes a condition *sufficient* for removing any incentive for a merger[7] between two firms within the same country.[8] There is no incentive for autarkic firms to merge within border; however, incentives exist for the trivial case of a duopoly when a merger to a monopoly is always profitable. This result is more general than analogous conditions identified in the earlier works of Salant *et al.* (1983) through Neary (2007) to the extent that our model nests a vertically related industrial structure.

Starting from the equilibrium industrial structure in autarky, with n firms at home and n^* firms in the foreign country, let us now turn to the incentives for mergers across countries. For ease of exposition, without loss of any generality, we assume hereinafter that foreign firms are relatively cost-efficient, that is, $c > c^*$. In the absence of vertical integration, a takeover of a home firm by a foreign firm, will be profitable *iff*

(13) $c > \xi_1 a + (1 - \xi_1)c^*$

where $0 < \xi_1 = \dfrac{(n + n^*)^2 - 2(n + n^*) - 1}{2n(n + n^*) + (n^* + 1)\left[(n + n^*)^2 - 1\right]} < \xi_0$.

Intuitively, a merger between high-cost and a low-cost firms increases efficiency by eliminating the high-cost firm and raises the price by increasing concentration. The profits of a low-cost foreign firm must increase significantly to justify its taking over a high-cost home firm when the cost differential is large. When this cost differential is sufficiently large, the foreign firm has a greater incentive to merge with the integrated home firm than to merge with a disintegrated home firm. A vertical merger can affect the incentives for competition in the input market. More specifically, the withdrawal of a vertically integrated firm from the input market weakens upstream competition. This raises the input price which, in turn, leads to a higher cost for the nonintegrated downstream firms.

The profits of the downstream unit of the integrated firm rise with a rise in its rivals' costs, and, subsequently, the integrated firm is better off withdrawing from

---

[7] The terms 'merger' and 'takeover' are used interchangeably in our model: a merger, in the absence of any tariff or transportation cost, effectively implies that one of the participating firms is closed down because there is no incentive for a firm to operate more than one plant. It may also be noted that mergers, in our setup, only relate to takeovers in the same sector.

[8] Neary (2007) had shown that a merger between two firms with the same unit cost (whether two home or two foreign firms) is never profitable provided $(n + n^*) > 2$. This result is more usual than that suggested by Salant *et al.* (1983), to the extent that it allows the unit costs of firms within a merger to differ from the unit costs of firms outside the merger.

the input market. As such, a vertical integration at home changes the strategic advantages for foreign firms. With the vertically integrated home firm operating at a lower cost relative to the disintegrated home firms, an increase in the profits of a foreign firm from a merger with an integrated home firm exceeds the increase in its profits from a merger with a disintegrated home firm, when there are fewer disintegrated firms at home in the premerger equilibrium.

The threshold sectors pinning down the extensive margins of trade[9], denoted by $\tilde{z}$ and $\tilde{z}^*$ at home and abroad respectively, can be determined (conditional on wages) by

$$(14) \quad W\beta(\tilde{z}) - \xi_{(\ )}a' - (1 - \xi_{(\ )})W^*\beta^*(\tilde{z}^*) = 0$$

$$(15) \quad W^*\beta^*(\tilde{z}^*) - \xi^*_{(\ )}a' - (1 - \xi^*_{(\ )})W\beta(\tilde{z}) = 0$$

This is depicted by ZZ in Figure 9.1 through 3, in which, given wages, the home country specializes in $z \in [0, \tilde{z}^*)$, the foreign country specializes in $z \in (\tilde{z}, 1]$, and production is diversified in $z \in [\tilde{z}, \tilde{z}^*]$.

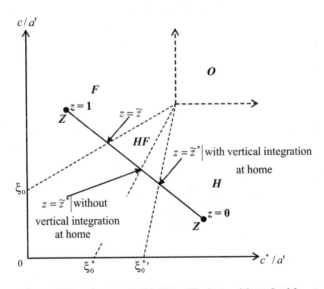

Figure 9.1 Premerger trading equilibrium with and without vertical integration at home

---

[9] The extensive margins of trade are defined in terms of the varieties exported from each country. See Beladi *et al.* (2013, 2015) and Chakrabarti *et al.* (2017).

When the cost of every firm exceeds a, in region O, then the good is not produced at all. In Region H, only the home can compete, and in Region F, only the foreign firms can compete. Region HF is a cone of diversification, wherein both home and foreign firms can coexist. When an upstream home firm becomes integrated with a downstream home firm, Region H (where exclusively home firms can compete) shrinks, and the cone of diversification HF (where both home and foreign firms can coexist) expands. In the premerger trading equilibrium, as seen in Figure 9.3, the extensive margin of trade shrinks in the face of vertical integration.

Cross-border mergers induce expansion and contraction of sectors, because high-cost firms in one country are bought out by low-cost foreign rivals in another. At any given wages, expanding firms will a) increase their output by only a fraction of the output of the firms that are taken over and b) have lower labor requirements per unit output than the contracting ones. Hence, the total demand for labor will fall, pressing wages down to restore equilibrium in the labor market, which, in turn, encourages hiring of labor at the intensive margin. The lower wages raise the profitability of high-cost firms, at the margin, placing them outside the reach of takeovers, thereby dampening the initial incentives for mergers. In Figures 9.2 and 3, a merger-induced fall in wages causes the ZZ locus to shifts toward the origin, which expands the range of sectors that remain in the HF region.

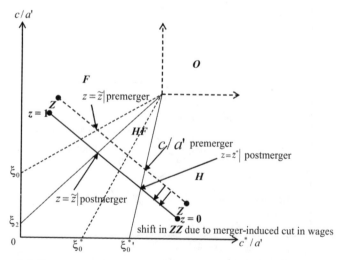

Figure 9.2 Postmerger trading equilibrium with vertical integration at home (foreign acquisition of a disintegrated home firm)

In sum, while a cross-border merger will mitigate the effect of vertical integration on the extensive margins of trade by facilitating specialization toward the direction of comparative advantage (i.e., moving production and trade patterns closer to what would prevail in a competitive Ricardian world), the impact of such a merger on the extensive margins of trade will be larger when a foreign firm acquires a disintegrated home firm compared to the impact when a foreign firm acquires a vertically integrated home firm.

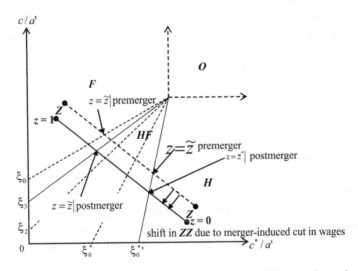

Figure 9.3 Postmerger trading equilibrium with vertical integration at home (foreign acquisition of an integrated home firm)

Discussion

The overall welfare effect, of a cross-border merger, remains ambiguous due to the conflicting impacts of cost reduction and price rise. Our VGOLE model can distinguish between the welfare effects of cross-border mergers involving a vertically integrated firm as opposed to mergers that do not involve vertical integration. This can be seen using the indirect utility function as follows:

$$U = \rho_1^2 - \lambda^2 \mu_2^P = a^2 - \int_{1/2}^{\tilde{z}} \lambda_p \left(W, W, z; \ n, n\right)^2 dz - 2\int_{\tilde{z}}^{1} \lambda_p \left(W, z; \ 0, n\right)^2 dz$$

Intuitively, mergers reduce wages, because they reallocate output to more efficient firms. This effect dampens the effect of vertical integration on the cone of diversification, because high-cost home firms benefit from lower wages. The reduction in wages also reduces the share of sectors, wherein foreign firms find takeovers of home firms profitable, but does not reverse them. Therefore, allowing for mergers shifts the global economy to an equilibrium in which the share of sectors with only foreign firms expands. Hence, they induce specialization according to comparative advantage. The magnitude of the effects depends on whether foreign firms merge with the vertically integrated or with the disintegrated domestic firms. Consequently, the welfare-augmenting (cost-reducing) effect of a cross-border merger between a disintegrated firm in one country and a vertically integrated firm in another is weaker than that of a merger between disintegrated firms across borders. Conversely, the welfare-dampening (price-raising) effect of a cross-border merger between a disintegrated firm in one country and a vertically integrated firm in another is stronger than that of a merger between disintegrated firms across borders. A couple of caveats of our VGOLE construct, which are worth underscoring, include the following: a) the number of firms is fixed and b) firm heterogeneity is absent. Allowing free entry and exit of firms can further enrich our insights into the gains from trade in relation to reallocations at industry equilibrium. We have endogenized firm survival maintaining that survival effects are the same for all firms of the same type: the condition for domestic firms' survival, for instance, does not depend on the number of domestic firms. This allows us to focus on the short-run effects of cross-border mergers. In addition, we assume that all firms within the same country have the same cost structure. The lack of heterogeneity is important for our modeling strategy, because it allows us to focus on cross-border mergers by abstracting from any incentives of within border mergers that can arise exclusively as a result of heterogeneity.

Conclusion

In this chapter, we have constructed a model that applies the analysis of an industry structure from the industrial organization literature, but at the same time keeps the general equilibrium analysis tractable and allows us to study specialization according to comparative advantage in the tradition of a typical neoclassical model of international trade. We have shown that embedding an upstream industry, from which downstream firms buy an intermediate good, adds an important dimension to a general oligopolistic equilibrium model, because vertical integration can act as a foreclosing device reducing upstream competition and, hence, raising the input price for the disintegrated downstream rivals. In particular, our VGOLE model highlights the importance of the interaction between efficiency and concentration, because a merger between high-cost and low-cost firms increases efficiency by eliminating the high-cost firms and raises price by increasing concentration. Consequently, the extensive margin of trade shrinks in the face of vertical integration. In the presence of a vertically integrated production structure, the impact of a merger on the extensive margins of trade will be magnified when the merger takes place between two disintegrated firms across borders compared to a merger between a disintegrated firm in one country and a vertically integrated firm in another. The empirical relevance of our results follows immediately. Brakman *et al.* (2013), when investigating the empirical connection between export performance and mergers, have observed a positive relationship between revealed comparative advantage and mergers. In light of our results, it then becomes imperative to ask if an observed relationship between exports and mergers is sensitive to the vertical structure of an industry. Some interesting extensions that we are working on involve the allowance for technology transfer (Mukherjee and Pennings , 2006), greenfield foreign direct investment (Mukherjee and Suetrong, 2009), and urban unemployment (Oladi and Gilbert, 2011), in our otherwise VGOLE model.

Appendix A

For any given z, in the premerger disintegrated equilibrium, each downstream firm produces

$$(A1) \quad y_i(n,n^*)\big|_D = \left(\frac{a - (n^* + 1)c + n^* c^*}{b(n + n^* + 1)} \right) \qquad \forall \quad i = 1,2,...,n$$

$$(A2) \quad y_i^*(n,n^*)\big|_D = \left(\frac{a - (n + 1)c^* + nc}{b(n + n^* + 1)} \right) \qquad \forall \quad i = 1,2,...,n^*$$

The industry output and price are

$$(A3) \quad \tilde{y}(n,n^*)\big|_D = \left(\frac{n(a - c) + n^*(a - c^*)}{b(n + n^* + 1)} \right)$$

$$(A4) \quad p(n,n^*)\big|_D = \left(\frac{a + nc + n^* c^*}{n + n^* + 1} \right)$$

In the premerger disintegrated equilibrium, the profit each downstream firm earns is

$$(A5) \quad \Pi_i(n,n^*)\big|_D = b\left(y_i(n,n^*)\big|_D \right)^2 \qquad \forall \quad i = 1,2,...,n$$

$$(A6) \quad \Pi_i^*(n,n^*)\big|_D = b\left(y_i^*(n,n^*)\big|_D \right)^2 \qquad \forall \quad i = 1,2,...,n^*$$

In the premerger equilibrium, the vertically integrated home firm $(M_1\text{-}R_1)$ produces

$$(A7) \quad y_1(n,n^*)\big|_I = y_1(n,n^*)\big|_D + \frac{1}{2}\left(\frac{(n - 1)(a - (n^* + 1)c + n^* c^*)}{(2 + n^*)(n + n^* + 1)b} \right)$$

Each disintegrated downstream firm at home produces

$$(A8) \quad y_i(n,n^*)\big|_I = \frac{1}{2} y_i(n,n^*)\big|_D \qquad \forall \quad i = 2,...n$$

Each disintegrated foreign downstream firm produces

$$(A9) \quad y_i^*(n,n^*)\big|_I = y_i^*(n,n^*)\big|_D + \frac{1}{2}\left(\frac{(n-1)(a-(n^*+1)c+n^*c^*)}{(2+n^*)(n+n^*+1)b}\right)$$

$$\forall \quad i = 1,2,...,n^*$$

The industry output and price are

$$(A10) \quad \bar{y}(n,n^*)\big|_I = \bar{y}(n,n^*)\big|_D - \frac{1}{2}\left(\frac{(n-1)(a-(n^*+1)c+n^*c^*)}{(2+n^*)(n+n^*+1)b}\right)$$

$$(A11) \quad p(n,n^*)\big|_I = p(n,n^*)\big|_D + \frac{1}{2}\left(\frac{(n-1)(a-(n^*+1)c+n^*c^*)}{(2+n^*)(n+n^*+1)}\right)$$

In the premerger equilibrium, with a vertically integrated firm at home, the profits of the downstream firms are

$$(A12) \quad \Pi_1(n,n^*)\big|_I = b\left(y_1(n,n^*)\big|_I\right)^2 = \left(1+\frac{(n-1)}{2(2+n^*)}\right)^2 \Pi_1(n,n^*)\big|_D$$

$$(A13) \quad \Pi_i(n,n^*)\big|_I = b\left(y_i(n,n^*)\big|_I\right)^2 = \frac{1}{4}\Pi_i(n,n^*)\big|_D \qquad \forall \quad i = 2,...n$$

(A14)

$$\Pi_i^*(n,n^*)\big|_I = b\left(y_i^*(n,n^*)\big|_I\right)^2 = \left(1+\frac{(n-1)\left(a-(n^*+1)c+n^*c^*\right)}{2(2+n^*)(a-(n+1)c^*+nc)}\right)^2 \Pi_i^*(n,n^*)\big|_D$$

$$\forall \quad i = 1,2,...,n^*$$

It is important to note that, in the face of vertical integration, the difference between the integrated firm's profit $\left(\Pi_1(n,n^*)\big|_I\right)$ and a disintegrated downstream firm's profit $\left(\Pi_i(n,n^*)\big|_I\right)$ exceeds the profit of the upstream monopolist (Π_M^U) as follows:

$$(A15) \quad \left[\Pi_1(n,n^*)\big|_I - \Pi_i(n,n^*)\big|_I\right] - \Pi_M^U = \left(\frac{(n+n^*+1)(n+2n^*+3)}{4(n^*+2)^2}\right) > 0,$$

that is, the gain from being part of a vertical integration is *sufficient* to induce integration in equilibrium.

In the absence of vertical integration, the net gain from a takeover of a disintegrated home firm by another disintegrated home firm is

$$(A16) \quad G_{HH-D} = b\left(y_i(n,n^*)\big|_D\right)^2\left[\left(1+\frac{1}{n+n^*}\right)^2 - 2\right] < 0 \text{ if } \left(n+n^*\right) > 2$$

$$\left(i = 1,2,...n\right)$$

Analogously, in the absence of vertical integration, the net gain from a takeover of a disintegrated foreign firm by another disintegrated foreign firm is

$$\text{(A17)} \quad G_{FF-D} = b\left(y_i^*(n,n^*)\big|_D\right)^2\left[\left(1 + \frac{1}{n+n^*}\right)^2 - 2\right] < 0 \text{ if } \left(n+n^*\right) > 2$$

$$\left(i = 1,2,...n\right)$$

When an upstream firm is integrated with a downstream firm at home (say, R_k), the net gain from a takeover of a disintegrated home firm by another disintegrated home firm is

$$\text{(A18)} \quad G_{HH-I}^{D-D} = b\left(y_i(n,n^*)\big|_I\right)^2\left[\left(1 + \frac{1}{n+n^*}\right)^2 - 2\right] < 0 \text{ if } \left(n+n^*\right) > 2$$

$$\left(i = 1,2,...n; \quad i \neq k\right)$$

When an upstream firm is integrated with a downstream firm at home (say, R_k), the net gain from a takeover of a disintegrated home firm by the integrated home firm is

$$\text{(A19)} \quad G_{HH-I}^{I-D} = -b\left(y_i(n,n^*)\big|_D\right)^2 \frac{(n+n^*-2)^2 + (n^*-1)(n+n^*-1)^2 + 1}{\left(2(n+n^*)(2+n^*)\right)^2} < 0$$

$$\left(i = 1,2,...n\right)$$

When an upstream firm is integrated with a downstream firm at home (say, R_k), the net gain from a takeover of a disintegrated foreign firm by another disintegrated foreign firm is

$$\text{(A20)} \quad G_{HH-I}^{D^*-D^*} = bA_1^2\left[\left(1 + \frac{1}{n+n^*}\right)^2 - 2\right] < 0 \text{ if } \left(n+n^*\right) > 2$$

$$\left(i = 1,2,...n^*\right)$$

where $A_1 = \left(\dfrac{a(n+2n^*+3) + c(3n+n^*+nn^*+1) - c^*(4n+3n^*+nn^*+4)}{2(2+n^*)(n+n^*+1)}\right)$

In the absence of vertical integration, the net gain from a takeover of a home firm by a foreign firm is

(A21)

$$G_{FH-D} = \frac{2n(n+n^*) + (n^*+1)\left[(n+n^*)^2 - 1\right]}{(n+n^*)^2(n+n^*+1)}\left(y_i(n,n^*)\big|_D\right)\left[c - \xi_1 a - (1-\xi_1)c^*\right]$$

$$\left(i = 1,2,...n\right)$$

where $0 < \xi_1 = \dfrac{(n + n^*)^2 - 2(n + n^*) - 1}{2n(n + n^*) + (n^* + 1)\left[(n + n^*)^2 - 1\right]} < \xi_0$.

When an upstream firm is integrated with a downstream firm at home (say, R_k), the net gain from a takeover of the integrated home firm by a foreign firm is

(A22) $G_{FH-I}^{D^*-I} = N_0\left(2(c - c)^* \, y_1(n, n^*)\Big|_I + b\Big(y_1(n, n^*)\Big|_I\Big)^2 \left[N_0 - (n + n^* - 2)\right]\right)$

where $N_0 = \left(\dfrac{(n + n^*)^2 + n^*(n^* + 4) + n + 2}{(n + n^*)(1 + n^*)(n + 2n^* + 3)}\right)$

When an upstream firm is integrated with a downstream firm at home (say, R_k), the net gain from a takeover of a disintegrated home firm by a foreign firm is

(A23) $G_{FH-I}^{D^*-D} = \dfrac{\Big(y_i(n, n^*)\Big|_I\Big)}{b'(n^* + 2)(n + n^* + 1)(n + n^*)^2 N_2}\left[c - \xi_2 a - (1 - \xi_2)c^*\right]$

$$(i = 2, ... n)$$

where $0 < \xi_2 = \left(1 - \dfrac{N_1}{N_2}\right) < \xi_0 < 1$

$N_1 = n + 4n^2 n^* + 5n^{*2} + 8n^2 + 2nn^{*3} + 6nn^{*2} + 6n^* + n^{*4} + 2n^{*3} + 14nn^* + n^2 n^{*2}$

$N_2 = 2nn^{*3} + n^2 n^{*2} + 2(4n^2 - 1) + 8nn^{*2} + 5n^2 n^* + 3n^{*2} + (n^{*4} - n^*)$

$$+3n^{*3} + 12nn^* + 2n$$

The difference between a foreign firm's gain from taking over a disintegrated home firm and a foreign firm's gain from taking over the integrated home firm is

(A24) $G_{FH-I}^{D^*-D} - G_{FH-I}^{D^*-I} = \dfrac{y_i(n, n^*)\Big|_I}{2b(n^* + 2)^2(n + 1)^2(n + n^*)N_3}\left[c - \xi_3 a - (1 - \xi_3)c^*\right]$

where $0 < \xi_2 < \xi_3 = \left(1 - \dfrac{N_3}{N_4}\right) < \xi_0 < 1$

$N_3 = 8n(n + 1) + n^*(3n^{*4} + 11n^{*3} + 16n^{*2} + 12n^* + 4) + nn^*(4n^{*3} + nn^{*2}$

$$+15n^{*2} + 4nn^* + 10n + 28n^* + 26)$$

$N_4 = (n^* + 1)[n^*(3n^{*3} + 11n^{*2} + 12n^*) + 6(n^2 + n - 1) + nn^*(4n^{*2} + nn^*$

$$+4n + 15n^* + 20) + 2]$$

Appendix B

Lemma 1. In the absence of vertical integration, closing down $(n - \tilde{n})$ home firms increases the output of all remaining firms (home as well as foreign) by

$$y_i(\tilde{n}, n^*)\big|_D - y_i(n, n^*)\big|_D = y_j^*(\tilde{n}, n^*)\big|_D - y_j^*(n, n^*)\big|_D = \left(\frac{n - \tilde{n}}{\tilde{n} + n^* + 1}\right) y_i(n, n^*)\big|_D$$

$$\forall i = 1, 2, ..., \tilde{n}; j = 1, 2, ...n^*.$$

Proof: Follows directly from A1 and A2.

Lemma 2. In the absence of vertical integration, closing down $\left(n^* - \tilde{n}^*\right)$ foreign firms increases the output of all remaining firms (home as well as foreign) by

$$y_i(n, \tilde{n}^*)\big|_D - y_i(n, n^*)\big|_D = y_j^*(n, \tilde{n}^*)\big|_D - y_j^*(n, n^*)\big|_D = \left(\frac{n^* - \tilde{n}^*}{\tilde{n}^* + n + 1}\right) y_j^*(n, n^*)\big|_D$$

$$\forall i = 1, 2, ..., \tilde{n}; j = 1, 2, ...n^*.$$

Proof: Follows directly from A1 and A2.

Lemma 3. When an upstream firm is integrated with a downstream firm (say, R_k) at home, closing down $(n - \tilde{n})$ disintegrated home firms increases the output of all remaining firms (home as well as foreign) by

$$y_i(\tilde{n}, n^*)\big|_I - y_i(n, n^*)\big|_I = y_k(\tilde{n}, n^*)\big|_I - y_k(n, n^*)\big|_I = y_j^*(\tilde{n}, n^*)\big|_I - y_j^*(n, n^*)\big|_I$$

$$= \left(\frac{n - \tilde{n}}{\tilde{n} + n^* + 1}\right) y_i(n, n^*)\big|_I$$

$$\forall i, k = 1, 2, ..., \tilde{n}; i \neq k; j = 1, 2, ...n^*$$

Proof: Follows directly from A7 through A9.

Lemma 4. When an upstream firm is integrated with a downstream firm (say, R_k) at home, closing down $\left(n^* - \tilde{n}^*\right)$ disintegrated foreign firms increases the output of

(*a*) the disintegrated home firms by

$$y_i(n, \tilde{n}^*)\big|_I - y_i(n, n^*)\big|_I = \frac{1}{2}\left(\frac{n^* - \tilde{n}^*}{n + \tilde{n}^* + 1}\right)\left(\frac{a + nc - (n + 1)c^*}{b(n + n^* + 1)}\right)$$

$$\forall i, k = 1, 2, ..., n; i \neq k$$

and

(*b*) the integrated home firm and the remaining disintegrated foreign firms by

$$y_k(n, \tilde{n}^*)\big|_I - y_k(n, n^*)\big|_I = y_j^*(n, \tilde{n}^*)\big|_I - y_j^*(n, n^*)\big|_I$$

$$= \left(\frac{n^* - \tilde{n}^*}{(n + \tilde{n}^* + 1)(2 + \tilde{n}^*)} \right) \left(\frac{\upsilon_1 a + \upsilon_2 c - \upsilon_3 c^*}{b(n + n^* + 1)(2 + n^*)} \right)$$

$$\forall j = 1, 2, ... \tilde{n}^*$$

where
$$\begin{cases} \upsilon_1 = (n + 1)^2 + n^*(n + \tilde{n}^* + 3) + \tilde{n}^*(n + n^* + 3) + 4 \\ \upsilon_2 = (n + 1)^2 + (n + 1)n^*\tilde{n}^* + 3(n^* + \tilde{n}^* + 1)n + n + n^* + \tilde{n}^* \\ \upsilon_3 = 2[(n + 1)^2 + (n + 1)(4 + n^*\tilde{n}^*) + n^*\tilde{n}^* + 2(nn^* + n^* + n\tilde{n}^* + \tilde{n}^*)] \end{cases}$$

Proof: Follows directly from A7 through A9.

References

Beladi, H., A. Chakrabarti, and S. Marjit. 2010. 'Cross-border Merger in a Vertically Related Industry and Spatial Competition with Different Product Varieties.' *Economics Letters* 109(2): 112–14.

_____. 2013. 'Cross-Border Mergers in Vertically Related Industries.' *European Economic Review* 59: 97–108.

_____. 2015. 'On Cross-Border Mergers and Product Differentiation.' *BE Journal of Economic Analysis and Policy: Advances* 15(1): 37–51.

Bertrand, O. and H. Zitouna. 2006. 'Trade Liberalization and Industrial Restructuring: The role of Cross-border Mergers and Acquisitions.' *Journal of Economics and Management Strategy* 15(2): 479–515.

Brakman, S., J. H. Garretsen, C. van Marrewijk, and A. van Witteloostuijn. 2013. 'Cross Border M&As and Revealed Comparative Advantage.' *Journal of Economics and Management Strategy* 22(1): 28–57.

Chakrabarti, A., Y. Hsieh, and Y. Chang. 2017. 'Cross-border mergers and market concentration in a vertically related industry: theory and evidence.' *The Journal of International Trade and Economic Development* 26(1): 111–30.

Child, J., D. Falkner, and R. Pitkethly. 2001. *The Management of International Acquisitions.* Oxford: Oxford University Press.

Dornbusch, R., S. Fischer, and P. A. Samuelson. 1977. 'Comparative Advantage, Trade and Payments in a Ricardian Model with a Continuum of Goods.' *American Economic Review* 67: 823–39.

Erel, I., R. C. Liao, and M. S. Weisbach. 2009. 'World Markets for Mergers and Acquisitions.' NBER Working Paper 15132.

Falvey, R. 1998. 'Mergers in Open Economies.' *The World Economy* 21: 1061–76.

Farrell, J. and C. Shapiro. 1990. 'Horizontal mergers: An equilibrium analysis.' *American Economic Review* 80: 107–26.

Finkelstein, S. 1999. 'Safe Ways to Cross the Merger Minefield.' In *Financial Times Mastering Global Business: The Complete MBA Companion in Global Business*, edited by G. Bickerstaffe and T. Dickson. London: Financial Times Pitman Publishing.

Head, K. and J. Ries. 1997. 'International Mergers and Welfare under Decentralized Competition Policy.' *Canadian Journal of Economics* 30: 1104–23.

Jovanovic, B. and P. L. Rousseau. 2003. 'Mergers as Reallocation.' Mimeo, New York University.

Lafontaine, F. and M. Slade. 2007. 'Vertical Integration and Firm Boundaries: The Evidence.' *Journal of Economic Literature* 45: 629–85.

Jones, R. W. and R. J. Ruffin. 2008. 'The Technology Transfer Paradox.' *Journal of International Economics* 75: 321–28.

Long, N. V. and N. Vousden. 1995. 'The Effects of Trade Liberalization on Cost-reducing Horizontal Mergers.' *Review of International Economics* 3: 141–55.

Lipton, M. 2006. 'Merger Waves in the 19th, 20th and 21st Centuries.' The Davies Lecture. Mimeo, New York University.

Mukherjee, A. and E. Pennings. 2006. 'Tariffs, Licensing and Market Structure.' *European Economic Review* 50(7): 1699–1707.

Mukherjee, A. and K. Suetrong. 2009. 'Privatization, Strategic Foreign Direct Investment and Host-country Welfare.' *European Economic Review* 53(7): 775–85.

Neary, J. P. 2003. 'Globalization and Market Structure.' *Journal of the European Economic Association* 1: 245–71.

_____. 2007. 'Cross-border Mergers as Instruments of Comparative Advantage.' *Review of Economic Studies* 4: 182–91.

Ordover, J. A., G. Saloner, and S. C. Salop. 1990. 'Equilibrium Vertical Foreclosure.' *American Economic Review* 80: 127–42.

_____. 1992. 'Equilibrium Vertical Foreclosure: Reply.' *American Economic Review* 82: 698–703.

Perry, M. and R. Porter. 1985. 'Oligopoly and the Incentive for Horizontal Merger.' *American Economic Review* 75: 219–27.

Qiu, L. D. 2010. 'Cross-Border Mergers and Strategic Alliances.' *European Economic Review* 54: 818–31.

Raff, H., M. Ryan, and F. Stähler. 2006. 'Asset Ownership and Foreign-Market Entry.' CESifo Working Paper 1676.

Reiffen, D. 1992. 'Equilibrium Vertical Foreclosure: Comment.' *American Economic Review* 82: 694–97.

Reuer, J. J., O. Shenkar, and R. Ragozzino. 2004. 'Mitigating Risk in International Mergers and Acquisitions: The Role of Contingent Payouts.' *Journal of International Business Studies* 35: 19–32.

Rey, P. and J. Tirole. 2005. 'Foreclosure.' In *Handbook of Industrial Organization, Volume* III, edited by M. Armstrong and R. Porter. Amsterdam: North-Holland Publishing.

Ruffin, R. and R. W. Jones. 2007. 'International Technology Transfer: Who Gains and Who Loses?' *Review of International Economics* 15: 209–22.

Salant, S., S. Switzer, and R. Reynolds. 1983. 'Losses due to merger: The Effects of an Exogenous Change in Industry Structure on Cournot-Nash Equilibrium.' *Quarterly Journal of Economics* 98: 185–99.

Sarker, S., J. Gilbert, and R. Oladi. 2008. 'Adjustment Costs and Immiserizing growth in LDCs.' *Review of Development Economics* 12: 779–91.

UNCTAD (United Nations Conference on Trade and Development). 2009. *World Investment Prospects Survey (WIPS) 2009–2011*. New York and Geneva: United Nations.

10

International Trade and Production Organization
A Review of Contemporary Literature

Meghna Dutta

Introduction

Over the second half of the century, the formation of several institutions involved in the reduction of tariff and nontariff barriers have advocated and promoted free trade between nations. The countries have also obliged either due to their acknowledgement of accrued benefits or because of sociopolitical compulsions. Consequently, the reduction in trade barriers by most countries has given international trade an impetus like never before. This reduction in barriers to international trade and investment and increasing global competition have driven producers across national borders to take advantage of lower costs abroad. Importantly, along with an increase in volume, there has also been a distinct change in the pattern of trade. The shift in trade pattern in favor of intraindustry trade led to an important question—can internal production organization of a firm or an industry alter the modalities of international trade?

The ease of doing international trade has played a crucial role in determining the international pattern of production and organizational forms. The proliferation of transnational production manifested via segmentation of production processes and coordination of the related activities has largely been possible because of reduction in trade barriers and innovations and improvements in information and communication technology. In addition, the new production organization has been aided by stricter protection of property rights and improved legal as well as business environment (Borrus and Zysman, 1997; Kaminiski and Ng, 2001). Notably, the segmentation of a single production process can be done in several ways. It is usually performed either by fragmenting and shifting a part of the production to a nonaffiliated, independent firm[1] or by collaborating with other firms, which can produce at a cheaper rate. The decision that the firm will take, to integrate or to outsource, depends on several costs and contingencies as transaction costs, asset specificity[2], completeness of contracts, etc. However, as Grossman and Helpman (2002, 1) put it, 'outsourcing is more prevalent in some industries than others', typically because the choice is not automatic and in reality depends upon the level of market competition, different cost considerations, input specificity, etc. The most significant feature of production fragmentation is that it allow firms to utilize cheaper external factors for some fragments of the value-added chain. Outsourcing some stages of production process to cheaper international location makes production less costly and, therefore, releases resources that could be directed elsewhere. Outsourcing and subcontracting of peripheral productions or selling and distributional activities allow firms to direct the scarce resources to their core business activities, thereby further enhancing competitive advantages and productivity (Olsen, 2006). Of late, these changes in production organization have significantly modified the erstwhile production relations. Outsourcing to the informal sector (Beneria and Floro, 2004) is an important outcome of such relocation. Needless to mention, the cost implications of fragmentation via outsourcing, subcontracting, or offshoring are different. Consequently, this rising informalization, as well as the shifting out of jobs to other countries, has resulted in political debates and disagreements in both the developed and the developing countries (Standing, 1999). The debate encompasses a range of topics including definitional issues (Bhagwati *et al.*, 2004), the number of jobs lost to developing countries in case of offshoring (Mankiw and Swaggel, 2006), distributional effects of fragmentation (Egger and Pfaffermayr, 2004; Feenstra and Hanson, 1996a, 1996b), and structural changes in the economy brought about by outsourcing (Nelson, 2005). As fragmentation becomes pervasive at the firm level, the underlying changes in trade and investment patterns, interrelations between factors of production and factor returns, etc., provide important perspective to the dynamics of production within and across countries.

The chapter is arranged as follows: The second section discusses related definitional complexities, the third section elaborates the existing literature on production organization, and the fourth section discusses some ideas related to international trade and production organization.

---

[1] This is often called outsourcing and, by definition, outsourcing, offshore outsourcing, and captive offshoring jointly constitute the process called production fragmentation (Jones and Kierzkowski, 2001).

[2] Asset specificity is defined as the extent to which the investments made to support a particular transaction have a higher value to that transaction than they would have if they were redeployed for any other purpose (McGuinness, 1994).

Definitional Complexities Related to Production Reorganisation

It should be emphasized that breaking down an integrated production process into separate stages opens up new possibilities for exploiting the gains from specialization (Deardorff, 2005). Therefore, it is important to distinguish between outsourcing and traditional arms-length transactions. Outsourcing entails a long-term relationship and involves the flow of stylized information in the form of detailed specifications on part of the customer as opposed to arms-length relationships (Curzon Price, 2001). Offshoring, on the other hand, only partially overlaps the definition of outsourcing (WTO, 2005). It refers to the process of obtaining goods and services from companies located outside the home country. In other words, outsourcing refers to the relocation of jobs and processes to external and independent providers regardless of the vendor's location. On the other hand, *offshoring* is relocation of jobs and processes to any foreign country irrespective of the provider being independent or affiliated with the firm. If a firm obtains intermediate inputs from its own plant in home country, it is called *domestic internal production*. However, if the firm takes over another firm at home and produces the intermediate output therein, it is called *domestic vertical integration*. Nevertheless, if such a plant is relocated to a foreign country for establishing a production affiliate abroad, then it is said to be a vertical foreign direct investment resulting in *captive offshoring* of intermediates (UNCTAD, 2004). Firms retain the ownership of the entire production process but locate portion of their activities abroad by setting up subsidiaries. When a firm decides to allow the production of a specific good or service to an independent subcontractor in the home country, it is called *domestic outsourcing*. In addition, *offshore outsourcing* occurs when a foreign unaffiliated provider sells intermediate goods or services to a domestic company (UNCTAD, 2004).

The definition of 'fragmentation' itself has also been a matter of debate. Egger and Falkinger (2001) have defined fragmentation using Q as the set of vectors of available primary factors of production, and $X = x^1 \times \ldots \times x^n$ as the set of possible intermediate goods. Thereafter, $f(q)$, $q \in Q$, and $x(q^1, \ldots, q^n) = (x^1(q^1), x^2(q^2), \ldots, x^n(q^n))$, $q^1, \ldots, q^n \in Q$ are the production functions. Thus, intermediate production processes x are said to be a fragmentation of integrated production f, if there exists a 'residual' technology $g(q^0, x)$, such that for all $q \in Q$, $f(q) = g(q^0, x(q^1, \ldots, q^n))$ for some $q^0, q^1, \ldots, q^n \in Q$.

Previously, Yeats (1998) had defined production fragmentation as the 'internationalization' of a manufacturing process, in which several countries participate at different stages of production of a good. Other studies have mostly focused on outsourcing to mean production fragmentation. Bhagwati *et al.* (2004) have defined Mode 1 of the WTO terminology as outsourcing. By this definition, trade in services involves arm-length supply of services, with the supplier and buyer remaining in their respective locations. Nonetheless, this sequential production, often termed 'vertical specialization,' has increased the verticality of trade[3] (Balasssa, 1967; Findlay, 1978a; Hummels *et al.*, 2001).

Regardless of the multiplicity of definition, it has been observed that by all measures, production fragmentation has increased. According to Yi (2003, 2), 'vertical specialization has grown by about 30 percent, and accounts for about one-third of the growth in trade, in the last 20–30 years.' This increase in the relative importance of production sharing also entails that countries have become interdependent. Therefore, the reorganization of production processes within and across national borders has undoubtedly added a new paradigm in international trade. However, as Helpman (2006) observed, 'the new generation of theories does not replace or supersede comparative advantage explanations of inter-sectoral trade and FDI flows, nor do they replace imperfect competition based explanations of intraindustry trade.' The contribution of the newer theories to international trade theory is with regard to the organizational choices of an individual firm, which addresses their make-or-buy dilemma and provides answers to questions, such as, which firms tend to operate internationally? how do they engage in foreign markets? What are the determinants of their organizational choices?

Review of Existing Literature

At the level of firm organization, production reorganization across national borders has raised new issues. Companies previously outsourced few ancillary activities such as production of basic components, maintenance-related jobs, or specialized legal work. However, currently, the trend has shifted toward outsourcing of major capabilities involving thousands of people, sensitive knowledge, and firm-specific technology (Burger, 2009). A large number of companies have been leveraging world-class capabilities from another company in order to improve the total value they can provide to their customers. The Jones and Kierzkowski (1990) framework presents a simple theoretical structure to understand global production sharing. It explains that international fragmentation should, in general, be beneficial because it is capable of enhancing the gains from trade.

---

[3] The verticality in trade has been given many names such as 'outsourcing' (Feenstra and Hanson, 1996a, 1996b, 1997), 'multistage production' (Dixit and Grossman, 1982), 'slicing up the value chain' (Krugman, 1995), (Jones and Kierzkowski, 1997), 'intraproduct specialization' (Arndt, 1997a), 'fragmentation of production' (Deardorff, 1998), and 'disintegration of production' (Feenstra, 1998).

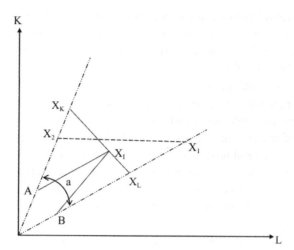

Figure 10.1 Production fragmentation

Figure 10.1, as presented by Jones and Kierzkowski (1990), illustrates the process of production fragmentation. To produce one dollar worth of Commodity X at given world prices, in an integrated manner, it requires A and B bundle of inputs (capital and labor). Before international fragmentation, these components could not be traded; therefore, there are only autarkic prices. Instead of trade prices, X_K and X_L indicate the capital–labor inputs, which would be required to produce $1 worth of the component, assuming that it is valued at local factor costs. These costs, in turn, depend on the local technology and world prices for other goods, which this economy may produce in the prefragmentation equilibrium. The factor requirement to produce $1 of final Good X in the integrated process is a weighted average of points X_K and X_L, with the weights showing the distributive value share of each segment in the integrated technology. Thus, the α-cone displays the cone of diversification spanned by the technologies for the component. After fragmentation becomes possible, trade price are determined for the separate segments of output. Because countries are assumed to differ in factor skills and technologies, a finer division of activities allows efficiency gain according to Ricardian theory of comparative advantage. Therefore, X_I, the formerly integrated process, is replaced by X_1 and X_2, which are the separate labor-intensive and capital-intensive segments, respectively, of producing Good X. They also assumed that the labor-intensive segment, X_1, is dominated by the capital-intensive segment X_2. They assumed so in the sense that less capital and less labor are required to earn $1 at new world prices, thereby producing segment X_2 as opposed to segment X_1.

Evidence support the spread of offshore outsourcing between a producer and an input provider. Three features of this practice are difficult to interpret within the domain of traditional trade theory and require new models. These include the unprecedented expansion in input trade across the boundaries of the firm (Borga and Zeile, 2004; Feenstra, 1998); the increasing share of imported intermediates in total inputs over the last three decades (Kleinert, 2003); and the spread of these trend across sectors and types of inputs (Helpman, 2006). As responses to these emerging trends, a new generation of theoretical approach has been developed to model the alternative patterns of firm-level activities as part of cross-border trade. Furthermore, the growing trend of international procurement of intermediate inputs through foreign direct investment could not be adequately explained by the traditional trade theories that did not take into consideration vertical fragmentation of production process and the make-or-buy decision facing firms.

The decision of firms to fragment their production processes has raised questions at both macro and micro levels. Regarding the macroaspects, scholars have studied the implications of fragmentation on trade flows, wages, and welfare. Arndt (1997b, 1998) and Jones (2000) have dealt with trade and wage inequality, and Deardorff (2001a, 2001b) have focused on the effect of international multistage production on wages and welfare. At the microlevel, fragmentation posed a question regarding which processes the firms should internalize and which they should outsource along with the rationales for choice of ownership structures of firms. Klette and Kortum (2004), in this regard, explained production reorganization by considering a market structure in which firms engage in Bertrand competition while the economy as a whole is of monopolistic competition type. They also assume that firms operate in an economy with continuum of differentiated goods of unit measure. Ericson and Pakes (1995) contributed to the micro-based growth theory by allowing for strategic interactions between the firms, which compete in the same market with regard to their R&D investment decisions and also allow for endogenous entry and exit of firms. Helpman (2006) and Antras (2005b) formulated models with heterogeneous firms, trading costs and incomplete contracts based on an earlier analysis of Melitz (2003). These models helped to address the issue of trade and production organization. Klette and Griliches (2000) use a differentiated product framework and the elements of the 'quality ladder models' introduced by Aghion and Howitt (1992), as well as by Grossman and Helpman (1991a, 1991b). However, it does not take into consideration the entry and exit decisions of firms.

Theoretical Frameworks Explaining Fragmentation of Production

Researchers in new trade theory have often combined trade theories with theories in industrial organization to bring forth new predictions. The possibility of organizing production processes across countries could change the pattern of comparative advantage and, hence, the levels and patterns of trade (Antras and Rossi-Hansberg,

2009). Jones and Kierzkowski (1997, 2001) had used a standard Heckscher–Ohlin framework, in which initially the production process was completed in a single stage. Thereafter, Jones and Kierzkowski (1997, 2001) moved on to describe the effects of fragmenting the production process into two intermediate stages with differing factor intensities. Trading the product of these two stages within an industry is similar to an improvement in the total factor productivity of the industry, which elucidates the effect of Hicks neutral technological change in Heckscher–Ohlin model. Ando (2006) had used the standard measure of intraindustry trade and compared it with the 25 percent threshold to identify vertical IIT and horizontal IIT.

$$\frac{1}{1+\alpha} \le \frac{P_{kj}^X}{P_{kj}^M} \le 1 + \alpha \; ; \alpha = 0.25 \tag{1.1}$$

where P_{kj}^X expresses the unit value of commodity j exported to the world by Country k, and P_{kj}^M is the unit value of Commodity j imported from the world by Country k.

While Jones and Kierzkowski (1990) looked at fragmentation and trade from the perspective of the country, Antras (2003) dealt with it from the point of view of the firm. Antras (2003) developed a model of a firm producing a continuum of varieties of two types of final goods, with each variety requiring a distinct intermediate input. The final good producer first decides whether to enter an industry and, if so, whether to purchase the input from an arms-length producer or from a vertically integrated division. To explain the empirical fact that capital-intensive goods are transacted within the boundaries of multinationals while labor-intensive goods are traded at arms-length, Antras (2003) extends the setting of Grossman–Hart (1986) by allowing for the capital expenditures to be transferred to the input supplier. According to Antras *et al.* (2005), outsourcing has a productivity-enhancing effect at a more aggregate level if offshoring would lead to the creation of new firms and the destruction of old ones[4]. This process is often associated with Schumpeter's theory of creative destruction, and numerous empirical studies have provided support for its positive impacts on productivity (Bartelsman *et al.* 2003). Contraction of trading firms has been treated differently in a newer perspective in the discussion of finite changes, as in Findlay and Jones (2000).

Deardorff (2001b) has introduced the possibility of fragmentation of production in both Ricardian and Heckscher–Ohlin structures for a small open economy, as well as a two-country world. In the same line, Jones (2006) captures the fact that

---

[4] For country-wise studies on this see literature pertaining to India (Dutta and Kar, 2013), Portugal (Carreira and Teixeira, 2008), Slovenia (Loecker and Konings, 2004), Finland (Maliranta, 2003), Estonia (Masso, Eamets, and Philips, 2004), and New Zealand (McMillan, 2004).

fragmented production process and the trade, therefrom, can be well explained by both Ricardian and Heckscher–Ohlin type models. If production activities are dispersed to different regions because workers in one area of the country tend to have different skills from those in another area, and the skills required in each production block differ so that dispersion of activity according to comparative advantage lowers the marginal costs of production, then it is a Ricardian-type explanation. On the other hand, if the production blocks are separated so as to locate the labor-intensive block in labor-abundant regions, then it is a Heckscher–Ohlin-type difference. In spite of the existing theories of comparative advantage and factor endowments providing some conceptual framework to explain the rationale and causality of international trade, the increasingly complex nature of fragmentation of trade seems to warrant a new analytical paradigm that goes beyond comparative advantage (Grossman and Rossi-Hansberg, 2008) or factor abundance (Baldone *et al.*, 2006). Van Long (2005) has discussed the effects of spillovers from outsourcing in a Cournot setting. He considered a foreign firm that outsources part of its production to another country, where the local rival firm produces an imperfect substitute. If outsourcing occurs, the foreign rival enjoys a positive spillover because outsourcing increases labor productivity in this country. He shows that outsourcing will be complete if both firms are monopolists in their markets, but will be incomplete, if the two goods are substitutes because the foreign firm would like to restrict the positive spillover to the local rival. Production fragmentation has also led to a spurt in the trade of intermediate goods. As Baldone *et al.* (2006) points out, 'with international fragmentation of production the number of traded goods no longer coincides with the number of final goods'. This suggests that trade patterns cannot be taken as indicators of comparative advantage in the production of final goods any more. Consequently, when exchange of intermediate good is allowed, the export of final goods by one country embodies not just the technology or some portion of the factors of production with which that country is endowed, but also the technology, know-how, and factors of other countries. Sanyal (1983), in this regard, determines the particular stage at which the vertical spectrum of the production process is broken so that each country can specialize in one part. He used two functions describing the 'intramarginal' technology in the two countries as follows:

$$a_X = f(x) \qquad f' > 0, \quad f'' > 0, \quad f(0) = 0, \quad f(1) = u \qquad (1.2)$$

$$b_X = g(x) \qquad g' > 0, \quad g'' < 0, \quad g(0) = 0, \quad g(1) = u \qquad (1.3)$$

The first equation describes technology in the home country, where a_x is the amount of labor needed to produce the good up to the stage x. As one moves toward the final stage, x is higher, and a_x is also higher. This is captured by the assumption that f' is positive. $f''>0$ implies that, for higher x, the rate at which a_x increases is also higher. Finally, at stage 1, a_x equals u. The second equation describes the technology used in the foreign country, which is interpreted in the same way except for the fact that g'' is negative, implying that, as the foreign country moves toward stage 1, b_x increases at a slower pace. At stage 1, b is equal to u, which reflects the assumption that the two countries share the same technology in terms of the total coefficients. Sarkar (1985) had showed in a two-country–two-good stationary-state model, in which the country with higher rate of interest specializes in the early stages of production. These countries can be roughly identified with the less-developed nations, where lower wage rates and higher capital costs lead to a comparative advantage in the early stages of the productive spectrum. Marjit (1987) also built a model in which different parts of an intermediate good are traded between two nations, and the intermediate good is then used to make two country-specific products. Marjit (1987) also showed that in a three-country, two-good, colonial world, immiserization can occur even when commodity terms of trade are given. This increasing fragmentation of trade has also led to the emergence of another strand of literature that puts forward the idea of intraindustry trade (Ando, 2006; Dluhosch, 2002; Zeddies, 2007) and discusses firm heterogeneity and their organizational choices (Antras and Helpman, 2003; McLaren, 2000; Grossman and Helpman, 2005).

The technological improvements, which had made fragmentation viable, have also altered the relative values of physical and human capital in favor of the later. This proposition had been extensively dealt with in Jones and Marjit (2001), which puts the rationale for regulating international trade and foreign investment in less-developed countries to the threats, which it poses to the wealth of the older generation. The rapid developments in information and manufacturing technology have also had a key role in fragmenting a single production process. This has resulted in a growing intermediate business–service trade that uses the time zone differences between countries and completes a job in a single working day (Marjit, 2007; Kikuchi and Marjit, 2010). However, the benefits from using time-zone differences have mostly remained confined to the service sector. Nonetheless, these innovations in communications technology have eased the linkage between the sliced production process through services, thereby substantially reducing the costs involved (Athukorala and Menon, 2010). Therefore, it can be safely asserted that the idea of production organization can be explained by the concept of increased reduction in marginal costs of production due to global production sharing, even though the cross-border spread of production involves new fixed costs, including services links, to ensure a smooth sequence in producing the final good. Besides, a more fragmented production process means that the fixed cost of service links gets spread over a larger output, allowing the firm to reap the benefits of lower average costs of production based on international specialization.

Empirical Evidence of Trade in Intermediate Goods

The increasing importance of production fragmentation has led to the formulation of several measures. Feenstra (1998) offered a detailed study of several measures of foreign outsourcing and argued that they have all increased since the 1970s. However, the absence of detailed and internationally comparable data makes evaluation of international fragmentation of production difficult.[5] Consequently, many studies (Feenstra and Hanson, 1996a; Jones *et al.*, 2005; Lawrence, 1994; Slaughter, 1995; Zeddies, 2007) have used data on trade in intermediate goods as a proxy to measure the levels of production fragmentation. But Feenstra and Hanson (1999) point out that the use of international trade in intermediate goods is a 'narrow measure' of outsourcing. Moreover, it is necessary to have detailed firm-level data on imports of intermediate goods and services, as well as information on the type of relationship between the buyer and supplier, in order to distinguish between offshore outsourcing and captive offshoring. Without the data on trading partner relationships, it is difficult to distinguish between the alternative variants of offshoring. What can only be measured is the extent of offshoring as a whole.

Nevertheless, other means of measuring fragmentation have been used by several researchers. Hummels *et al.* (1998) obtained the import content of export from Input–Output tables and used this measure of vertical specialization to identify cases in which production is carried out in at least two countries and the goods crossed international border at least twice. Hummels *et al.* (2001) using the aforementioned measure observed that, as of 1990, vertical specialization accounts for 20 percent of merchandise exports in the OECD countries. Smaller countries and those outside the OECD group, such as Ireland, Korea, Taiwan, and Mexico, have vertical specialization shares as high as 40 percent of exports. However, this measure only captures a special case of offshoring. In addition, this measure is relevant only when the offshored goods are further used for production of final goods that are then exported. Besides, this does not take into account the case when a country exports intermediate goods to another country, which in turn uses them as input in the production of export goods (Hummels *et al.*, 2001; WTO, 2008). Using the measure of vertical specialization, Yi (2003) observed that a reduction in tariff rates increased vertical specialization, which can explain over 50 percent of the rise in world trade. Gorg (2000) reports that between 1988 and 1994, around 20 percent of US exports to the EU were for inward processing, that is, they were exported to the EU for processing and were subsequently exported outside the EU. Head and Ries (2002) have investigated the influence of offshore production

---

[5] Data available for studying international trade and FDI have been extensively discussed in Feenstra *et al.* (2010).

by Japanese multinationals on domestic skill intensity using firm-level data. They concluded that working through foreign affiliates in low-income countries raises the skill intensity at home; however, this effect falls as investment shifts toward high-income countries. This observation was in accord with the idea that vertical specialization by multinationals contributes to the upgradation of skill domestically. Baldone (2006) has presented an index based on the Balassa index of revealed specialization as follows:

$$R_{ji} = \frac{\left(\dfrac{F_{ij}}{F_{dj}}\right)}{\left(\dfrac{F_{iEU}}{F_{dEU}}\right)} \tag{1.4}$$

where R_{ji} is the index of revealed propensity of Country j measured with respect to the flow of type i.[6]

F_d measures final trade flows
F_i measures temporary trade flow of type i
EU is the whole European Union
j refers to the j-th country in EU

For each country and with respect to each type of flow, this index measures the propensity to undertake processing trade as the share of each temporary flow relative to final flows, using the average EU propensity as a benchmark.

However, empirical research in identifying the determinants of outsourcing remains very limited. In this regard, Kimura (2001) and Tomiura (2004) have used data for the Japanese manufacturing industry, Gorg and Hanley (2004) for the Irish electronics industry, Girma and Gorg (2004) for the UK manufacturing industries, and Holl (2004) for the Spanish manufacturing industry to find out the relative importance of factors in deciding the intensity of outsourcing by a firm. Of these studies, Gorg and Hanley (2004) and Girma and Gorg (2004) tried to infer the factors that may affect the level of outsourcing, whereas Holl (2004) focused on the determinants of the probability that a firm takes the decision of outsourcing using a probit model. Hansson (2005) studied Swedish multinational enterprises (MNEs) during the years 1990–1997 and found a significantly positive impact of increased employment share in the affiliates of these MNEs located in non-OECD

---

[6] It refers to the following four different types of trade flows: (1) temporary exports of goods by a EU country to be processed in a non-EU member; (2) reimports by the EU of the processed goods; (3) temporary imports of goods to be processed in the EU; and (4) re-exports of those goods to the country of origin outside the EU. The first two flows measure the *outward processing trade*; the last two flows measure the *inward processing trade*.

countries with regard to skill upgradation in Swedish parent MNEs. Verhoogen (2008) proposed quality-upgrading mechanism as a new means of linking trade and wage inequality in developing countries and investigated its empirical implications in panel data on Mexican manufacturing plants.

Some Contemporary Issues Related to Trade and Fragmentation

This section discusses issues that are fragmentation facilitator as wage inequality, capital inflow in the form of foreign direct investment.

Trade, Production Fragmentation, and Wage Differentials

The fundamental justification behind the profitability of slicing up of an entire production process is the idea of taking benefit of wage differentials between the developed and developing countries (Ando, 2006). Its short-run and long-run impacts on the factor returns, in the source as well as the host country, pose important economic as well as political questions. Feenstra and Hanson (1996a) had showed that starting from an equilibrium with immobile capital and then subsequently allowing capital to move from home to foreign country raises (lowers) rental charges of capital at home (abroad). It also tends to expand the range of intermediate goods outsourced to foreign country, thereby lowering relative demand for unskilled labor in both countries and raising relative wage of skilled labor in both countries. They have also shown that even when the relative wage of unskilled workers falls in both countries, their real wages need not fall due to a drop in the prices of final good. These results hold regardless of whether the increased outsourcing is due to a capital flow, growth in the capital endowments abroad at a rate exceeding that at home, or simply because of better technological progress abroad than at home. Whether the change in relative wages is due to international trade or not can be computed from the Heckscher–Ohlin–Vanek model, which looks into the change in factor content of trade and associated changes in factor prices. This was justified by Deardorff and Staiger (1988) who showed the following:

$$(w^2 - w^1)(F^2 - F^1) \geq 0 \qquad (1.5)$$

where w^i are equilibrium wages in a country in two equilibria $i=1,2$, and F^i is the factor content of exports for that country. The aforementioned equation is interpreted as saying that a higher content of imports for some factor k, $F_k^2 < F_k^1 < 0$ so $(F_k^2 - F_k^1) < 0$, will tend to be associated with a falling wage for that factor, $(w_k^2 - w_k^1) < 0$. The same would be true for the direct import of a factor, as with immigration.

Harris (2001) developed a model that provides an alternative explanation for the expansion of fragmentation other than those based on factor price differences and factor intensity differences. It emphasizes the role of fixed cost and increasing returns associated with international trade networks, in particular with communication networks. Arndt (1997a) shows that contrary to a standard Heckscher–Ohlin model, intraproduct specialization by both countries raises nominal and real wages in both. Amiti (2005) develops a model with vertically linked industries embedded in a two-factor Heckscher–Ohlin model to analyze the effects of trade liberalization on the location of vertically linked industries that differ in factor intensities. Unlike the H–O model, the real return to both factors falls in the labor-abundant home country and rises in the capital-abundant foreign country when agglomeration forces initially take effect. This is followed by an increase in the real returns to all factors throughout the agglomeration phase of trade liberalization until the fragmentation phase begins. During the fragmentation stage, the real returns to the abundant factor in each country increases, while the real return to the scarce factor falls in each country. Therefore, the total world utility increases throughout the whole phase of trade liberalization, because the gains in the foreign country outweigh any losses that may occur in the home country. Leamer (1998, 2000) argues that studying volumes of trade, factor bias of technological change, and factor content of trade to explain what effects factor prices is incorrect. On the other hand, Krugman (2000) criticizes these studies asserting that trade volumes are not irrelevant because it is inconsistent with the argument of large distributional effects from trade. He asserts that the factor bias of technological change is only immaterial in the case where such change takes place in a small open economy and where technical change occurs only in that economy. Finally, Krugman proves that the use of a factor content approach to surmise the effects of trade on factor prices is justified when carefully applied. From another study on OECD countries, Krugman (1995) concluded that trade explains a fairly small fraction of the rise in wage inequality, because although the imports of labor-intensive manufactures have grown rapidly, these imports were considered too small a share of income to explain the massive increase in wage differentials[7].

According to Marjit and Kar (2005),

$$\hat{w} = \frac{\theta_{KX}}{\theta_{LX}} \frac{\theta_{SY}}{\theta_{KY}} \hat{w}_S, \tag{1.6}$$

that is, wage inequality decreases with skilled labor emigration if, and only if, capital's share in Sector X exceeds that in Sector Y where, X uses unskilled labor and capital, whereas Y uses skilled labor and capital.

---

[7] The same conclusion was also reached by Borjas *et al.* (1992), as well as Lawrence and Slaughter (1993).

In the context of the effect of outsourcing on wages in the North and South countries, Glass and Saggi (2001) showed that outsourcing lowers the relative wage in the North. According to Helpman (2011), if the assumption that all individuals are alike is rested, then trade may be harmful to some without government intervention. In studying the effect of outsourcing on the wages of skilled and unskilled labor, Feenstra and Hanson (1996a, 1996b, 1999) had considered the effects of labor market adjustments and showed that international outsourcing increases the relative wage of high skilled labor in both the insourcing and the outsourcing countries. Moreover, they had put forth skill-biased technical change as an explanation for the relative decline in low-skilled labor demand and, hence, in relative wages of the low-skilled laborers. Feenstra (1998) had formulated a factor endowment model, in which one final good is produced by a continuum of intermediate inputs ranked by skill intensity. In this model, increased international outsourcing shifts the production of intermediate goods from the North to the South. This is so because from the North's stance, these were unskilled activities, whereas from the South's perspective, these are skill-intensive activities. The resulting rise in the relative demand for skilled labor in both the countries widens the wage gap in both the regions. Extending this structure of Feenstra and Hanson, Xu (2000) considers an economy with two sectors, each producing a final good. In sharp contrast to Feenstra and Hanson (1997), Xu (2000) finds that international outsourcing does not necessarily generate skill-biased labor demand shifts in either the host or the source economy. Feenstra (2007) had concluded that as outsourcing leads to an increase in productivity of firms, the prices of final goods will fall, and if the fall in price is greater than the fall in unskilled wage, the real wages of unskilled workers would increase. This conclusion was more strongly asserted by Grossman and Rossi-Hansberg (2008). Deardorff (2001a, 2001b) shows by a combination of Ricardian and Heckscher–Ohlin models that the effects of international outsourcing depend on the nature of fragmentation, particularly on the factor intensities of the production stages that have been relocated abroad, and concludes that the increase or decrease in a country's welfare due to international outsourcing depends on the terms of trade effect. Deardorff (2001a) also states that international outsourcing can eventually lead to factor price equalization.

However, according to Zeddies (2007), even though differences in labor costs between countries are believed to have promoted production fragmentation, factor price differences are only a necessary and not a sufficient condition.

Production Fragmentation and Foreign Direct Investment

An obvious consequence of fragmentation is the movement of foreign capital. As more and more firms resort to fragmentation, firm boundaries dissolve, and foreign investment flows freely between nations, which had become easier after most countries in the world had conceded to the positive effects of liberalization. This question became increasingly relevant with literatures confirming that foreign direct investment (FDI) is among the fastest growing economic activities around the world (Helpman, 2006). UNCTAD (2011) reported that in 2010 the developing economies had generated record levels of FDI outflows and predicted that global FDI will recover to its precrisis level in 2011, increasing to $1.4 – 1.6 trillion, and approaching its peak in precrisis level in 2013.[8]

However, as discussed before, it is evident that production fragmentation can be undertaken in different forms. In which form will the host firm source a part of its production process depends immensely on the quality of the institutional framework in the sourced countries (Grossman and Helpman, 2005). A firm will resort to outsourcing and offshoring if institutions are good, and suppliers are able to enforce the contracts instead of underinvesting through FDI (WTO, 2008; Grossman and Helpman, 2003). Antras and Helpman (2007) had showed that when there is a possibility of existence of various types of contracts across industries and countries, better institutional frameworks for contracting in the South will increase the likelihood of offshoring, but would reduce the relative prevalence of either FDI or foreign outsourcing. The issue of incomplete contract has both ex-post and ex-ante consequences, and, therefore, it plays a critical role in deciding how a firm should fragment a single production process; should it resort to direct investment or should it outsource? According to Hart (1995), to counter these problems, a firm often prefers mergers, which, however, can prove to be counter-productive. Levchenko (2007) shows that the share of US imports in goods with complex production processes increased by 0.23 when a country improves institutional quality from the bottom 25 percent to the top 75 percent level. Antras (2003) predicted that FDI is the preferred form of investment to source intermediate inputs for capital-intensive sectors, whereas arm-length trade is the preferred option for labor-intensive sectors. He reasoned that in capital-intensive sectors, the relation-specific investment of the producer is more important. Consequently, the producer chooses to integrate in order to keep a higher share of the profits and to get the right incentive to adequately invest in the relationship with a supplier. Antras and Helpman (2003) showed that in sectors where the production of the final good is component intensive, outsourcing prevails over vertical integration. On the other hand, in sectors where the final good producer provides 'headquarters-intensive services', all four organizational forms can coexist. The prevalence of one form over another depends on the distribution of productivity across firms within the

---

[8] Here crisis refers to the subprime crisis of 2006–2007, which had a world-wide recessionary effect.

sector. In particular, in decreasing order of productivity, the most productive firms will engage in FDI, firms with a medium-high level of productivity will offshore internationally, and firms with a medium–low level of productivity will integrate all activities within the firm, with no outsourcing. Finally, the least productive firms will either be driven out of the market or will outsource in the domestic market (Antras and Helpman, 2003; WTO, 2008).

FDI that flows in when parts of production processes are shifted to other countries is documented to have the potential to serve several purposes. The literature endorses FDI to be a growth-inducing factor via technology diffusion (Barro and Salai-Martin, 1995). According to Blomstrom (1991), FDI can affect the host country's productivity growth in both setting up of business operations and providing technological opportunities to local firm. There also remains a possibility of indirect productivity gain if the technology spills over to the local unorganized sector firms; this issue we will verify in the third chapter. Krugman (1979) points out that FDI can augment the growth of the host country through capital accumulation and incorporation of new inputs and technology into the production function of the host country. Not only through integration, FDI is found to be growth enhancing when it is coupled with other less specific types of knowledge transfers, which takes the form of quasi-investment arrangement such as leases, contracts, and joint ventures (de Mellow and Sinclair, 1995).

References

Aghion, P. and P. Howitt. 1992. 'A Model of Growth through Creative Destruction.' *Econometrica* 60(2): 323–51.

Amiti, M. 2005. 'Location of Vertically Linked Industries: Agglomeration versus Comparative Advantage.' *European Economic Review* 49(4): 809–32.

Ando, M. 2006. 'Fragmentation and Vertical Intra-industry Trade in East Asia.' *North American Journal of Economics Finance* 17(3): 257–81.

Antras, P. 2003. 'Firms, Contracts and Trade Structure.' *The Quarterly Journal of Economics* 118(4): 1375–418.

————. 2005a. 'Incomplete Contracts and the Product Cycle.' *The American Economic Review* 95(4): 1054–73.

————. 2005b. 'Property Rights and the International Organization of Production.' *The American Economic Review* Volume 95(2): 25–32.

Antras, P. and E. Helpman. 2003. 'Global Sourcing.' *Journal of Political Economy* 112(3): 552–80.

————. 2007. 'Contractual Frictions and Global Sourcing.' CEPR Discussion Paper No. 6033.

Antras, P. and E. Rossi-Hansberg. 2009. 'Organizations and Trade.' *Annual Review of Economics* 1: 43–64.

Antras, P., L. Garicano, and E. Rossi-Hansberg. 2005. 'Offshoring in a Knowledge Economy.' NBER Working Paper 11094.

Arndt, S. W. 1997a. 'Globalization and the Open Economy.' *North American Journal of Economics and Finance* 8(71–79).

—————. 1997b. 'Globalization and the Gains from Trade.' In *Trade, Growth and Economic Policy in Open Economies*, edited by K. Jaeger and K. J. Koch. New York: Springer-Verlag.

Athukorala, P. C. and J. Menon. 2010. 'Global Production Sharing, Trade Patterns, and Determinants of Trade Flows in East Asia.' ADB Working Paper Series on Regional Economic Integration No. 41.

Balassa, B. 1967. *Trade Liberalization among Industrial Countries*. New York: McGraw-Hill.

Baldone, S., F. Sdogati, and L. Tajoli. 2006. 'On Some Effects of International Fragmentation of Production on Comparative Advantages, Trade Flows, and the Income of Countries.' CESPRI Working Paper 187.

Barro, R. J. and X. Sala-I-Martin. 1995. *Economic Growth*. Singapore: McGraw Hill.

Bartelsman, E., S. Scarpetta, and F. Schivardi. 2003. 'Comparative Analysis of Firm Demographics and Survival: Micro-level Evidence for the OECD Countries.' Working Paper 348. Paris: OECD.

Beneria, L. and M. S. Floro. 2004. 'Labour Market Informalization and Social Policy: Distributional Links and the Case of Homebased Workers.' Vassar College of Economics Working Paper 60.

Bhagwati, J., A. Panagariya, and T. N. Srinivasan. 2004. 'The Muddles over Outsourcing.' *Journal of Economic Perspectives* 18(4): 93–114.

Blomstrom, M. 1991. 'Host Country Benefits of Foreign Investment.' In *Foreign Investment, Technology and Economic Growth*, edited by D. G. McFetridge. Toronto and London: Toronto University Press.

Borga, M. and W. J. Zeile. 2004. 'International Fragmentation of Production and the Intra Firm Trade of U.S. Multinational Companies.' BEA Working Paper 0013. Washington, DC: U.S. Bureau of Economic Analysis.

Borjas, G., R. Freeman, and L. Katz. 1992. 'On the Labour Market Effects of Immigration and Trade.' In *Immigration and the Work Force*, edited by G. Borja and R. Freeman. Chicago, IL: University of Chicago Press.

Borrus, M. and J. Zysman. 1997. 'Wintelism and the Changing Terms of Global Competition; Prototype of the Future?' BRIE Working Paper 96B. Berkeley: University of California, Berkeley.

Burger, A. 2009. *Dynamic Effects of International Fragmentation of Production: Empirical Analysis of Slovenian Manufacturing Firms*. PhD dissertation, University of Ljubljana, Slovenia.

Carreira, C. and P. Teixeira. 2008. 'Internal and External Restructuring over the Cycle: A Firm based Analysis of the Gross Flows and Productivity Growth in Portugal.' *Journal of Productivity Analysis* 29(3): 211–20.

Curzon Price, V. 2001. 'Some Causes and Consequences of Fragmentation.' In *Fragmentation: New Production Patterns in the World Economy*, edited by H. Kierzkowski and S. W. Arndt. Oxford: Oxford University Press.

Deardorff, A. V. 2001a. 'Fragmentation across Cones.' In *Fragmentation: New Production Patterns in the World Economy*, edited by S. W. Arndt and H. Kierzkowski. Oxford: Oxford University Press.

—————. 2001b. 'Fragmentation in Simple Trade Models.' *North American Journal of Economics and Finance* 12: 121–37.

—————. 2005. 'A Trade Theorist's take on Skilled Labor Outsourcing.' *International Review of Economics and Finance* 14(3): 259–71.

Deardorff, A. and R. Staiger. 1988. 'An Interpretation of the Factor Content of Trade.' *Journal of International Economics* 24: 93–107.

de Mellow, L. R. and M. T. Sinclair. 1995. 'Foreign Direct Investment, Joint Ventures and Endogenous Growth.' Mimeo, University of Kent.

Dixit, A. K. and G. M. Grossman. 1982. 'Trade and Protection with Multistage Production.' *Review of Economic Studies* 49(4): 583–94.

Dluhosch, B. 2002. 'Intra-Industry Trade and Fragmentation in Economic Integration.' Working Paper, University of FAF, Hamburg.

Dutta, M. and S. Kar. 2013. 'Does Outsourcing Enhance Multifactor Productivity? Evidence from Indian Manufacturing Industries.' Mimeo, Centre for Studies in Social Sciences, Kolkata, India.

Egger, H. and J. Falkinger. 2001. 'A Complete Characterization of the Distributional Effects of International Outsourcing in the Heckscher- Ohlin Model.' CESifo Working Paper 573.

Egger, P. and M. Pfaffermayr. 2004. 'Two Dimensions of Convergence: National and International Wage Adjustment Effects of Cross-border Outsourcing in Europe.' *Review of International Economics* 12(5): 833–43.

Ericson, R. and A. Pakes. 1995. 'Markov-perfect Industry Dynamics: A Framework for Empirical Work.' *Review of Economic Studies* 62(1): 53–82.

Feenstra, R. C. 1998. 'Integration of Trade and Disintegration of Production in the Global Economy.' *Journal of Economic Perspectives* 14(4): 31–50.

Feenstra, R. C. 2007. 'Globalization and its Impact on Labor.' Presented at the Global Economy Lecture, Vienna Institute for International Economic Studies.

Feenstra, R. C. and G. H. Hanson. 1996a. 'Foreign Investment, Outsourcing and Relative Wages.' In *Political Economy of Trade Policy: Essays in Honour of Jagdish Bhagwati,* edited by R. C. Feenstra *et al.* Cambridge, MA: MIT Press.

———. 1996b. 'Globalization, Outsourcing, and Wage Inequality.' *The American Economic Review* 86(2): 240–45.

———. 1997. 'Foreign Direct Investment and Relative Wages: Evidence from Mexico's Maquiladoras.' *Journal of International Economics* 42: 371–93.

———. 1999. 'The Impact of Outsourcing and High-Technology Capital on Wages: Estimates for the United States, 1979–1990.' *The Quarterly Journal of Economics* 114(3): 907–40.

Feenstra, R. C., *et al.* 2010. 'Report on the State of Available Data for the Study of International Trade and Foreign Direct Investment.' NBER Working Paper 16254.

Findlay, R. 1978a. 'An Austrian Model of International Trade and Interest Rate Equalization.' *Journal of Political Economy* 86: 989–1008.

Findlay, R. and R. W. Jones. 2000. 'Factor Bias and Technical Progress.' *Economics Letters* 68: 303–08.

Girma, S. and H. Gorg. 2004. 'Outsourcing, Foreign Ownership and Productivity: Evidence from UK Establishment Level Data.' *Review of International Economics* 12: 817–32.

Glass, A. J. and K. Saggi. 2001. 'Innovation and Wage Effects of International Outsourcing.' *European Economic Review* 45: 67–86.

Gorg, H. 2000. 'Fragmentation and Trade: US Inward Processing Trade in the EU.' *Review of World Economics* 136(3): 403–22.

Gorg, H. and A. Hanley. 2004. 'Does Outsourcing Increase Profitability?' *The Economic and Social Review* 35(3): 367–87.

Grossman, S. J. and O. D. Hart. 1986. 'The Costs and Benefits of Ownership: A Theory of Vertical and Lateral Integration.' *Journal of Political Economy* 9(2): 169–89.

Grossman, G. M. and Helpman, E. 1991a. *Innovation and Growth in the Global Economy.* Cambridge, MA: MIT Press.

————. 1991b. 'Quality Ladders in the Theory of Growth.' *Review of Economic Studies* 58(1): 43–61.

————. 2002. 'Integration versus Outsourcing in Industry Equilibrium.' *The Quarterly Journal of Economics* Vol. 117: 85–120.

————. 2003. 'Outsourcing versus FDI in Industry Equilibrium.' *Journal of the European Economic Association* 1(2/3): 317–27.

————. 2005. 'Outsourcing in a Global Economy.' *Review of Economic Studies* 72(1): 135–59.

Grossman G. M. and E. Rossi-Hansberg. 2008. 'Trading Tasks: A Simple Theory of Off-shoring.' *The American Economic Review* 98(5): 1978–97.

Hansson, P. 2005. 'Skill Upgrading and Production Transfer within Swedish Multinationals in the 1990s.' *Scandinavian Journal of Economics* 107(4): 673–92.

Harris, R. G. 2001. 'A Communication-Based Model of Global Production Fragmentation.' In *Fragmentation: New Production Patterns in the World Economy,* edited by S. Arndt and H. Kierzkowski. Oxford: Oxford University Press.

Hart, O. 1995. *Firms, Contracts and Financial Structures.* Oxford: Oxford University Press.

Head, K. and J. Ries. 2002. 'Offshore Production and Skill Upgrading by Japanese Manufacturing Firms.' *Journal of International Economics* 58(1): 81–105.

Helpman, E. 2006. 'Trade, FDI, and the Organization of Firms.' *Journal of Economic Literature* 44(3): 589–630.

————. 2011. *Understanding Global Trade.* Cambridge, MA: Harvard University Press.

Holl, A. 2004. 'Production Subcontracting and Location: Panel Data Evidence from Spanish Manufacturing Firms.' Mimeo: University of Sheffield.

Hummels, D., J. Ishii, and K. M. Yi. 2001. 'The Nature and Growth of Vertical Specialization in World Trade.' *Journal of International Economics* 54(1): 75–96.

Hummels, D., D. Rapoport, and K. M. Yi. 1998. 'Vertical Specialization and the Changing Nature of World Trade.' *Economic Policy Review* 4(2): 79–99.

Jones, R. W. 2000. *Globalization and the Theory of Input Trade.* Cambridge, MA: MIT Press.

————. 2006. 'Production Fragmentation and Outsourcing: General Concerns.' Presented in the inaugural SCAPE Workshop held at the National University of Singapore.

Jones, R. W. and H. Kierzkowski. 1990. 'The Role of Services in Production and International Trade: A Theoretical Framework.' In *The Political Economy of International Trade,* edited by R. Jones and A. Krueger. Oxford: Blackwell Publishers.

————. 1997. *Globalization and the Consequences of International Fragmentation.* Geneva: University of Rochester and Graduate Institute of International Studies.

————. 2001. 'A Framework for Fragmentation.' In *Fragmentation and International Trade,* edited by S. Arndt and H. Kierzkowski. Oxford: Oxford University Press.

Jones, R. W., H. Kierzkowski, and C. Lurong. 2005. 'What does Evidence Tell Us about Fragmentation and Outsourcing.' *International Review of Economics and Finance* 14: 305–16.

Jones, R. W. and S. Marjit. 2001. 'The Role of International Fragmentation in the Development Process.' *The American Economic Review* 91: 363–66.

Kaminiski, B. and F. Ng. 2001. 'Trade and Production Fragmentation: Central European Economies in EU Networks of Production and Marketing.' Working Paper 2611. The World Bank Trade Development Research Group.

Kikuchi, T. and S. Marjit. 2010. 'Growth with Time Zone Differences.' *Economic Modelling* 28: 637–40.

Kimura, F. 2001. 'Fragmentation, Internalization, and Inter-firm Linkages: Evidence from the Micro Data of Japanese Manufacturing Firms.' In *Global Production and Trade in East Asia*, edited by L.K. Cheng and H. Kierzkowski. Boston: Kluwer Academic Publishers.

Kleinert, J. 2003. 'Growing Trade in Intermediate Goods: Outsourcing, Global Sourcing, or Increasing Importance of MNE Networks?' *Review of International Economics* 11(3): 464–82.

Klette, T. J. and Z. Griliches. 2000. 'Empirical Patterns of Firm Growth and R&D Investment: A Quality Ladder Model Interpretation.' *Economic Journal* 110(463): 363–387.

Klette, T. J. and S. Kortum. 2004. 'Innovating Firms and Aggregate Innovation.' *Journal of Political Economy* 112(5): 986–1018.

Krugman, P. 1979. 'A Model of Innovation, Technology Transfer and the World Distribution of Income.' *Journal of Political Economy* 87: 253–63.

_____. 1995. 'Growing World Trade: Causes and Consequences.' *Brookings Papers on Economic Activity* 1: 327–77.

_____. 2000. 'Technology, Trade and Factor Prices.' *Journal of International Economics* 50: 51–71.

Lawrence, R. 1994. 'Trade, Multinationals and Labour.' NBER Working Paper 4836.

Lawrence, R. and M. Slaughter. 1993. 'International Trade and American Wages in the 1980s: Giant Sucking Sound or Small Hiccup?' *Brookings Papers on Economic Activity* 2: 161–226.

Leamer, E. 1998. 'In Search of Stolper–Samuelson Linkages between International Trade and Lower Wages.' In *Imports, Exports and the American Worker,* edited by S. Collins. Washington, DC: Brookings Institute.

_____. 2000. 'What is the Use of Factor Contents?' *Journal of International Economics* 50(1).

Levchenko, A. A. 2007. 'Institutional Quality and International Trade.' *Review of Economic Studies* 74(3): 791–819.

Loecker, J. K. De and J. Konings. 2004. 'Creative Destruction and Productivity Growth in an Emerging Economy: Evidence from Slovenian Manufacturing.' CEPR Discussion Paper No. 4238.

Maliranta, M. 2003. 'Micro Level Dynamics of Productivity Growth: An Empirical Analysis of the Great Leap in Finnish Manufacturing Productivity in 1975–2000.' Mimeo, The Research Institute of the Finnish Economy, No. 38.

Mankiw, N. G. and P. Swagel. 2006. 'The Politics and Economics of Offshore Outsourcing.' Harvard Institute of Economic Research Working Papers 2120.   ·

Marjit, S. 1987. 'Trade in Intermediates and the Colonial Pattern of Trade.' *Economica* 54(214): 173–84.

_____. 2007. 'Trade Theory and the Role of Time Zones.' *International Review of Economics and Finance* 16: 153–60.

Marjit, S. and S. Kar. 2005. 'Emigration and Wage Inequality.' *Economics Letters* 88(1): 141–45.

Masso, J., R. Eamets, and K. Philips. 2004. 'Creative Destruction and Transition: The Effects of Firm Entry and Exit on Productivity Growth in Estonia.' IZA Discussion Paper No. 1243.

McGuinness, T. 1994. 'Markets and Managerial Hierarchies.' In *Markets, Hierarchies and Networks,* edited by G. Thompson *et al.* London: Sage Publication.

McLaren, J. 2000. 'Globalization and Vertical Structure.' *The American Economic Review* 90(5): 1239–54.

McMillan, J. 2004. 'Quantifying Creative Destruction Entrepreneurship and Productivity in New Zealand.' Motu Working Paper 04–07.

Melitz, M. J. 2003. 'The Impact of Trade on Intra-Industry Reallocations and Aggregate Industry Productivity.' *Econometrica* 71(6): 1695–725.

Nelson, D. 2005. 'Outsourcing and the Political Economy of Globalization: A Discussion Note.' Presented at the workshop *The Political Economy of Globalization: How Firms, Workers, and Policymakers Are Responding to Global Economic Integration*, Princeton University.

Olsen, K. B. 2006. 'Productivity Impacts of Off-shoring and Outsourcing.' Science Technology and Industry Working Paper 2006/1.

Sanyal, K. 1983. 'Vertical Specialization in a Ricardian Model with a Continuum of Stages of Production.' *Economica* 50(197): 71–78.

Sarkar, A. 1985. 'A Model of Trade in Intermediate Goods.' *Journal of International Economics* 19(1–2): 85–98.

Slaughter, M. J. 1995. 'Multinational Corporations, Outsourcing, and American Wage Divergence.' NBER Working Paper 5253.

Standing, G. 1999. *Global Labour Flexibility: Seeking Distributive Justice*. New York: St. Martin's Press.

Tomiura, E. 2004. 'Foreign Outsourcing and Firm-level Characteristics: Evidence from Japanese Manufacturers.' Hi-Stat Discussion Paper No. 64. Institute of Economic Research, Hitotsubashi University, Tokyo.

UNCTAD (United Nations Conference on Trade and Development). 2004. *World Investment Report: The Shift towards Services*. Geneva: UNCTAD.

_____. 2011. *World Investment Report: Non-Equity Modes of International Production and Development*. Geneva: UNCTAD.

Van Long, N. 2005. 'Outsourcing and Technology Spillovers.' *International Review of Economics and Finance* 14: 297–304.

Verhoogen, E. A. 2008. 'Trade, Quality Upgrading, and Wage Inequality in the Mexican Manufacturing Sector.' *The Quarterly Journal of Economics* 123(2): 489–530.

WTO (World Trade Organisation). 2005. 'Offshoring Services: Recent Developments and Prospects.' *World Trade Report*. Geneva: WTO.

_____. 2008. 'Trade in Globalizing World.' *World Trade Report*. Geneva: WTO.

Xu, B. 2000. 'The Relationship between Outsourcing and Wage Inequality under Sector Specific FDI Barriers.' Working Paper, University of Florida.

Yeats, A. J. 1998. 'Just How Big is Global Production Sharing?' World Bank Policy Research Working Paper 1871.

Yi, K. M. 2003. 'Can Vertical Specialization Explain the Growth of World Trade?' *Journal of Political Economy* 111(1): 52–102.

Zeddies, G. 2007. 'Determinants of International Fragmentation of Production in the European Union.' IWH Discussion Paper 15, Halle Institute for Economic Research.

11

Negative Production Externalities, Labor Market Imperfection, and Production Tax Policy in a Developing Economy

Sarbajit Chaudhuri

Introduction and Motivation

The production of a 'dirty good' generates pollution that creates harmful effects on the health of the population, thereby lowering the efficiency of the workforce. Because the negative externalities are not internalized, the production of such a commodity should be controlled by introducing a Pigouvian production tax in order to increase social welfare. This is a standard consequence noted in the literature related to the small open economy. However, the available literature tends to assume that there are no other distortions in the economy. The simple economic argument for such an assumption is that such a tax on producers lowers production of the dirty commodity and diverts economic resources toward the production of clean commodities. The tax does not affect consumer prices, and the amount of excess demand for the 'dirty' commodity by consumers can be easily met through imports of the good from the international market at the given price. The tax revenue collected by the government is transferred to consumers in a lump-sum fashion. Hence, the socially optimal Pigouvian tax rate in a small open economy is unambiguously positive. Herein, we have set aside the problems relating to measurement and implementation of the tax mechanism and other alternatives to deal with 'pollution' and concentrate on the Pigouvian tax principle solely from the perspective of social welfare.[1]

---

[1] For issues relating to measurement and implementation problems of the Pigouvian tax principle and alternative ways to deal with negative externalities, one may go through Baumol (1972), Boettke (2012), Vaughn (1980), Barthold (1994), Coase (1960), Carlton and Loury (1980), Kohn (1986), Fullerton (1997), Fullerton and Metcalf (1998), Bovenberg and Mooij (1994), Goulder, Parry, and Burtraw (1997), Sandmo (2008), etc.

Two pertinent questions arise at this juncture, which are as follows: (i) is the optimal Pigouvian tax in a small open economy strictly positive even in the presence of other distortion(s), for example, labor market distortion? and (ii) does the sign of the optimal tax anyhow depend on the magnitude of negative externalities that the production of the dirty good generates?

This theoretical piece attempts to provide answers to the aforementioned questions in terms of a 2×2 full-employment small open-economy model with exogenous labor market imperfection. The import-competing sector (Sector 2) produces a manufacturing commodity that causes health hazards, thereby lowering the efficiency of the workers. In Sector 2, workers receive an exogenously given higher wage than their counterparts in Sector 1.[2] Thus, we have exogenous labor market imperfection in Sector 2. In such a scenario, there is a Pigouvian production tax on the production of good in Sector 2, which aims at tackling negative externalities generated by the production of Commodity 2. In this setting, we have shown that although the socially optimal production tax lowers the degree of labor market distortion, it may not necessarily be positive. Besides, it crucially hinges on both the degree of labor market imperfection and the scale of negative externalities that production of the dirty commodity generates. These results have some important policy implications in the context of a small open-developing economy.

The Model

A small open economy is considered with the following two sectors: an agricultural sector (Sector 1) and a manufacturing sector (Sector 2). Sector 1 is an informal sector that produces an agricultural commodity, X_1, by means of labor (L) and capital of type K. Sector 2 is the formal sector producing a final manufacturing commodity, X_2, using the same two homogeneous inputs. Capital (labor) is perfectly (imperfectly) mobile between the two sectors. Let r denote the economy-wide return to capital. Sector 2 faces an imperfect, labor market where workers receive an exogenously given wage, W^*, while the wage rate in the informal sector, W, is market determined with $W^* > W$. The labor allocation mechanism is as follows. Workers first compete for getting jobs in Sector 2, where the wage rate is high. However, those who cannot get employment in that sector are automatically absorbed in Sector 1, which provides a competitive and lower wage. Hence, we have exogenous labor market distortion.[3] Sectors 1 and 2 are the exports and

---

[2] See footnote 3.

[3] The existence of high wage in the formal sector can be explained in different ways. However, in the literature on trade and development, it has most commonly been explicated either in

importing-competing sectors of the economy, respectively. Commodity prices are given by the small open-economy assumption. The Walras' law is taken care of by the trade-balance condition.

Sector 1 is assumed to be non-polluting[4], but the production of Commodity 2 generates pollution that affects the efficiency of workers. It is assumed that the efficiency of a representative worker, h, is inversely related to the level of pollution in the economy. Environmental pollution leads to health hazards[5], thus adversely affecting the worker's efficiency. Although in this model the manufacturing sector creates pollution, it is assumed that pollution affects the efficiency of not only those workers engaged in Sector 2 but the entire workforce. This is because both the sectors operate at close vicinity so that environmental degradation affects the entire working population equally. Thus, the average efficiency of the workers, h, is considered to be a positive function of the total amount of production of Commodity 2 and is given by

$$h = h(X_2); h'(.) < 0 \qquad (1)$$

Because the production of the manufacturing commodity creates external diseconomies, its free market production is not optimal. Therefore, there should be a Pigouvian production tax on the polluting sector from the perspective of social welfare. The producers have to pay a production tax at the ad-valorem rate, z, for the production of Commodity 2. Hence, the effective price of Commodity 2 received by its producers is $P_2^* = P_2(1 - z)$.

We assume Sector 2 to be capital-intensive in value sense, which implies that $\dfrac{a_{K2}}{W * a_{L2}} > \dfrac{a_{K1}}{Wa_{L1}}$. Here, a_{ji} denotes requirement of the jth input required to produce

---

terms of strict implementation of the minimum wage law of the government or collective bargaining on the part of labor unions with their employers or in terms of efficiency wage considerations of the employers in this sector. Although Harris-Todaro (1970) and Bhagwati and Srinivasan (1971, 1974) have considered high wage in the formal sector as a consequence of government fiat, Stiglitz (1976) has explained it in terms of efficiency wage considerations. On the other hand, Calvo (1978), Quibria (1988), Chau and Khan (2001), and Chaudhuri (2016) have explicated that the high wage in the urban sector (formal sector) is the outcome of trade union behavior.

[4] This is a simplifying assumption. A typical agricultural sector also vitiates the environment through the use of chemical fertilizers and pesticides. However, the amount of pollution generated by the agricultural sector is insignificant relative to that produced by the manufacturing sector.

[5] For example, air pollution can lead to irritation, breathing problems, and lung diseases; water pollution causes the contamination of drinking water; improper management of waste disposal is associated with the proliferation of significant human pathogens. All of these factors have adverse effects on the health of an average worker, thereby reducing her/his work efficiency.

1 unit of output of the ith sector for $j = L$, K and $i = 1$, 2. All other assumptions of the Heckscher–Ohlin–Samuelson model including CRS with positive but diminishing marginal productivity to each input holds. Labor is measured in efficiency unit. Finally, Commodity 1 is considered to be the numeraire.

At this stage, it should be pointed out that Sector 2 uses $a_{L2}X_2$ efficiency units of labor apart from capital in its production to produce X_2 units of Commodity 2. The production of Commodity 2 lowers the average efficiency of the workers through pollution. If X_2 rises by 1 percent, Sector 2 employs λ_{L2} percent of the labor force additionally while it lowers the labor force in efficiency unit by ε_h percent at the margin, where $\varepsilon_h = \left(\dfrac{dh(.)}{dX_2} \cdot \dfrac{X_2}{h(.)} \right) < 0$ is the elasticity of the labor efficiency function, $h(X_2)$, with respect to X_2, and λ_{L2} is the proportion of effective labor endowment (measured in efficiency unit) employed in Sector 2. We assume that ε_h is constant. Effectively, Sector 2 utilizes $(\lambda_{L2} + |\varepsilon_h|)$ proportion of the total labor force of the economy measured in efficiency unit. Hence, Sector 2 in effect uses more labor vis-à-vis what it directly requires in production. This gives rise to the necessity of classifying sectors in terms of **efficiency-adjusted physical sense**.

Because $W^* > W$, our assumption that Sector 2 is more capital-intensive in relation to Sector 1 in **value sense** automatically implies that Sector 2 is capital-intensive in **physical sense** as well, that is, $\dfrac{\lambda_{K2}}{\lambda_{L2}} > \dfrac{\lambda_{K1}}{\lambda_{L1}}$. However, herein, only the uses of direct labor in production are taken into consideration. We concentrate on the case where Sector 2 is more capital-intensive than Sector 1 even in **efficiency-adjusted physical sense**, that is, $\left(\dfrac{\lambda_{K2}}{\lambda_{L2} + |\varepsilon_h|} \right) > \left(\dfrac{\lambda_{K1}}{\lambda_{L1}} \right)$. It is not problematic to assume Sector 2 to be capital-intensive in both **value sense** and **efficiency-adjusted physical sense** so long as $|\varepsilon_h|$ is low. Problems arise when $|\varepsilon_h|$ is sufficiently high so that Sector 2 becomes labor-intensive in **efficiency-adjusted physical sense**. It is not difficult to check intuitively that the results get altered in this peculiar case.

The General Equilibrium Structure

Given the assumption of perfectly competitive markets, the usual price–unit cost equality conditions relating to the sectors of the economy are given by the following two equations.

$$Wa_{L1} + ra_{K1} = 1 \qquad (2)$$

$$W^* a_{L2} + ra_{K2} = (1 - z)P_2 = P_2^* \qquad (3)$$

Complete utilization of labor and capital imply, respectively

$$a_{K1}X_1 + a_{K2}X_2 = \bar{K} \tag{4}$$

$$a_{L1}X_1 + a_{L2}X_2 = h(X_2)\bar{L} \tag{5}$$

where $\bar{K}$ denotes the exogenously given stock of capital. On the other hand, $\bar{L}$ is the labor endowment of the economy in physical unit, while $h(X_2)\bar{L}$ denotes the effective labor endowment measured in efficiency unit.

Determination of factor prices and output levels from equations (2)–(5) are obvious. All the endogenous variables come out as functions of the system parameters including the policy variable, the production tax rate, z.

In this small open economy, we measure social welfare in terms of national income valued at domestic prices, Y, which is given as follows.[6]

$$Y = X_1 + P_2X_2 \tag{6}$$

This may alternatively be written in the following form.

$$Y = X_1 + (1 - z)P_2X_2 + zP_2X_2 \tag{6.1}$$

It is to be noted that in the presence of the production tax, the producer price of Commodity 2 becomes $(1 - z)P_2$. Thus, the government earns tax revenue of the amount of zP_2X_2, which is transferred to the consumers in a lump-sum manner.

Comparative Statics

Totally differentiating equations (2)–(5), the following proposition can easily be derived.

Proposition 1: A production tax on Commodity 2 leads to the following: (i) a decrease in the return to capital, r; (ii) an increase in the competitive wage, W; (iii) a reduction in intersectoral wage differential; (iv) increase in wage–rental ratios; (v) an expansion (a contraction) of Sector 1 (Sector 2); and (vi) a decrease in the number of workers employed in Sector 2, $L_2(= a_{L2}X_2)$.

---

[6] Optimum social welfare depends on the commodity prices faced by the consumers and national income. When the commodity prices change, there are two effects on welfare—price effect and income effect. In such cases, national welfare should ideally be measured in terms of a strictly quasi-concave social welfare function, because both the price and income effects can be captured by this function. However, in a small open-economy, which is a price-taker at the international market and where there is no non-traded final commodity, national income at domestic prices can be used as a good proxy for social welfare, because it can capture the income effect. Hence, in our case, national income at domestic prices may be used for measuring social welfare, because here commodity prices faced by the consumers do not change due to the production tax on Commodity 2.

The consequences of an increase in z on W and r arise due to the ***Stolper–Samuelson effect***, while those on X_1 and X_2 occur following the ***Rybczynski-type effect***.[7,8] Note that Sector 2 is more capital-intensive vis-à-vis Sector 1 in both its

---

[7] It is important at this stage to explicate the difference between a **pure *Rybczynski effect*** and a *Rybczynski-type effect* because the latter concept is not well known in the trade literature. It is recognized that in a Heckscher–Ohlin model, two sectors can be classified in terms of relative factor intensities. In a higher-dimensional (for example in a three-sector) Heckscher–Ohlin model, there are three sectors and three factors of production, say labor (L with given endowment, $\overline{L}$), capital (K with given endowment, $\overline{K}$), and land (N with given endowment, $\overline{N}$). Suppose that Sector 1 and Sector 2 use L and K, whereas Sector 3 uses labor and the sector-specific input, land. Now, Sector 1 and Sector 2 when considered together would look like a miniature Heckscher–Ohlin model, which is called a Heckscher–Ohlin subsystem (HOSS). Hence, labor is mobile across all of the three sectors, whereas capital is mobile between Sector 1 and Sector 2. In the HOSS, the two sectors can, therefore, be classified in terms of relative factor intensities. Suppose that Sector 1 (Sector 2) uses labor (capital) more intensively vis-à-vis Sector 2 (Sector 1) with respect to capital (labor). Now suppose that the economy's endowment of capital increases, ceteris paribus. Consequently, Sector 2 expands and Sector 1 contracts, because Sector 2 is more capital-intensive relative to Sector 1. This effect is called the pure '*Rybczynski effect*'. On the other hand, if the economy's land endowment grows, Sector 3 must expand, because land is specific to this sector. Nonetheless, for expansion of Sector 3, more labor is required that must come from the HOSS. Hence, the supply of labor to the HOSS decreases, which causes Sector 1 to contract and Sector 2 to expand, because the former sector is more labor-intensive relative to Sector 2. We note that Sector 1 (Sector 2) contracts (expands) although the economy's endowments of labor and capital have not changed. We call this the '*Rybczynski-type effect*'. There are some works on trade and development that have talked about this effect. See for example, Chaudhuri (2014) and Chaudhuri and Biswas (2016).

[8] It is to be pointed out that even in a 2×2 Heckscher–Ohlin model, there might arise a *Rybczynski-type effect* following a change in the relative commodity prices if production technologies are of the variable-coefficient type. Let us explain this as follows. We know that this structure satisfies the decomposition property, so that the two-factor prices are determined from the two-zero profit conditions. Hence, factor prices depend only on commodity prices and not on factor endowments. Besides, we also know that the input coefficients, a_{ji}s, depend only on factor prices apart from the technological parameters. Now, if the relative price of the labor-intensive commodity (Commodity 1) rises, ceteris paribus, the wage rate, W, rises while the return to capital, r, falls both in absolute and relative terms. This is the ***Stolper–Samuelson effect***. Because the wage–rental ratio, (W/r) rises, producers in both of the sectors would substitute labor by relatively cheaper capital. Consequently, the labor–output ratios in the two sectors, that is, a_{L1} and a_{L2}, decrease while the capital–output ratios, that is, a_{K1} and a_{K2}, increase. At the initial output levels, X_1 and X_2, there would be an excess supply of labor and a shortage of capital, which would pave the way for a *Rybczynski-type effect* leading to an expansion of the labor-intensive Sector 1 and a contraction of the capital-intensive Sector 2. The *Rybczynski-type effect* takes place despite there being no changes in the economy's factor endowments. Hence, we say that a ***Stolper–Samuelson effect*** contains an element of

value sense and *efficiency-adjusted physical sense*. In addition, the wage rate in Sector 2 is exogenously fixed at W^*. An increase in the ad-valorem production tax rate on Commodity 2, z, lowers its effective producer price, $(1 - z)P_2$. Consequently, r falls and W rises (see equation 3 and equation 2, respectively). The intersectoral wage differential, $(W^* - W)$, falls. Wage–rental ratios in both the sectors increase, which drive the producers to substitute labor by capital. Consequently, the labor–output ratios, a_{Li}s, decrease, and the capital–output ratios, a_{Ki}s, increase. This leads to an expansion of Sector 1 and a contraction of Sector 2 following a *Rybczynski-type effect*.[9] The aggregate employment of labor in Sector 2 (**in efficiency unit**), $L_2(=a_{L2}X_2)$, decreases.

Let us now examine the welfare consequence of the production tax. Differentiating equations (2)–(5) and (6.1), the following expression can be derived.[10]

$$(\frac{dY}{dz}) = -[(\frac{1}{1-z})(\frac{\lambda_{L1}\bar{A}_2 + \lambda_{K1}\bar{A}_1}{|\lambda|})[(W^* - W)L_2 + (zP_2X_2 - Wh(.)\bar{L}|\varepsilon_h|)]] \qquad (7)$$

$$(+) \qquad\qquad (+) \qquad\qquad\qquad (+)$$

In equation (7), $\bar{A}_2$, $\bar{A}_1$ and $|\lambda|$ are positive terms that have been defined in Appendix 2. The other notations have already been defined. From equation (7), the following proposition can now be established.

Proposition 2: An increase in the ad-valorem rate of production tax on Commodity 2 worsens welfare if $zP_2X_2 \geq Wh(.)\bar{L}|\varepsilon_h|$.

Proposition 2 can be verbally explained in the following fashion. We have already explained above how the production tax leads to contraction of Sector 2, both in terms of output and employment. Note that Sector 2 is the higher wage-paying sector relative to Sector 1. The higher (lower) wage-paying sector now absorbs less (more) workers than previously. Hence, the aggregate wage income falls. This we call the *labor reallocation effect (LRE)*, which produces a negative effect on social welfare. On the other hand, as the polluting sector contracts, health hazards decrease, and detrimental effects of negative externalities ease. This raises the

---

Rybczynski effect if production techniques are of the variable coefficient type. However, in the case of fixed-coefficient technologies, factor coefficients are technologically given, and they do not respond to changes in the relative commodity prices. Therefore, in such a case, the question of the *Rybczynski-type effect* does not arise, and the output levels do not change.

[9] In the present case, an increase in the rate of ad-valorem production tax on Commodity 2 raises the relative producer price of the labor-intensive Commodity 1, that is, $[1/(1 - z)P_2]$. What happens subsequently has already been explained in detail in footnote 8.

[10] This has been derived in Appendix 2.

average efficiency, h, of the workers. Note that h is a decreasing function of X_2. Consequently, the effective labor endowment of the economy measured in efficiency unit, $h(.)L$, rises.[11] The increase in the effective labor force creates additional wage income. This we call the ***labor endowment effect (LEE)*** that works favorably on welfare. Besides, an increase in z owing to contraction of Sector 2 lowers the tax revenue of the government and, hence, the amount of transfer payments to consumers. For the want of a better term, we call it the ***tax revenue effect (TRE)***. TRE lowers national income (see equation 6.1). Thus, social welfare deteriorates if the combined negative effect of ***LRE*** and ***TRE*** is stronger than the positive ***LEE***. This happens under a sufficient condition: $zP_2X_2 \geq Wh(.)\overline{L}|\varepsilon_h|$.[12] This condition implies that the ***TRE*** is at least not weaker than the ***LEE***. It may, however, be noted that one can easily derive a couple of alternative sufficient conditions subject to which the results hold.

We now proceed to find out the socially optimal rate of the Pigouvian tax. Setting $\left(\dfrac{dY}{dz}\right) = 0$ from equation (7), we find the following condition.

$$[(W^* - W)L_2 + (zP_2X_2 - Wh(.)L|\varepsilon_h|)] = 0 \tag{8}$$

From equation (8), it is easily seen that the magnitude of the socially optimal Pigouvian tax rate, denoted z^*, is as follows.

$$z^* = [(\frac{Wh(.)\overline{L}}{P_2X_2})|\varepsilon_h| - (W^* - W)(\frac{a_{L2}}{P_2})] \tag{9}$$

Hence, the magnitude of the socially optimal Pigouvian tax rate on the production of Commodity 2 depends positively on $|\varepsilon_h|$ and negatively on the intersectoral wage differential, $(W^* - W)$.

Let us now check whether the optimal production tax rate on the dirty commodity (Commodity 2) in the economy, z^*, is indeed positive. Putting $z = 0$ in equation (7), one obtains the following expression.

$$[(\frac{dY}{dz})]_{z=0} = -[(\frac{\lambda_{L1}\overline{A}_2 + \lambda_{K1}\overline{A}_1}{|\lambda|})\{(W^* - W)L_2 - Wh(.)L|\varepsilon_h|\}] \tag{10}$$

$$(+) \qquad\qquad (+) \qquad\qquad\quad (+)$$

---

[11] One might think of a ***Rybczynski effect*** taking place which has, however, already been taken care of within the ***Rybczynski-type effect*** because of our assumption that Sector 2 is more capital-intensive vis-à-vis Sector 1 in ***efficiency-adjusted physical sense***, that is,

$$\left(\frac{\lambda_{K2}}{\lambda_{L2} + |\varepsilon_h|}\right) > \left(\frac{\lambda_{K1}}{\lambda_{L1}}\right).$$

[12] See Appendix 2.

From equation (10), the following proposition readily follows.

Proposition 3: The socially optimal production tax rate, z^*, is negative (zero) (positive) if and only if $(W^* - W)L_2 > (=)(<)WhL|\varepsilon_h|$.

We explain Proposition 3 as follows. To see whether the socially optimal production tax rate is positive or not, we shall have to start from a situation where the initial tax rate is zero, that is, $z = 0$. Now suppose that the tax at a very small rate $dz > 0$ is introduced. Quite naturally, the *TRE* would be zero, because we are starting from $z = 0$. However, the negative *LRE* and the positive *LEE* would be there. The socially optimal tax rate is negative (zero) (positive) if the magnitude of the *LRE* is stronger (equal to) (less) than the *LEE*.

Two important observations are in order. First, as explained earlier, $|\varepsilon_h|$ is the absolute value of the elasticity of the efficiency function of labor with respect to the level of production of the dirty good. The dirtier the Commodity 2, the higher would be the value of $|\varepsilon_h|$ and, hence, the strength of the *LEE*. This implies that the probability that the production tax policy would improve social welfare and that the optimal tax rate would be positive increases with an increase in the degree of dirtiness (measured by the value of $|\varepsilon_h|$) of Commodity 2. Second, the larger (smaller) the intersectoral wage differential $(W^* = W)$, the higher would be the strength of the *LRE* and, hence, the magnitude of negative impact on welfare due to the tax. Now, labor market reform, which in this model means lowering W^*, reduces the intersectoral wage gap and, hence, the magnitude of the *LRE*.[13] It, therefore, increases the efficacy of the tax policy in increasing social welfare. In the extreme case, when there is no labor market distortion, we have $W^* - W$. Consequently, there would be no negative *LRE*. There would remain only the positive *LEE*. In this situation, the optimal production tax rate is unambiguously positive.[14] This leads to the final proposition of the model.

Proposition 4: The probability that the production tax policy would be effective in addressing the problem of negative externalities and, hence, in improving social welfare increases with an increase in the degree of dirtiness of the commodity. This possibility also increases if the tax policy is accompanied by a policy of labor market reform.

---

[13] If the higher wage in Sector 2 is due to trade union factors, which is often a feature of the developing economies such as India, the government may undertake different labor market regulatory measures, for example, partial or complete ban on resorting to strikes by the trade unions, as well as reformation of employment security laws to curb union power. All these tend to lower W^*.

[14] See Appendix 3.

Discussion

There are two types of distortions in this model: negative production externalities and labor market distortion. Both of them are connected to Sector 2. It is well known in the literature on trade and development that in an economy that is plagued with multiple distortions, any policy change designed to correct a particular distortion is likely to increase the degree(s) of other distortion(s). Hence, the net outcome on welfare might be ambiguous.[15] The production of Commodity 2 generates pollution that lowers the efficiency of each worker, thereby lowering the effective labor endowment of the economy measured in efficiency unit. On the other hand, the institutionally given wage rate in Sector 2, W^*, is greater than the competitive wage in Sector 1, W. This prevents the free intersectoral mobility of labor and leads to intersectoral wage differential.

A Pigouvian tax on Commodity 2 is an instrument to deal with negative externalities. It lowers production by the distorted sector and diverts economic resources toward the production of the environmentally clean good (Commodity 1). This lowers the pollution level and raises the endowment of labor measured in efficiency unit by increasing their efficiency. This is how the policy improves welfare. On the other hand, it lowers welfare by increasing the welfare cost that arises out of the existence of labor market distortion. Because the level of employment of labor in the higher wage-paying sector falls, the aggregate wage income of the workers decreases, thus affecting social welfare adversely. The net result of the production tax on social welfare, therefore, remains inconclusive. Anyway, it is clear that there should be another policy instrument that directly takes care of the labor market distortion to improve economic efficiency. Such a policy ideally would be labor market reform that curbs the labor unions' power and leads to a decrease in the intersectoral wage differential. However, it goes without saying that implementation of labor market reform is a highly politically sensitive issue. Hence, the possibility of imposition of this policy is questionable in a democratic setup. Consequently, for attaining the second best situation beside production tax on the dirty commodity, one can think in terms of providing a wage subsidy to producers in Sector 2.

Conclusion

In this chapter, using a 2×2 full-employment general equilibrium model for a small open-developing economy with negative externalities and labor market imperfection, we have shown that a Pigouvian tax on the polluting sector may not be

---

[15] See Lipsey and Lancaster (1956), Bhagwati (1971), and Batra (1973) in this context.

the right instrument to deal with negative externalities and improve social welfare. The socially optimal tax rate may not necessarily be positive. Besides, the degree of dirtiness of the commodity, whose production emanates negative externalities, plays a very crucial role in determining the sign of the socially optimal tax rate. We have advocated that the tax policy should be accompanied by labor market reform for improving economic efficiency, thereby leading the economy toward the first-best scenario, that is, the Pareto-optimal situation.

Appendix 1: Some useful results

Differentiating equations (2) and (3), it is straightforward to find that

$$\hat{r} = -\left(\frac{Z\hat{z}}{\theta_{K2}}\right)$$

$$\hat{W} = \left(\frac{\theta_{K1}}{\theta_{K2}\theta_{L1}}\right)Z\hat{z} \tag{A.1}$$

where $Z = (z/1-z) > 0$.

Differentiating equations (4) and (5), using (A.1), simplifying and writing in a matrix notation one gets the following:

$$\begin{bmatrix} \lambda_{L1} & (\lambda_{L2} + |\varepsilon_h|) \\ \lambda_{K1} & \lambda_{K2} \end{bmatrix}\begin{bmatrix} \hat{X}_1 \\ \hat{X}_2 \end{bmatrix} = \begin{bmatrix} A_1\hat{z} \\ -A_2\hat{z} \end{bmatrix} \tag{A.2}$$

where $A_1 = \left(\frac{Z\lambda_{L1}S_{LK}^1}{\theta_{L1}\theta_{K2}}\right) > 0$ \hfill (A.3)

$$A_2 = \left(\frac{Z\lambda_{K1}S_{KL}^1}{\theta_{L1}\theta_{K2}}\right) > 0$$

Here, S_{ji}^k is the elasticity of the jth factor coefficient in the kth sector with respect to the ith factor price for $k = 1, 2$ and $j, i = L, K$. For example, the elasticity of the labor coefficient in Sector 1, a_{L1}, with respect to the return to capital, r, denoted S_{LK}^1, is $S_{LK}^1 = \left(\frac{\partial a_{L1}}{\partial r}\frac{r}{a_{L1}}\right)$. Similarly, the elasticity of a_{L1} with respect to the wage rate, W, is $S_{LL}^1 = \left(\frac{\partial a_{L1}}{\partial W}\frac{W}{a_{L1}}\right)$. Because the production functions are homogenous of degree 1, the factor coefficients are homogeneous of degree zero. Hence, we have $((S_{LL}^1 + S_{LK}^1) = 0$. Because the two factors are substitutes, and there is positive but diminishing marginal productivity of each factor, we have $S_{LK}^1 > 0$ and $S_{LL}^1 < 0$. This also applies in the case of factor coefficients in Sector 2. Finally, '^' denotes proportional change. For example, $\hat{G}$ means $\dfrac{dG}{G}$.

Solving (A.2), we get the following expressions:

$$\hat{X}_1 = \left(\frac{1}{|\lambda|}\right)[\lambda_{K2}A_1 + (\lambda_{L2}|\varepsilon_h|)A_2)]\hat{z}$$

$$\hat{X}_2 = -\left(\frac{1}{|\lambda|}\right)(\lambda_{L1}A_2 + \lambda_{K1}A_1)\hat{z} \qquad \text{(A.4)}$$

where $|\lambda| = [\lambda_{L1}\lambda_{K2} - (\lambda_{L2} + |\varepsilon_h|)\lambda_{K1}] > 0$

Appendix 2: Expressions for change in welfare

Differentiating equation (6.1), one gets

$$dY = [dX_1 + P_2^*dX_2 + zP_2dX_2] \qquad \text{(A.5)}$$

Here, note that $X_1 = F^1(L_1, K_1)$ and $X_2 = F^2(L_2, K_2)$ are the two production functions, while the full-employment conditions for the two inputs are as follows: $L_1 + L_2 = h(X_2)\bar{L}$ and $K_1 + K_2 = \bar{K}$

After differentiating the production functions, equation (A.5) may be expressed as follows:

$$dY = dX_1 + P_2dX_2 = [(F_L^1dL_1 + F_K^1dK_1) + P_2^*(F_L^2dL_2 + F_K^2dK_2) + zP_2dX_2]$$

$$= [WdL_1 + rdK_1 + W * dL_2 + rdK_2 + zP_2dX_2]$$

$$= [(W * -W)dL_2 + (Wh'(.)\bar{L} + zP_2)dX_2 + r(dK_1 + dK_2)]$$

or, $dY = [(W * -W)dL_2 + (Wh'(.)\bar{L} + zP_2)dX_2] \qquad \text{(A.6)}$

Now the aggregate employment of labor in Sector 2, denoted L_2, is given by

$$L_2 = a_{L2}X_2 \qquad \text{(A.7)}$$

Differentiating (A.7), using (A.1) and (A.4) and simplifying, one can derive the following expression.

$$\hat{L}_2 = -[\frac{(\lambda_{L1}A_2 + \lambda_{K1}A_1)}{|\lambda|}]\hat{z} \qquad \text{(A.8)}$$

Using (A.4) and (A.8) and simplifying from (A.6), the following expression can be obtained.

$$\left(\frac{dY}{dz}\right) = -\frac{(W*-W)L_2}{(1-z)}\left(\frac{\lambda_{L1}\bar{A}_2 + \lambda_{K1}\bar{A}_1}{|\lambda|}\right)$$

$$-\left(\frac{X_2}{1-z}\right)\left(\frac{\lambda_{L1}\bar{A}_2 + \lambda_{K1}\bar{A}_1}{|\lambda|}\right)(Wh'\bar{L} + zP_2)$$

$$\text{or,} \left(\frac{dY}{dz}\right) = -\left(\frac{1}{1-z}\right)\left(\frac{\lambda_{L1}\bar{A}_2 + \lambda_{K1}\bar{A}_1}{|\lambda|}\right)[(W*-W)L_2 + (zP_2X_2 - Wh(.)\bar{L}|\varepsilon_h|)]$$

$$(+)$$

$$(A.9)$$

where, $\bar{A}_1 = (A_1 / Z), \bar{A}_2 = (A_2 / Z); Z = (\frac{z}{1-z}) > 0$

From (A.9), it follows that

$$\left(\frac{dY}{dz}\right) < 0 \quad \text{if} \quad zP_2X_2 \geq Wh(.)\bar{L}|\varepsilon_h| \tag{A.10}$$

Appendix 3: Socially optimal Pigouvian tax rate

Putting, $z = 0$ in equation (A.9), we find that

$$\left[\left(\frac{dY}{dz}\right)\right]_{z=0} = -\left[\left(\frac{\lambda_{L1}\bar{A}_2 + \lambda_{K1}\bar{A}_1}{|\lambda|}\right)\{(W*-W)L_2 - Wh(.)\bar{L}|\varepsilon_h|\}\right] \tag{A.11}$$

From (A.11), it is quite clear that the sign of $\left[\left(\frac{dY}{dz}\right)\right]_{z=0}$ is ambiguous. It depends on the degree of labor market distortion $(W* - W)$ and the magnitude of $|\varepsilon_h|$.

In the absence of any labor market distortion, we have $W* - W$. Then from (A.10), it follows that

$$\left[\left(\frac{dY}{dz}\right)\right]_{z=0} = -\left[\left(\frac{\lambda_{L1}\bar{A}_2 + \lambda_{K1}\bar{A}_1}{|\lambda|}\right)Wh'\bar{L}X_2\right] > 0 \tag{A.11.1}$$

$$(+) \qquad (-)$$

References

Barthold, T. A. 1994. 'Issues in the design of environmental excise taxes.' *The Journal of Economic Perspectives* 8(1): 133–51.

Batra, R. N. 1973. *Studies in the Pure Theory of International Trade*. London: Macmillan.

Baumol, W. J. 1972. 'On taxation and the control of externalities.' *American Economic Review* 62(3): 307–22.

Bhagwati, J. 1971. 'The generalized theory of distortions and welfare.' In *Trade, Balance of Payments and Growth*, edited by J. N. Bhagwati, R. W. Jones, R. A. Mundell, and J. Vanek. Amsterdam: North-Holland Publishing.

Bhagwati, J. N. and T. N. Srinivasan. 1971. 'The theory of wage differentials: production response and factor price equalization.' *Journal of International Economics* 1(1): 19–35.

_____. 1974. 'On reanalyzing the Harris-Todaro model: policy rankings in the case of sector-specific sticky wages.' *American Economic Review* 64: 502–08.

Boettke, P. 2012. *Living Economics*. The Independent Institute, Universidad Francisco Marroquin.

Bovenberg, A. L. and R. A. Mooij. 1994. 'Environmental levies and distortionary taxation.' *The American Economic Review* 84(4): 1085–89.

Calvo, G. 1978. 'Urban unemployment and wage determination in LDCs: trade unions in the Harris-Todaro model.' *International Economic Review* 19(1): 65–81.

Carlton, D. W. and G. C. Loury. 1980. 'The limitations of Production taxes as a long run remedy for externalities.' *Quarterly Journal of Economics* 95(3): 559–66.

Chau, N. H. and M. A. Khan. 2001. 'Optimal urban employment policies: notes on Calvo and Quibria.' *International Economic Review* 42: 557–68.

Chaudhuri, S. 2016. 'Trade unionism and welfare consequences of trade and investment reforms in a developing economy.' *Metroeconomica* 67(1): 152–71.

_____. 2014. 'Foreign capital, non-traded goods and welfare in a developing economy in the presence of externalities.' *International Review of Economics and Finance* 31: 249–62.

Chaudhuri, S. and A. Biswas. 2016. 'Endogenous labour market imperfection, foreign direct investment and external terms-of-trade shocks in a developing economy.' *Economic Modelling* 59(C): 416–24.

Coase, R. H. 1960. 'The problem of social cost'. *Journal of Law and Economics* 3(1): 1–44.

Fullerton, D. 1997. 'Environmental levies and distortionary taxation: comment.' *The American Economic Review* 87(1): 245–51.

Fullerton, D. and G. Metcalf. 1998. 'Environmental taxes and the double dividend hypothesis: did you really expect something for nothing?' *Chicago Kent Law Review* 73: 221–56.

Goulder, L. H., I. W. H. Parry, and D. Burtraw. 1997. 'Revenue-raising versus other approaches to environmental protection: The critical significance of preexisting tax distortions.' *The RAND Journal of Economics* 28(4): 708–31.

Harris, J. R. and M. P. Todaro. 1970. 'Migration, unemployment and development: a two-sector analysis.' *American Economic Review* 60: 126–42.

Kohn, R. E. 1986. 'The limitations of Production taxes as a long run remedy for externalities: comment.' *Quarterly Journal of Economics* 101(3): 625–30.

Lipsey, R. G. and K. Lancaster. 1956. 'The general theory of second best.' *The Review of Economic Studies* 24(1): 11–32.

Quibria, M. G. 1988. 'The Harris-Todaro model, trade unions and the informal sector: a note on Calvo.' *International Economic Review* 29: 557–63.

Sandmo, A. 2008. 'Production taxes.' *The New Palgrave Dictionary of Economics, Second Edition*.

Stiglitz, J. E. 1976. 'The efficiency wage hypothesis, surplus labor, and the distribution of income in the LDC.' *Oxford Economic Papers* 28: 185–207.

Vaughn, K. 1980. 'Does it matter that costs are subjective?' *Southern Economic Journal* 46(3): 702–15.

12

Tax-Financed Public Transfers
A Mechanism for Double Taxation

Baisakhi Marjit, Sugata Marjit, and Saibal Kar

Introduction

A well-known and well-accepted policy of the government is to tax the rich and provide welfare benefits to the poor who cannot sustain minimum acceptable standards of living consistent with human and social dignity. Although such a practice is in vogue in all countries in the world, the quality and quantity of intervention varies widely. Governments may use current taxes and borrowing to finance its activities, including provisions for transfer of payments. The recipients of transfers generally constitute that group of people who do not pay direct and indirect taxes of various kinds, as may be prevalent in the economy. While indirect taxes are user taxes and, therefore, everybody has to bear it regardless of income level, it should not be restrictive to assume that the transfer recipients either consume a small amount leading to generation of smaller tax revenue, or they consume goods and services that are outside such tax nets. Regarding the use of inputs, it is also unlikely that such individuals engage in purchase of raw materials and hiring of labor that would attract indirect taxes. In fact, individuals from poor households in several countries depend on subsidized food grains, fuel, and public services. This could apply equally well for the public distribution system in India to allocation of food stamps in the United States. Services availed in public hospitals and subsidized public transports are mostly exempt from the payment of indirect taxes.

Therefore, the purpose of this chapter is to remind us that if transfer payments made out of taxes lead to escalation of unskilled wages in the labor market and if tax payers are forced to hire non-tax-paying workers for certain household activities, effectively there will be double taxation. The double taxation operates first through a higher tax rate implemented directly and indirectly, and thereafter through the higher wage rate of non-tax-paying workers, as propelled by public transfer programs. Ignoring the general equilibrium effect of this phenomenon reflects an incomplete and imprecise economic judgment.

The example that we consider is true for households in many developing countries, but if we expand this limited example to the case of home production in general, then following Becker (1965) allocation of time for such activities remains a much more generic subject. In our case, the motivation arises from the fact that households in urban areas register a considerable demand for support workers to carry out many activities of home production. This may include substantial requirement of caregivers for ailing parents, babysitters for kids, etc. In most countries, relatively unskilled workers (or those still pursuing skill training) are engaged in these activities. Previously, household production theory helped to determine how economic factors, such as market wages and lump-sum transfers, affect the household's internal division of labor, and how changes in the home production technology affect decisions about participating in labor market (see Greenwood and Vandenbroucke, 2005). The participation in the labor market has also traversed long passages. The transformation of labor rights in many countries (see Goldin, 1994 for the United States) over the last century allowed individuals to re-evaluate wage–work balance facilitated by shorter hours, sick leave, security on the job, unemployment safety nets, etc. At the same time, the countries have seen a widening of the wage structure and a rising trend in inequality, with specific types of skills being rewarded much more than traditional skills, for example. In some labor markets, such as in the United States, this has reduced working hours and raised weekly leisure by 6–9 hours for males and 4–8 hours for females, particularly owing to decline in time spent for home production (see Aguiar and Hurst, 2007). This does not, however, nullify the long-believed evidence that Americans work longer hours than most people around the world (Hamermesh, 2014). In fact, a series of papers by Prescott (2004), Alesina, Glaeser, and Sacerdote (2006), Prescott, Rogerson, and Wallenius (2009), etc., have argued that higher levels of income taxes explain why Europeans spend a smaller share of their lifetimes at work than average Americans. Clearly, an important (but possibly underappreciated) element of these studies is the assumption that tax revenues are refunded to households in the form of a lump-sum subsidy. This is justified on the grounds that welfare states are usually the dominant form of governance in some western European countries. Thus, higher tax effectively amounts to a *compensated wage decrease* in these studies. Conversely, instead of refunding tax revenues to households, if European governments used tax revenue on some non-welfare projects, such as manufacturing nuclear armaments, then one would no longer necessarily expect higher taxes to reduce labor supply. This chapter also commences on this aspect and argues that if individuals pay taxes, continue to work longer hours, and are unable to allocate sufficient time for home production, an alternative arrangement must be made. If outside market for old-age support or childcare is underdeveloped, then inhouse arrangement shall need to factor in the reservation wage of potential workers. In this chapter, the reservation wage of the support staff depends on how taxes paid by households are spent by the government. We explore one possibility, namely, government transfers to non-tax-paying individuals. This is a generic form of public support, G, available in almost all economic structures related to what we discuss here.

Naturally, important applications of household production theory is also available for developing countries, where rural households often divide their time between, say, tending their own land and providing agricultural labor to the market. However, this is distinctly different from urban practices even in developing countries, where wage premium for skill is quite high, while surplus unskilled labor keeps unskilled wages low, allowing for such household support as mentioned above (also see Kar and Marjit, 2009, in which such occupations are part of informal arrangements and have to do with levels of poverty in a developing country). Often coined as *life-care services* (Ireland and Riccardi, 2003), these home production activities are also gendered, so much so that, women and girls solely bear the responsibility for housework and childcare in a family. Domestic work is seen to impede women's and girls' efforts to obtain education and participate in paid work (Findlay and Wright, 1996).

Importantly, some predictions of home production theory are *independent of the form of the utility function*. Overall, the related literature predicts that a rise in public transfers (G) could lower the amount of hours put in the market if leisure is normal. Conversely, if leisure is inferior in consumption and the effect is strong, it might outweigh the income effect and lead to more hours being put in the labor market. This is not unusual for individuals from very low-income groups. We argue that the availability of G is responsible for raising the reservation wage of such individuals. It has been statistically confirmed and often used as a symbol of success for the largest employment guarantee program in the world, that is, the National Rural Employment Guarantee Act (NREGA) in India, which has raised the rural, as well as overall, wage rate of labor. This means that the cost of hiring unskilled workers in the urban areas, as well as that for standard agricultural work, has increased. If taxes are used for financing such activities, taxpayers would be subjected to double taxation, because they have to pay higher wage for domestic support toward household work and related services. It is clear that the partial equilibrium consequence of a rise in the tax rate for generating more revenue to facilitate transfer payments may underestimate the wider effects. It is so because taxes as a source of transfer payments itself may impose additional burden of tax through general equilibrium wage effects. However incorrect (politically speaking) it might be to highlight such an issue, this remains an important economic phenomenon that can hardly be neglected in view of optimal allocation of resources and time within a typical household. Ideally, if taxes could be used for financing transfers that would leave the opportunity cost of recipients unaffected, such double incidence of taxation would be less likely. The results in this chapter would show that the political implications of what prevails as a public policy might not be complex, since the size of welfare recipients is always much larger in most developing countries ensuring a steady political support. Indeed, it could be increasing in some of the developed countries as well. This makes the direction of the political choice relatively straightforward.

Typically, transfers may not affect the equilibrium wage in the labor market, specifically the market-determined competitive wage, if the supply curve of labor is infinitely elastic. In other words, if we consider the historical world of Lewisian unlimited supply of labor, then political choice of public transfers receives greater credence in favor of improving the conditions of the poor in a democracy, without any side effects. Under these circumstances, any rise in demand would only mean more job creation. The analytics of such informal labor market in developing countries have been discussed at length in Marjit and Kar (2011). Notwithstanding, labor shortage arises from various frictions in such markets, one of which is public transfers. Despite relative unavailability of market-based or publicly provided solutions for old-age homes and childcare (the provision is still a very urban phenomenon, few in number, available in pockets, and expensive), the impact of public transfers on household's ability to hire private support is less visible as a social concern. Indeed, the persistence of poverty and attempts at helping them out of it always provide breathing space to state policies. In addition, the prevalence of corrupt practices leads to erroneous identification of welfare recipients in developing countries. For India, there is accepted evidence that a large share of the rich households in rural areas in parts of India manage to hold onto BPL (Below Poverty Line) identity cards and qualify for transfers (Jalan, Marjit and Santra, 2016). Under the circumstances, the political benefits from redistribution can never be undermined.

Finally, with rigid short-run supply curve of labor and sticky demand for household jobs, transfer expenditure will raise the urban wage. In the model we develop, we take a vertical labor supply and a Nash wage bargaining process to prove our point starkly in terms of a small-scale general equilibrium model. We wish to highlight that because taxpayers are relatively few, sharing the responsibility of revenue generation and yet bearing the additional burden of higher wages due to government's policy, the transfers should not be considered as Pareto improvement. In fact, the chapter further shows that the transfer system is regressive, in the sense that poorer tax payers are hit harder by the generosity of the state to welfare recipients.

The Model and Results

A small open economy produces and exports a skilled good at the world price P_S to the rest of the world. The skilled population has varying skills, and the commodity in question requires only skilled labor as input. The model is conceived of as a Ricardian extension. The competitive structure yields,

$$w_s(z) a_s(z) = P_S \tag{1}$$

$a'_S < 0$. The skilled population has a mass equal to 1 indexed in $z \in [0, 1]$, as in the standard model of continuum in international trade similar to Dornbush, Fisher, and Samuelson (1977), Wilson (1980), Marjit and Yu (2008), Marjit and Beladi (2009), Bandopadhyay, Marjit, and Yang (2014), etc. Unskilled population L is absorbed in a sector, X, and has diminishing marginal productivity. At a given P_X unskilled wage is given by,

$$w = f'(L), f' > 0, f'' < 0 \tag{2}$$

and
$$w_S(0) > w \tag{3}$$

The innovation of this model allows us to introduce a household sector in which skilled laborer needs to provide caregiver support to the elderly and children in the household. As argued previously, we assume that the private or public facilities for daycare and old-age homes are poor substitutes for inhouse care offered to the old and very young within a given family. For each skilled worker, there is one old or young dependent in a given household. The country structure we have in mind also ensures that $L \gg S$, that is, the endowment of unskilled labor far exceeds that of skilled labor. These dependents are not in the labor market. Thus, if the skilled individual attends to this activity in person, then α fraction of $w_S(z)$ is expended from her/his income. If the individual hires a caregiver to attend to this responsibility, then she has to pay w as the market wage for the unskilled worker. We do not distinguish between the types and quality of caregivers in this model. The determination of w in this model is an outcome of the Nash bargaining between post-tax skilled and unskilled wages in the presence of an outside opportunity available to the unskilled in the form of public transfers. Nash bargaining model of wage determination for the general context is available in Booth (1995).

We assume that the government in this country taxes only skilled workers. In the first case, we assume that the entire tax revenue is used by the government and, therefore, its presence in the system, as far as the purpose of this chapter goes, is redundant. The effective after-tax wage determination then follows from the Nash bargaining model, with 't' ($0 < t < 1$) as the proportional tax imposed on the skilled wage.

$$V = \left[w_S\left(z\right)\left(1-t\right)\left(1-\alpha\right) - w \right]\left[w - w_0 \right] \qquad (4)$$

In equation (4), the reservation wage of the caregivers is w_0. However, note that, with both L and S held fixed, w_0 is a constant.[1] Setting $\dfrac{dV}{dw} = 0$ with equal weights assigned to the bargaining powers of skilled and unskilled workers in equation (4), we get,

$$w = \frac{1}{2}\left(1-\alpha\right)\left(1-t\right)w_S\left(z\right) + \frac{1}{2}w_0 \qquad (5)$$

Here, $\dfrac{d^2V}{dw^2} < 0$. We define effective skilled wage as

$$w_S^e\left(z\right) = w_S\left(z\right)\left(1-t\right) - \frac{1}{2}\left(1-\alpha\right)\left(1-t\right)w_S\left(z\right) - \frac{1}{2}w_0$$

Or, $$w_S^e\left(z\right) = w_S\left(z\right)\left(1-t\right)\left[1 - \frac{1}{2}\left(1-\alpha\right)\right] - \frac{1}{2}w_0 \qquad (6)$$

It implies that if the skilled individual cannot avoid hiring an external help for caregiving, then the effective skilled wage must be reduced by the amount payable to the unskilled worker for this support. The distinction of this structure with the practice of old-age homes or daycare facilities for the children is that the individual has to directly factor in the consequence of the reservation wage, which might increase in the face of a direct transfer received by such workers. In case of (scarcely available) old age homes, the burden of such increase in the reservation wage of unskilled caregivers is pooled and shared by several households. This lowers per household burden and incurs a smaller amount of welfare loss. The effective skilled wage should still be lower, but not as low as in the case of private care. Moreover, if daycare facilities exist in a competitive market as might be common in developed countries, the price (fee) for such support will be lower compared to noncompetitive (monopoly) pricing as in equation (4).

The second case is, therefore, at the core of what this chapter addresses. Consider that the government transfers the entire tax collected. In other words, if the mass of skilled workers is held at 1, then $T = t\bar{w}_S$, where $\bar{w}_S = \int_0^1 w_S\left(z\right)dz$. This transfer

---

[1] Indeed, as mentioned briefly, a policy such as the rural employment guarantee scheme popularized in India since 2004, called the National Rural Employment Guarantee Act (NREGA), is founded on the principle that up to 100 days of daily wage work shall be allocated in several (rural) districts in India. The demand for such jobs comes from workers self-selecting into this opportunity if they do not have round-the-year employment. The daily wage was predetermined by the government in each state of the country according to local demand and supply.

is made to the unskilled workers directly, and this raises the reservation wage of the unskilled workers from w_0 to $\left(w_0 + \dfrac{t\bar{w}_S}{L} \right)$.

Therefore, the effective skilled wage in the tax-transfer regime is given by:

$$w_{ST}^e (z) = w_S (z)(1 - t)\left[1 - \frac{1}{2}(1 - \alpha)\right] - \frac{1}{2}w_0 - \frac{1}{2}\frac{t\bar{w}_S}{L} \tag{7}$$

and

$$w_{ST}^e (z) < w_S^e (z) \tag{8}$$

In addition, $w_{ST}^e (0) > w_0 + \dfrac{t\bar{w}_S}{L}$ (9)

We have the following proposition.

Proposition I: *In a system where redistribution from tax revenue directly enhances the reservation wage of the unskilled, the skilled workers have an effective double burden of* $\dfrac{1}{2}\dfrac{t\bar{w}_S}{L}$

Proof: It follows from equations (6), (7), and (8).

Proposition II: *The additional tax burden is regressive.*

Proof: Let us consider $\dfrac{w_{ST}^e (z)}{w_S (z)}$ as the ratio of effective post-tax wage to true wage of the skilled workers. We know that,

$$w_{ST}^e (z) = w_S^e (z) - \frac{1}{2}\frac{t\bar{w}_S}{L} \tag{10}$$

or

$$R(z) \equiv \frac{w_{ST}^e (z)}{w_S (z)} = \frac{w_S^e (z)}{w_S (z)} - \frac{1}{2}\frac{t\bar{w}_S}{L} \cdot \frac{1}{w_S (z)}$$

$$R(z) = \frac{1}{2}(1 - t)(1 + \alpha) - \frac{1}{2}\frac{w_0}{w_S (z)} - \frac{1}{2}\frac{t\bar{w}_S}{L} \cdot \frac{1}{w_S (z)} \tag{11}$$

It is obvious that $R'(z) > 0$, as $w_S'(z) > 0$. QED

Equation (11) shows that for a continuum of skill measured over z, the effective skilled wage to true skilled wage rises with skill, despite the transfers made by the government to the unskilled workers. Therefore, although the transfer raises the reservation wage of the unskilled workers, skilled persons who are at the higher rungs of the skill ladder face lesser challenge to accommodate the higher opportunity cost of caregiving. Conversely, skilled workers who are closer to the margin would find it difficult to accept the claim for higher wage by unskilled workers owing to transfers made by the government. This gives the public transfer as non-labor income a regressive nature and may be welfare reducing for a large section of the workers who are skilled, but not super skilled, so as to largely assuage such impact. Indeed, for skilled workers at the margin with need to employ caregivers, it is possible to expect a switchover to the group of unskilled workers, who receive unconditional transfers and become net suppliers of such labor. The welfare implications for this transition could be varied.

Conclusion

This chapter showed that the use of government transfers for supporting minimum income for large number of unskilled workers translates into higher opportunity cost in the labor market. One way to relate this policy of income support with the larger literature could be a comparison with the effects of efficiency wage. It too raises the opportunity cost. In other established studies drawing on the implementation of efficiency wage, it has been shown that the aggregate demand for labor is most likely to fall. It would then imply that some individuals or firms, as the case might be, would not be able to register positive demand for labor or simply end up hiring less than before. In our model, availability of public transfers allows workers to a fallback option, which often lies at the core of such policy design. The implementation of NREGA program in India has offered an equivalent outcome. The strictly positive fallback option allows the bargaining power of such workers to be higher. This too could be an objective of a government policy in poor countries, where availability of no alternative often pushes unskilled workers to the receiving ends of policy and negotiation, alike. We showed that when skilled workers pay taxes and also need to hire unskilled welfare recipients as household support, the provision of public transfers may end up imposing double taxes on the skilled workers. Consequently, given a distribution of skill, it is then possible that some of the skilled workers shall not be able to hire the support. It would be true for skilled workers in the lower tail of the distribution. Interestingly, the unskilled wage obtained from the Nash bargaining solution is not responsive to which skilled household the worker finds a job. In other words, if the richer skilled households are willing to commit more to attract workers, it may start a wage war. For all practical purposes, such wages are usually open to negotiations, unless preset by an intermediary, say, a nurse supplying agency. These considerations in future can enrich the scope of this simple model.

Finally, we showed that the transfers create a regressive burden on the distribution of skill—the lower is the skill level, the higher is the burden on the household. Consequently, the limits of transfers become important in deciding how it influences the group of welfare recipients as compared to the taxpayer.

References

Alesina, A., E. Glaeser, and B. Sacerdote. 2006. 'Work and Leisure in the U.S. and Europe: Why So Different?' In *NBER Macroeconomics Annual 2005*, edited by M. Gertler and K. Rogoff. 20: 1–100.

Aguiar, M. and E. Hurst. 2007. 'Measuring Trends in Leisure: The Allocation of Time Over Five Decades.' *Quarterly Journal of Economics* 122(3): 969–1006.

Bandyopadhyay, S., S. Marjit, and L. Yang. 2014. 'International oligopoly, barriers to outsourcing and domestic employment.' *Canadian Journal of Economics* 47(4): 1372–86.

Booth, A. 1995. *The Economics of the Trade Union*. Cambridge: Cambridge University Press.

Browning, M., F. Bourguignon, P. A. Chiappori, and V. Lechene. 1994. 'Incomes, and Outcomes: A Structural Model of Intra-Household Allocation.' *Journal of Political Economy* 102: 1067–96.

Card, D. and P. K. Robins. 2005. 'How Important Are "Entry Effects" in Financial Incentive Programs for Welfare Recipients? Experimental Evidence from the Self-Sufficiency Project.' *Journal of Econometrics* 125: 113–39.

Dornbusch, R., S. Fischer, and P. Samuelson. 1977. 'Comparative Advantage, Trade, and Payments in a Ricardian Model with a Continuum of Goods.' *American Economic Review* 67(5): 823–39.

Findlay, J. and R. Wright. 1996. 'Gender, poverty and the intra–household distribution of resources.' *Review of Income and Wealth* Series 42(3): 335–51.

Goldin, C. 1994. 'Labor Markets in the Twentieth Century.' NBER Historical Working Paper 58.

Greenwood, J. and G. Vandenbroucke. 2005. 'Hours Worked: Long-run Trends.' NBER Working Paper 11629.

Hamermesh, D. 2014. 'Not Enough Time?' *The American Economist* 59(2).

Jalan, J., S. Marjit, and S. Santra, eds. 2016. 'India's Fiscal Policy: Past, Present, and the Way Forward.' In *India Public Finance and Policy Report*. New Delhi: Oxford University Press.

Ireland, R. and A. Riccardi. 2003. 'Household Services as Life Care: An Alternative View of Household Services in the Legal System.' *Journal of Legal Economics* 109–18.

Kar, S. and S. Marjit. 2009. 'Urban Informal Sector and Poverty.' *International Review of Economics and Finance* 18(4): 631–42.

Marjit, S. 2008. 'Skill Formation and Income Distribution in a Three Class Small Developing Economy.' In *Emerging Issues in International Trade*, edited by S. Marjit and E. Yu. n.p.: Emerald Publishers.

Marjit, S. and H. Beladi. 2009. 'International and Intra-national Trade: A Continuum Approach.' *Japanese Economic Review* 60(3): 320–32.

Marjit, S. and S. Kar. 2011. *The Outsiders: Economic Reform and Informal Labour in a Developing Economy*. New Delhi, London: Oxford University Press.

Prescott, E. 2004. 'Why Do Americans Work So Much More Than Europeans?' *FRB Minneapolis Quarterly Review* 28(1): 2–14.

Prescott, E., R. Rogerson, and J. Wallenius. 2009. 'Lifetime Aggregate Labor Supply with Endogenous Workweek Length.' *Review of Economic Dynamics* 12: 23–36.

Wilson, C. A. 1980. 'On the General Structure of Ricardian Models with a Continuum of Goods: Applications to Growth, Tariff Theory, and Technical Change.' *Econometrica* 48(7): 1675–702.

Contributors

Anwesha Aditya is Assistant Professor at the Indian Institute of Technology, Kharagpur. She has received International Economic Research Annual Award from the Export-Import (EXIM) Bank of India for her PhD dissertation.

Rashmi Ahuja is Assistant Professor at Lal Bahadur Shastri Institute of Management in Delhi. She completed her PhD from the University School of Management and Entrepreneurship, Delhi Technological University.

Hamid Beladi, Janey S. Briscoe Endowed Chair in Business, Associate Dean of Research and Professor of Economics, is a prolific writer in international economics and finance, and edits reputed journals.

Eric W. Bond is the Joe L. Roby Professor of Economics at Vanderbilt University since 2003. His specializations include trade theory and applied microeconomics. His work has appeared in all the frontier journals of economics.

Avik Chakrabarti is Associate Professor at the University of Wisconsin-Milwaukee. His specializations include international trade and investment, international finance, industrial organization and economic systems.

Tonmoy Chatterjee is Assistant Professor in the Department of Economics, Ananda Chandra College, Jalpaiguri, India. His research interests include applications of trade theory in health and development issues.

Sarbajit Chudhuri is Professor and Head of the Department of Economics, University of Calcutta. Specialized in general equilibrium trade theory, he has written extensively on many issues.

Meghna Dutta is Assistant Professor of Economics at the Indian Institute of Technology, Patna. She is specialized in the area of international trade and industrial organization.

Priya Brata Dutta earned his PhD from the Indian Statistical Institute, works as Assistant Professor at Visva Bharati, Santiniketan, and publishes mainly in the field of trade and development.

Kausik Gupta is Professor of Economics at the University of Calcutta. He has served as Vice Chancellor of WB State University. His research interests include international trade and environment.

Ronald Winthrop Jones is an influential international trade theorist over last five decades. He is Professor of Economics, Emeritus, at the University of Rochester. He was elected as the Distinguished Fellow by the American Economic Association in 2009 and is a member of the National Academy of Sciences.

Saibal Kar is Professor of Economics at the Centre for Studies in Social Sciences, Calcutta (CSSSC) and Research Fellow at IZA Bonn. He has several papers and books in labor economics and international trade.

Sajal Lahiri is the Vandeveer Chair Professor of Economics and Distinguished Scholar at Southern Illinois University. He has published in all leading journals on trade, development and public economics.

Baisakhi Marjit is an editor. She publishes commentaries in economics, literary critiques, and current affairs.

Sugata Marjit is the RBI Professor of Industrial Economics at the Centre for Studies in Social Sciences, Calcutta (CSSSC). He has won numerous awards and has published papers on trade, industrial organization, and development in top journals.

Sudeshna Mitra works at the Department of Economics, St. Paul's C.M. College, Kolkata. Her research interests include international economics.

Noritsugu Nakanishi is Professor of Economics at Kobe University, Japan. His research interests include international economics and game theory. He is the recipient of Kojima Kiyoshi Prize of the Japan Society of International Economics.

Index